MANX SCHOOLS

PAST, PRESENT AND PROPOSED

an anthology

written and illustrated by

RONALD S.ELY

*   *   *

Published 2003 by Ronald.S.Ely.

Cover design from an original by Mr Ely
(Dhoon School. Drawn January 1985)

*   *   *

Printed in Leicester
by
Sceptre Print Limited

Distribution by
R. S. Ely
43 Quenby Lane
Ripley
DE5 3NN

ISBN 0-9546506-0-3

MANX SCHOOLS
Past, Present and proposed.

*   *   *

"Only time can cure a person of childhood and youth,
which are truly ages of imperfection in every respect."
(Balthazar Gratien. 1646)

*   *   *

A Dedication

Some of the present generation of Manx folk may not be fully aware of the important part played in the provision of schools and basic education on the Isle of Man by the early church; similarly, only a few of the new residents who have arrived within, say, the last ten years or so, will be aware of the fact. Yet, the church, and churchgoers of the Isle of Man, between them, provided the only formal method of education available to most of the island children for over three hundred years.

As a whole, the churches may not have been completely selfless in the promotion of schools during the those early years, but the history of Manx Education would have been much poorer without the sincere effort put into the church schools by all members of the various communities on the Island.

and an Appreciation

My thanks to the various Head Teachers who have assisted by providing information, to Dr Peter Davey and Dr Ros Stott for advice, to the Librarian Archivist of Douglas Museum, Roger Simms, and to his staff for their willing assistance, also, to John Cain, Director of Education., for guidance regarding official records.

R.S.Ely. 2003.

CONTENTS

ILLUSTRATIONS

" Familiarizing oneself with one's children, getting them to talk about all manner of things, treating them as sensible people and winning them over with sweetness, is an infallible secret for doing what one wants with them. They are young plants which need tending and watering frequently; a few words of advice offered at the right moment, a few marks of friendship and affection given now and then, touch them and bind them. A few caresses, a few little presents, a few words of cordiality and trust make an impression on their minds, and they are few in number that resist these sweet and easy methods of making them persons of honour and probity." (Abbé Goussault 1693)

*   *   *

MANX SCHOOLS

Past, Present and Proposed.

An introduction.

My interest in Manx schools began soon after I came to the Isle of Man as a holidaymaker during the late 1960s and early 70s; those early visits were highlighted by the number of voyages I made aboard that fine sea-boat of fond memory, the 1965 version of the 'Ben my Chree'.

My first trip to the Island was as a complete stranger. I knew nothing of the place, or its people; the mere fact that it was a popular holiday destination was good enough for me !

Wrongly, I had assumed that the Isle of Man was primarily a rural place in which the towns and their schools would be of a modest size; I was taken by surprise when I saw the spacious and well built schools in and around Douglas.

In April 1987, my wife Edwina and I retired from our employment in England and decided to make our home in the Isle of Man. I would have preferred to do so decades before but the needs of a growing family prevented any such move. We know that our decision was right.

On my early travels around the Island, I noticed the many schools which continued to serve sparsely populated country districts and small village communities and I couldn't help wondering whether the parents, whose children attended these smaller schools, really appreciated the thoughtfulness of the Manx Education authorities who were allowing such schools to continue in use for the benefit of a small number of local children ?

It was just because these small rural schools <u>were</u> still in use that I came to realise how fortunate I was; I had come to the Island just in time to help record the passing of an age so far as the the older Manx school buildings were concerned.

In several instances I was too late; a number of the older schools had been sold and converted into workshops or private residences and several have been altered so much that they are hardly recognisable as ever having been schools.

We tend to take school buildings for granted, you might even think that they are unlikely subjects for an artist, (especially when some of the newer schools strongly resemble industrial buildings !) yet I have enjoyed drawing the older schools.

Prints of some of my pen and ink drawings are included within this book and I hope that you will enjoy looking at them too.

Mostly, my drawings are of the older and smaller schools and there are three good reasons for this :-

Firstly:-

In a number of instances, it is the smaller of those same schools which must, inevitably, be closed or rebuilt within a few years because of their age, lack of modern facilities, gradual decay, and, more important, the ever declining number of true rural families WITH CHILDREN. In addition, some of the smaller schools are unable to meet the current standards of space necessary for present day methods of education and recreation.

The welfare of youngsters must come first and for this reason some of the old schools have closed to children within the few years since I drew them.

Secondly:-

All my original drawings are to the same overall dimension, about 238mm x 148mm. You might consider that these dimensions are rather small, but it is a good size within which to draw the smaller buildings and quite big enough for pen and ink drawings.

Thirdly:-

It has been a labour of love because I do appreciate the efforts made by Manx people of the past in finding sufficient monies with which to provide and maintain a large number of small schools spread throughout the Island. By so doing, the Manx made sure that children living in rural parts of the Isle of Man would receive an adequate education and not be penalised unduly just because they did not live in one of the towns.

I hope that the drawings included within this book will provide a small but lasting memorial to the adults, the children, and the teachers, who regularly went to country schools in an age when distance was a matter of concern, when roads were poor and public transport was almost unheard of.

All of them knew from experience that, at times,a three mile walk to and from school, every schoolday, through gales and rain, snow, storm or broiling sunshine could be a journey which was very hard for a child to face.

The story recounted in this book has been put together without any particular bias other than for it to be considered a small part of the social history of the Isle of Man.
In the words of G.M.Trevelyan :-
"Social history might be described as the history of a people with the politics left out. Without social history, economic history is barren and political history is unintelligible."

*   *   *

For the most part I have used available information concerning the schools as they were during the late nineteenth and early twentieth centuries, a period which, as far as modern Manx education is concerned, included 'the formative years'.

*   *   *

Several schools have prepared booklets describing their own particular history, if these and similar chronicles could be gathered together for reference in one central place they would be useful tools for historians of the future. If such booklets could also be expanded so as to include the current and past viewpoints of teachers, children and their parents, so much the better.
At present, unfortunately, so much seems to be missing; the detail is probably somewhere, but where ? I believe that the subject really should be covered in some depth with especial thought being given to the early schools from, say, 1600 to 1900.
It is possible that a real tragedy has already taken place because so many of the Island schools mentioned in my text have disappeared almost without trace and with little or no accessible written history.
In some instances it is already too late to gather information other than from surviving school log books (and they tend to be skimpy at times) or by closely scrutinising copies of early newspapers, because there are very few living persons who can truly recall the day to day way of life within many of the earlier schools.

I have not attempted the complete history of any individual school, such a subject would be far too big for this particular book. Nevertheless, if there is some particular nugget of information that you happen to possess concerning some of the earliest schools, something which is not recorded in this book, I would be so delighted to hear of it through the publisher.
Similarly, if you discover an error of fact it will be my own fault. Do, please, let me know what it is so that I can rectify the fault wherever and whenever possible. Thank you.

R.S.Ely.

FOOTNOTES AND REFERENCES

I have avoided footnotes but the sources of many items are listed within the Bibliography, page 227 onward.

Reference numbers to these sources are given in the text within brackets in this manner :-   [??] .

*   *   *

SCHOOL INSPECTORS

Ladies and Gentleman, please note that I have used the initials HMI to signify School Inspectors irrespective of whether they were those originally appointed by the Diocese, the English authorities, or those appointed or employed by the Manx Education Board/Council etc.

In most instances the observations and reports made by the Inspectors' have been printed in this book in bold lettering.

*   *   *

The outline Map of the Isle of Man is reproduced by kind permission of Manx National Heritage.

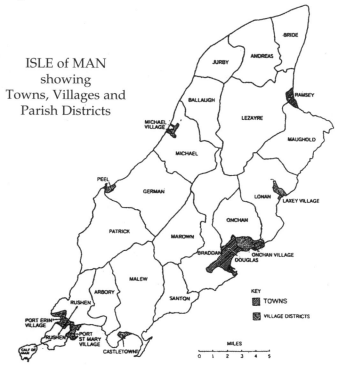

ISLE of MAN
showing
Towns, Villages and
Parish Districts

BRIDE
ANDREAS
JURBY
BALLAUGH
RAMSEY
MICHAEL VILLAGE
LEZAYRE
MICHAEL
MAUGHOLD
PEEL
GERMAN
LONAN
LAXEY VILLAGE
ONCHAN
PATRICK
MAROWN
BRADDAN
ONCHAN VILLAGE
DOUGLAS
MALEW
ARBORY
SANTON
KEY
RUSHEN
TOWNS
PORT ERIN VILLAGE
VILLAGE DISTRICTS
RUSHEN
PORT ST MARY VILLAGE
CALF OF MAN
CASTLETOWN
MILES
0   1   2   3   4   5

" Thank you for condemning the education of labourers.
I, who farm the land, need agricultural workers and not tonsured clerics.
The lower classes should be guided, not educated; they are not worthy to be
educated."
(Voltaire when congratulating La Chatolais)

*   *   *

Chapter one

TIMES PAST - 16th/17th centuries

Elizabethan laws provided for a master to teach the 'pettyes' of each village in
England. (The term 'petty' was interchangeable with 'parochial' and was taken
from the French 'petits' - for the small or young ones)
    At that time the word 'baby' denoted children of school age; the others came to
be divided as 'little ones', 'middle ones' and 'big ones' or 'lytell babes' and 'lytell
children'.

*   *   *

From an early date the leadership of the Church of England was interested in
education, the Bishops' realising that education in depth was a necessary
requirement in order that the clergy could become erstwhile leaders with the
knowledge and ability to cope with almost every religious and secular problem. To
assist in their programmes of education there were a relatively large number of
grammar schools in England within which students could receive a good
grounding - but none in the Isle of Man.

Before he fell from favour, Cardinal Wolsey (1475-1530) had planned a Cardinals'
College at Oxford which was to have a Dean, sixty senior canons and forty petty
canons, all to be drawn from a network of Grammar Schools which he planned to
endow throughout England.
    This was an ambitious scheme, especially so when we consider that the
population of the whole country had not recovered from the ravages of the Black
Death. Whilst the figure for the population stood at 3.7 million in 1348, it had
dropped to 2.1 million in 1400 and, even by 1524, was still less than 2.4 million.
    Unfortunately, Wolsey's whole scheme tottered upon his demise; only one of his
planned Grammar Schools came into existence, and that was largely through the
efforts of the lawyer, Thomas Cromwell (1485-1540), this school was in Ipswich,
Wolsey's home town.

Out of the residue of Wolsey's scheme, Henry VIII endowed Christ Church, Oxford, and matched it with the foundation of Trinity at Cambridge, both enterprises designed so as to further the royal domination of Universities and to encourage the education of the elite.

That the church made full use of the educational facilities then available, can be ascertained from a remark made by a man who was usually a severe critic of the clergy for their morals and politics, - John Seldon (1584-1654) - when he said, "All confess there never was a more learned clergy."

All of them spoke and understood Latin and most were also learned in at least one other of the classical tongues. In turn, the main Protestant churches struggled to make a University Degree a necessary qualification for ordination; suffice to note that in 1603 the Lincoln diocese alone had 646 graduate clergy.

*   *   *

During the early 1600's, education in the Isle of Man drifted along in a desultory manner much the same as it had been doing for ages past.

In 1586 Bishop John Meryck had made the remark that Manx clergy were, "generally natives and had their whole education on the Island", but, he did add, "they are not taxed with ignorance".

Unfortunately, just under half a century later, in 1634, an official paper stated that:-

"All the Manx clergy except two or three are illiterate men, brought up in the Island in secular professions."

In 1639 Bishop Richard Parre wrote concerning the Isle of Man clergy :- "Most of the Ministers are of no better ability than to read distinctly divine service". He added that the Island was destitute of means of learned education.

A ray of light appeared on the scene in 1650, when William Blundell wrote, considering the clergy of the Island:- "Their Ministers are not unlearned, and I spoke to many. I did not converse with anyone but found him both a scholar and discreet."   [M12b]

There is evidence suggesting that a few schools existed in different parts of the Island from well before the 1600s'; these schools were for fee paying children but the standard of teaching was poor, as was the accommodation.

Most Manx children were unable to attend these earliest of schools, which, perhaps, was just as well, because most parents did not want their children to go to school. Their children, like those in England, were of far more use in the home or on the land; from the parents' point of view the children were taught useful things at home and made to appreciate the values of everyday life therein much better than in any schoolhouse.

During Bishop William Foster's Visitation of the Island's parish churches in 1634, he asked :-

"Do any schoolmasters keep school without license ?".

In five parishes - rather less than a third of the diocese -, three were without a schoolmaster and only one actually admitted the existence of a school master.

However, it is probable that those parishes which included a town were, indeed, provided with a schoolmaster and, in some of the rural parishes, the vicar kept school, *but some parishes were without any means for the elementary education of their children.*

*   *   *

Lord Fairfax ruled the Island under English suzerainty from 1652 to 1660 (under the Commonwealth) and one of his commissioners reported as follows :-

"The Bishop's lands and Jurisdictions are devolved to the Lord of the Isle; who for better encouragement and support of the Ministers of the Gospel and for the promoting of learning hath conferred all this revenue upon the Ministers as also for maintaining Free Schooles .... at Castletown, Peel, Douglas and Ramsey."

No information is available concerning these free schools beyond the bare fact of their existence, but, by 1661 there were also a number of Parish schools.   [M12b]

It was against this sort of background that Bishop Isaac Barrow made his way to the Isle of Man in 1663.

Quickly discovering that the Manx were a virtually uneducated people and his locally born clergy not much better, it soon became his firm intention to make schooling readily available to all, so that in future years all Manx people could receive some education.

If it was humanly possible the Bishop wanted free education for every child who was able and willing to attend a school and, in 1669, so as to make a start with the process of organised education, the Bishop instigated the establishment of a 'petty', or Parochial School in every parish. So it was, that soon after the Bishop's arrival on the Island the casual Manx approach to schooling was changed for good.

The Bishop's intentions were farsighted; he looked forward to a time when there would be a three tier system of schooling guided at every stage by the Church, which would be available to every Manx child, irrespective of that child's station in life. The parochial or 'petty' school was to be the starting place for every child, being, in effect, a primary school through which any child could progress to separate grammar schools and from thence, if particularly able, on to an academic school which would prepare pupils for the Ministry of the Church or, perhaps, the legal profession.

Such far sighted thinking, and the action taken, could have put education on the island in a leading position, but, through no fault of his own, Bishop Barrow's idea of providing such a comprehensive system of education on the Isle of Man was not to be met until well into the twentieth century.

The failure of subsequent Bishops' to implement in a proper manner the three tier system he had envisaged was a tragedy, because, if the original ideas had been followed through as intended, all Manx people would have been well educated far in advance of any such happenings elsewhere in Britain.

Indeed, at a time when it was unheard of to provide an elementary or general education of children in England, the Island could actually have become one of the top places for education.

Who knows ? If an Academy had been established on a sound footing within the Isle of Man during those early years, it might even have spawned a University ? The possession of such a prestigious establishment in the 17th or 18th century would have placed the Isle of Man in the forefront of education for centuries. Such an establishment would also have brought in much needed revenue from potential students overseas who would, assuredly, have flocked to an established Academy or University on the Island ?

Strangely enough, the idea had been thought of before.

The Seventh Earl of Derby, James I, who ruled the Island from 1627 to 1651, also planned the foundation of a college of university rank, he wrote :-

"I had a design...to set up an university without much charge which may oblige the nations round about us. It may get friends into the country and enrich the land."

But, of course, nothing came of his idea   [12b]

For those interested in such matters I would remind you that a decision was made at an early date which should have ensured that all Church of England Schools on the Isle of Man were to be open to every child no matter what religious or other background the child might or might not have.

In these earliest of Manx C of E schools, whilst the children might be encouraged to take part in religious events and teachings, the original intention was that they should not be compelled to conform with the dogma of the church.

Bishop Barrow may have laid the groundwork for the petty schools but the population as a whole was far from convinced of the need.

Most people coped well with life as they knew it, they were quite happy for their children to follow in their own footsteps and, as a consequence, voluntary attendances at the earliest of the Petty schools were disappointingly low.

Bishop Barrow's endeavours to provide schooling would certainly have come to nought without a certain amount of compulsion and it was fortunate that Charles Stanley, the eighth Earl of Derby, Lord of Man from 1660 to 1672, also agreed with the concept of elementary education, because it was he who encouraged compulsory attendance.

The Earl Charles was a friend of Bishop Barrow and real progress started in 1672 when a big stick was employed to make sure that education had a chance of succeeding; he compelled his tenants to send their children to school under severe penalties for non-compliance :-

> "All farmers and other tenants in my Isle of Mann of what degree or quality soever doe and shall send their eldest sonnes and all other children to such pettie schools as soon as they are capable, wherein if any doe faile or be remiss .....(they) shall not onely be fined severely, but their children made uncapable of bearing any office or place of trust ... for want of such literature and education."

Records show that the order was followed through, fines were enforced and school masters were not allowed to neglect their pupils with impunity.

To put things into some sort of time perspective, remember that Bishop Isaac Barrow did not arrive on the Island until 1663, petty schools were not instigated until 1669, and Earl Charles's first attempts at compulsory attendance did not begin until 1672, by which time the original voluntary nature of school attendance had been proved unworkable.

It was the Earl who made the clergy responsible for educating children in their parishes and, furthermore, he ordered the parents of children on his estates to send them to school.

Without this initial care shown by the interested leadership of the church *and the Lord of Man* during the 17th century, it is doubtful whether many Manx children, other than those of the wealthy few, would have received any formal education at that time, or during the following two centuries.

Behind the establishment of church schools on the Island at that time there were just two simple motives and they are best summarised as being:-

" To educate to the best ability of the Teachers, Masters and Mistresses involved, so that a child might better itself".

*   *   *

Throughout the next two centuries, it was left to the Manx churches of the Church of England, almost unaided, to provide schools and supply the teachers with which to educate the children.

It must be admitted that the schools of the period were generally of a poor quality, but then, it is hard to see how they could have been otherwise, the Island was so wretchedly poor, but, at least, the church and the people did try.

For a large part of this time the schools had another serious problem; this lay in the fact that almost the whole population spoke in the Manx tongue alone; the language was adequate for the spoken word but it was a language that was virtually unwritten; there was nothing whatsoever written in Manx that could be used for text book purposes.

The problem extended further, should the children be taught in Manx or English ? At first sight there did not seem to be any particular benefit in doing other than to teach in Manx but the decisions eventually reached favoured a perceived need to educate in English.

Manx fishermen and seamen were frequently meeting and doing business with English speaking peoples and, in their own insular dealings, the Manx were meeting more and more people from England, a country with real and growing power, but, no matter which language should be taught eventually, the debate hardly mattered at first because there were no Manx to English or English to Manx text books, neither were the teachers bilingual.

The earliest teachers in the church sponsored schools were the Manx clergy, most but not all of whom spoke Manx. Even between themselves there were occasions when some of the clergy had great difficulty in communicating, let alone with the children who were supposed to be under their instruction.

It has been said that a Vicar who could only speak in Manx, when speaking to another who only spoke English, only managed to communicate because both understood Latin.

When other teachers came to be employed who could only speak or write in English, the difficulties for both teacher and the Manx speaking scholars can easily be imagined. The problems of communication must have seemed to be almost insurmountable.

At a Convocation held in 1683, the clergy agreed to pay "Ten Pownes a piece" to Parson John Harrison, the Rector of Kirk Bride, and John Christian, the Curate of Kirk Andreas, for having caused, "a constant and diligent schoole to be kept in their churches for five years past."

That action was followed up when the Convocation of 1685 distributed sums of money to clergy, the acceptance of which made them responsible to keep a school in their respective parishes.

The Convocation encouraged the creation of schools at :-

Kirk Christ. Rushen.	Kirk Arbory.	Kirk Santon.
Kirk Marown.	Kirk Braddan.	Kirk Conchan.
Kirk Lonan.	Kirk Maughold.	Kirk Michael.
Jurby.	Kirk Christ. Lezayre.	

The following schools were already in existence :-

Castletown Petty School. Douglas Petty School. Ramsey Petty School.

Kirk Bride.	Kirk Andreas.	Ballaugh.
Kirk Patrick.	Kirk German.	[M13b]

*   *   *

It was Bishop Thomas Wilson who paid for St. Matthew's Gospel to be printed in Manx; this was a limited edition of 53 copies which were printed solely for the use of the clergy, the first to be printed in the Manx language.

With the help of Dr.Thomas Bray, the Bishop went on to establish parochial libraries in 1699; whenever he visited England he brought back books, this was done so as to help raise the standard of education and understanding among the clergy who could, in turn, share their knowledge with the children they taught.

Later, in 1731, a Convocation made each vicar responsible for the library in his own parish, a requirement subsequently given legal backing by Tynwald in 1734. (Unfortunately, despite this legal action, the libraries have all disappeared.)

During the eighteenth century the Bible and the Prayer Book were in print in the Manx language. These works existed solely because of the earlier zealous endeavours of Bishop Mark Hildesley. When this Bishop came to the Island in 1756, he took the trouble to learn some of the Manx language so that he could make himself more generally understood by the people and, in 1758, he followed up this action by, "declaring a great desire of having the Church catechism printed in the Manks tongue by itself,".

His intention and hope was that this and other translations would be:- "For the instruction and comfort of such persons as do not understand the English language."

Bishop Hildesley made a good start by having the Gospels printed in Manx during 1763, this was followed by a translation of the Old Testament and the remaining books of the Bible.

The Bishop had discovered willing and able translators amongst his clergy, possibly because they needed to teach in the Manx and English within their schools, as well as dual preaching in their churches. Before long, a large number of the clergy were taking part in translating the Bible into the Manx.

Most of the work was divided up so that individual clergymen would translate just one particular book of the Bible.

The classical scholar who did most of the checking and editorial work on these translations was Philip Moore (1705-1783) who, for 47 years, was Chaplain and Schoolmaster at St Matthews, he was assisted by Dr Kelly to whom the Bishop was deeply indebted for the excellence of his work.

The cost of printing such a complex publication was beyond the means of the Bishop but, providentially, the Society for Promoting Christian Knowledge gave immediate help when, in 1762, they handed the Bishop £100 toward the publication followed by donations from various "charitable persons" in England.

BUT, both, Dr John Kellys' Manx Dictionary and his Manx Grammar were primarily compiled at the Bishop's request for his own use.

In 1764 the SPCK published a pamphlet in which it reported of the Manx people that, "Of a population of 20,000 the greater part speak no English."

It was not until 1804 that the first Grammar by Dr John Kelly was actually published and then, just a few years later, in 1835, Archibald Creegan's Manx dictionary appeared.

Born in Colby, the son of a cooper, Creegan had been trained as a stone mason; he compiled his dictionary quite independently of Dr Kelly - whose work he had not known about - it took him twenty years to collect his list of words .

Unfortunately. these dictionaries appeared too late to really influence the decisions previously made concerning teaching in English.

The church persevered in educating children to the best of its ability; even more so during the late nineteenth and early twentieth century when, in collaboration with the National Society and, later, the Manx authorities, the Church of England in the Isle of Man played the major part in providing most of the schools within which a basic education was provided for all children on the Island.

In 1847/8, Robert John Eden, the Bishop Aukland, asked the Council for Education in London to send an Inspector to report on the Manx schools. Canon Moseley came, and one of the things he reported was that 26 of the schools had neither maps or blackboards. This was a failing which was followed up by the Bishop, who, during March 1850, appointed his own Diocesan Inspectors to visit and report regularly on the Parish Schools.

By 1875 it was reported that most people on the Isle of Man spoke both Manx and English and, as a measure of progress in education from the 1600s, it was also reported that there were only 190 people on the Island who spoke solely in the Manx tongue, 12,340 were bilingual and spoke both Manx and English, a figure that dwarfs the present day bilinguists.

There were great advantages in having the ability to speak in both tongues because, for the Manxman with courage and foresight, the English language, coupled with the Manx, opened up new horizons for employment across the seas at a time when there was not all that much work available on the Island.

Eventually, of course, as other denominations increased their membership on the Island, so they, too, played a useful part in general education by providing their own schools.

Within this book I have only mentioned a few of the things with which the various Bishops' were concerned regarding education on the Isle of Man up to about 1900. However, their actions do need to be viewed within a wider perspective because all Bishops' were involved with church and political matters far more than they were with the Schools. In some way and at some time the involvement of the Bishops' in other matters affected almost every man, woman and child on the Island, no matter what their field of endeavour.

A good way in which to learn more of this involvement is to read Canon John Gelling's fine book entitled :-

"A history of the Manx Church, 1698 to 1911."

"There is no such whetstone, to sharpen a good wit
and encourage a will to learning, as is praise."
(Roger Ascham 1515-1568)

*   *   *

Chapter two

The Formative Years. 17th, 18th & 19th Centuries.

The controlling British Governments of the day had no deeply committed interest so far as the matter of education was concerned in the Isle of Man; the various Governments were too preoccupied with serious problems of their own.

There were so many other things which seemed to be much more important, for these were the years of strife which were leading to civil wars, the Commonwealth, various disturbances within the Government and others within the House of Lords.

In any case, there was so little in the way of elementary education in England that there was hardly any likelihood of attention being given to the provision of elementary schools on the Isle of Man.

The Scots passed excellent laws in 1633 and 1696, which ordained that a well appointed school should be set up in every parish and be maintained by local rates. Unfortunately, while the laws were worth believing in, the reality in Scotland was very different.

In England, at the start of the civil war, during 1643, two thirds of all males and nine tenths of all females could not write their names.

As it happened, by winning the civil war, the Puritans were able to give some consideration to the subject of education. This did not happen at once, of course, but it is a fact that during the time of the Commonwealth, the Puritans believed in particular in the education of the young: Whilst they were in power far more was done for the extension of education in England than had ever been attempted previously, private schools began to have a greater importance and schemes were drawn up for universal elementary education and a third university, but.... the return of the Royalists and the 'Restoration' proved to be the undoing of all this good groundwork.

The new rulers had their own ideas, amongst which a reduction in taxes had high priority; the cost of education for the mass of the population was definitely not included within any of their plans. The drive for educational, social and legal reform was halted, and the country went back to traditional rule by a conservative landed elite. Following the Act of Uniformity even the Grammar Schools of England became and were considered to be utterly inefficient from 1662 to 1870.

[M12b]

During the life of Queen Anne, (1664-1714), many parishes in England had no school at all and, when a school could be found, too often it was a dark, draughty, dirty hovel where the master or mistress usually lived on starvation wages.

At the end of Queen Anne's reign there were 5,000 children attending charity schools in London but throughout the rest of England there were only 20,000 such fortunates out of a total population of about 5 million..   [18]

In spite of abortive attempts by charitable persons to found an educational system in the eighteenth and nineteenth centuries, no organized provision for the education of the lower orders existed in England and Wales before the second half of the nineteenth century.   [7]

*   *   *

In the Isle of Man it was different; the church had made a positive start with the elementary education of children *and despite considerable problems the schools did continue.*

During the formative years, attendances at Manx petty schools were far from regular; this was because, in the early 17th century, most of the Manx population was still engaged in rural employment, the fishing industry or smuggling, all of which occupations were interchangeable in so far as most of the men-folk were concerned; many parents still preferred to keep their children working at home or on the farm, only a few could imagine or foresee any benefit arising from the schooling of their children.

It was often the case that some of the children who did attend the first schools only did so when their parents had no other work for them to do. In fact, the same parental attitude was to persist right up to and well into the first few decades of the twentieth century with children still being kept away from school to assist in the fields. This attitude led to a lack of continuity and a corresponding despondency on the part of the masters, especially the clergy, some of whom certainly believed that their abilities could be employed better elsewhere rather than in taking a school class.

By 1675, each parish had an established "free" school and in these early "Petty" schools the local church minister was expected to do the teaching; his stipend was increased for this specific purpose and he was required to teach "for the perfecting of their children and fitting them for the Grammar School."

A Grammar School indeed ! Yes, a Grammar School.

At Castletown, within a building on the site of the future St Mary's Church, a grammar school had been founded by Bishop Barrow. The fond hope of all concerned was that it would, in time, become the first academic school on the Isle of Man.

Leaders of the Church were behind Bishop Barrow in this endeavour and at Church convocations held in 1685 and 1703 they gave a formal standing to his initiatives.

The Grammar School was to be:-

" for the support of young persons designed for the ministry."

Unfortunately, and for various reasons, the school never became an academy and was not really a success as a Grammar School.

*   *   *

'Petty' schools were established as part of the church and most of the early schools were held _within_ the various parish churches. There were early safeguards; for example, no one was allowed to teach without the Bishop's licence and during the short era of Bishop Baptista Levinz (1684-93) we learn that the clergy licence to teach cost 2/6d whilst that for laymen was one shilling.

It became a sad fact that within a relatively few years there were no longer many 'free' places in the schools. Problems caused by the cost of maintaining the schools and school buildings, as well as employing teachers, forced an ongoing burden on to the parents - the payment of school fees.

In 1704, Bishop Thomas Wilson (1698-1755) sought the status of an Act of Tynwald to make his education regulations more effective. An Act was passed and academic studies started on the Isle of Man. For this purpose a small number of students were gathered under William Ross, they were to work in the upper part of the new 1706 Library at Castletown. The lower part of the Library was used by the House of Keys.

Unfortunately, this 'Academy' did not thrive either.

Later still, academic studies for a selected few were also pursued at Bishopscourt, but this was never a true Academic school because it dealt primarily with matters theological; nevertheless, several of its pupils did progress well, most, but not all, becoming clergymen.

Bishop Wilson continued to promote education and by virtue of large additions to endowments, and monies received from the trustees of an "Academic Fund", he was able to start a Grammar School in Douglas which was placed under the charge of the Chaplain of the new St. Matthew's Church.

Old Library
and House of Keys
Castletown

Castletown Library - Opened 1707. A short lived academic school was
started on the first floor. Drawn September 1999.

This Douglas School was in addition to the Castletown Grammar School.(which had previously been removed to the 13th century Chapel of St. Mary in 1671.)

Unfortunately, Bishop Wilson took a further step which, within a few years, led to a great falling off in the standard of education.

Up to the time of this Bishop the relatively well educated clergy had been responsible for teaching within all the petty schools; you will recall that their stipends had been increased for this very purpose. Bishop Wilson relieved the educated clergy of their teaching duties by allowing the appointment of masters or mistresses to take charge of the schools - the stipends did not revert to their previous levels.

Almost inevitably these new teachers were only paid a pittance, they became appointees, poorly paid teachers who were required to "instruct the children in learning and good manners, to be diligent in teaching them the Church Catechism and their prayers", and to, "bring them up in the fear of God.".

Sadly, the majority of teachers so appointed were themselves poorly educated and standards fell rapidly; as a consequence, the basic education of Manx children suffered shamefully and needlessly, for nearly 150 years.

In another action, which, in many cases, further removed the minister from the school, Bishop Wilson signified that schools should be removed from all churches into buildings of their own and, to emphasise his argument, he made the Church Wardens of each Parish responsible for providing a school.

Admittedly, the Bishop did have good reason for forcing through this particular action. Children were showing a considerable lack of respect for the places of worship within which they were being taught and untold damage was caused in several churches by the youngsters. It was probably for this same reason that the Bishop would not agree to the Petty School and the Grammar School being under the same roof in Castletown.

Despite these problems, the ordinary people of the Isle of Man showed a commendable attitude toward the education of their children from the late 1700s onward because, despite the relative poverty endured by the majority of the population, *together with the poor standard of education,* most of their children did attend schools. Simple education did continue - but it was hard for it to do so. There was Island wide poverty which made it very difficult for schools to be funded; most schools depended almost entirely on whatever fees they could raise.

Very few schools had any sort of endowment and the few which did have something behind them were not usually provided with adequate means for the repair or proper maintenance of the school buildings themselves. It was a natural consequence of being in a poor country with no major source of wealth, teaching standards and the quality of school buildings were poor and they seemed to be getting worse.

School fees payable by the majority of parents were proving to be an essential requirement and in an attempt to regularise the standard of fees, the church Convocation did, on February 3rd 1703, pass Canon no 9 - later passed by Tynwald in 1704 - which included, in effect, the following, that :- "all children have to be sent to school. Parents neglecting to do so to pay the Schoolmaster one shilling a quarter - a lesser fine where children have attended irregularly........ at harvest time when the children are needed in the fields and are unable to attend school, they are to attend the Parish church an hour before evensong on the third Sunday in the month to be taught by the Schoolmaster."

Each Vicar was expected to visit his school once a quarter and report on the progress of each child.

In addition to a meagre salary, the Schoolmasters at this time received sixpence a quarter from the parents of every child taught to read, and ninepence for each child taught to write, although parents genuinely unable to pay were not expected to do so.

*   *   *

Despite such an early and tragic failure by different Bishops to follow through from the excellent start made by Bishop Barrow, Manx folk do have every reason to be proud of the history of education on the Island because, despite the many problems that were encountered at various times, schooling did continue throughout the 17th and 18th centuries with the result that the Isle of Man was often well in advance of the neighbouring islands.

Unfortunately, during the 19th century, Manx education slipped badly, the overall authority seemed to be satisfied by maintaining minimal standards and there was no incentive to aim for higher standards.

At the beginning of the 20th century Manx schools made little headway, but then, under a dynamic Council of Education, Manx schools gradually caught up with and passed the educational expertise elsewhere. By the middle of the century the Isle of Man had taken the lead in some respects when compared to England and in recent years a further lead has been taken in several aspects of education for the children.

There are two excellent books by the Rev Hinton Bird.,which illustrate the historical facts very well indeed.

Within these books he has followed through the political course of education on the Island in some depth, the story makes fascinating reading and should not be missed.

His books are obtainable from any bookshop and are entitled :-

" An Island that led - The History of Manx Education."

(There are two paper back volumes)

"I should sell my last shirt, if I had nothing else, to see my children on the
same level as all the others of their age and rank."
"They must not be brought into the world to humiliate us
with their ignorance and behaviour."
(General de Martange. 1756-1782)

*   *   *

Chapter three

Progress

As Douglas grew in size over the years, Castletown gradually lost its' commercial importance; the population of the old capital continued to grow slowly whilst that of Douglas increased steadily. Such changes were to have a considerable effect on the respective schools, both past and present.

Here are a few examples showing the population growth:-

Year	Castletown	Douglas
1726	785	810
1784	1318	2850
1831	2062	6776

Largely because of its fine natural harbour, which was ideal for Manx trade between the Island and Scotland, England, Wales and Ireland (legal or otherwise), Douglas was destined to become the only town on the Isle of Man with a sizeable population, the town was also a very good base for the fishing fleet.

Fairly regular employment was to be found in the fishing fleet as well as within the ancillary trades which grew around that fleet. Employment was also to be had in and around the prosperous harbour with its valuable import and export trades. It was these same trades which were to create people of wealth, many of whom were soon expressing a willingness to pay more for a better education of their children.

The town's fairly rapid development did lead to a few private schools being provided for the merchants' children, but it was in later years that such private schools were given a boost when, after the Napoleonic wars and as a direct result of the cheapness of living in Douglas, the town became a popular place for an increasing number of "half-pay" officers.

The "half-pay" men were usually long term Naval or Military officers who had served for many years but for whom no service commissions or appointments seemed likely in the foreseeable future; they were placed on half-pay in semi-retirement and, as most of them had no experience of a civilian occupation, they had the dual problems of obtaining employment somewhere and/or, a place in which to live at moderate cost, but, of course, the location still needed to be commensurate with their 'exalted' social position as ex-officers !.

These ex-officers needed to be careful in their choice of a town or place in which to live because most of them could not afford to remain in England, yet both they, and their wives, did so want to maintain the standard of life they had become used to as officers, gentlemen and their ladies. They set up residences for their families in and around Douglas and, with the usual snobbery that existed between differing ranks of officers and their wives, they soon expressed a similar preference for their children, they wanted them to attend fee paying private schools.

In response to the demand, a large number of small privately owned schools of various capabilities came to be opened in Douglas as well as in a few of the other towns throughout the Island. Some of these private schools were rather risky ventures which did not last very long nor leave much of an impression, but others gradually grew and became fairly important in their own particular field; these lasted well.

In later years, however, it was a sad fact that, more often than not, closure of a private school would follow the demise of a particularly gifted Master or Teacher; usually his or her death was a serious matter, the loss caused an almost insoluble problem because, in private schools, continuity with good teaching staff was always difficult.

*   *   *

Meanwhile, in England, there was a continuing struggle between those who wanted the state to provide elementary education and those who would not agree to such a premise under any consideration; a good start to the provision of elementary education for English children seemed to be as far away as ever.

In 1819, Sturgess Bourne was proposing the establishment of industrial training schools as an alternative to the then existing type of family allowance, which was formed of alms and Parish Relief, saying that:- 'the money was often squandered, and not applied to the benefit of the children.' Instead, he considered that if the money was spent on education and training it would benefit not only the children, but the ratepayers and the country as a whole. In opposition, George Philips insisted that children must not be compelled by the state to go to school.

It didn't matter, the British government wasn't really interested and the following item illustrates the lack of any great depth of thought that was being given to the subject !!!

In 1833 a factory act was being discussed by the Government, one clause of which would have provided for the education of factory children. _At the same time_, in the other House, the Lords were rejecting a clause which would have given authority to establish schools. This rejection was rather unfortunate because it meant that even if the factory act _had_ been passed by the Government the children would not have had any schools to go to !

In the same year, the Economists were not disinterested in their advocacy of education, but, when they discussed what children should be taught, their spokesman, John Ramsey McCullough, suggested that the children:- "Ought to be made acquainted with the duties enjoined by religion and morality and with the circumstances which occasion that gradation of ranks and the inequality of fortunes which usually exist." (*Such pomposity* !)

The Economists argued that by giving a child a proper training he would be able to earn a good living when he grew up; relieving the ratepayer in the process.

- But the economists were talking about industrial training, not schools; they did not advocate education for its value to a child but solely to fit the child to serve society.

The Rev Thomas Whately, when speaking of "judicious education", meant, as he went on to explain, "Religious education", and by religious education he meant instruction in the precepts of the Church of England.

The Evangelicals were fervent supporters of "free" schools, but to almost all of them 'education' only meant instruction in the scriptures in accord with their beliefs.

The British Government did not want to get involved with the thorny and possibly expensive problem of whether or not to provide elementary education for all children and they had good reason, because, despite Governmental apathy, schools <u>were</u> beginning to appear, and, by the mid 18th century a number of differing educational systems had emerged in England such as Robert Raikes Sunday Schools, Hannah More's schools for the children of the poor in the West Country, the establishments of Joseph Lancaster and Andrew Bell and a number of church schools.

It was in 1801, that Joseph Lancaster founded the system named after him of undenominational schools in urban districts. Much of the teaching in his schools was done by older children acting as monitors and it was from this start that there emerged, in 1808, the Lancastrian Society which continued his work. (Joseph emigrated to America in 1818) Later, these schools were maintained by the British and Foreign Schools Society which tended to help in the setting up of schools of a non-conformist character.

In 1811 the National Society began the institution of conformist Church Schools in every parish in England, control being in the hands of the clergy. At this time the Society's full name emphasised it's intentions: -

"The National Society for Promoting the Education of the Poor in the Principles of the Church of England."

Neither the British and Foreign or the National Society schools had much of an organised education system to start with, (especially when compared with our own, nowadays) but their pupils did have a very real familiarity with the Bible and we are told that this tended to raise their imaginations above any vulgarity of mind. - I wonder ? !

"National" schools came into their own pre-eminent sphere largely because the British Parliament, whilst not wishing to get involved in the matter of providing education, did, eventually, accept the need to provide government funding with which to help provide basic schools for the elementary education of all children. This actually happened in 1833; the sole intention of the government being to provide assistance toward the initial financing of elementary schools, nothing more.

Members of the House voted £20,000 to assist in the establishment of elementary schools but, at the same time, the government made it clear that it did <u>not</u> want to get involved in the arguments which were bound to ensue when it came to sorting out the ticklish problem of deciding where and to whom the money should be paid out.

What the government did do, in effect, was to share the whole sum between the National Society and the British and Foreign Society with an instruction to distribute the grants in as fair a manner as possible.

It must be mentioned that both societies <u>did</u> use the money carefully and wisely. Normally, they would only give grant aid toward the construction of a school when local subscriptions toward the cost of a new school were at least half the sum of the grant likely to be made by the society.

*   *   *

On the Isle of Man, the next step in the general development of education was the gradual introduction of "Lancaster" and "National" schools. Most of these were designed as replacements for the old, life expired petty schools, some of which were very old indeed and/or decrepit.

When, for example, we read of the "National School" in Ramsey or Douglas or Dhoor, we must remember that, so far as the Isle of Man was concerned, the term 'National' had nothing to do with the status of the school relative to the Island's own identity, it was the generic name given to all of the Manx schools which came to be opened with the backing and financial assistance of the Church of England through the "National Society".

By the time that plans were started for the building of National Schools on the Isle of Man, the intentions of the National Society were widely known and clearly stated, they were as follows:-

"That this Society receives schools into union with itself on condition that the children are instructed in the principles of the Church of England, subject to the superintendence of the parochial clergyman, and that they attend the Established Church. The managers of such schools have to report annually to the Society with reference to the state and progress of their schools."

Dhoon School

Dhoon School - Opened 1876. Drawn January 1985 with one mobile classroom and before enclosed toilet facilities were provided

The stated requirement that "they *(the children)* attend the Established Church", was, of course, far removed from Bishop Barrow's idea of education for all irrespective of background and in Britain as a whole, the stated intentions of the National Society came to be viewed as forms of discrimination, they were to become a major plank in the campaigns which were eventually fought for the provision of undenominational schools, schools which would accept all children and would not require them to be committed to any one particular creed.

In the meantime, however, there was no other responsible body able or willing to undertake the enormous task of providing schools in every parish.

(As a matter of interest; during 1843, a Factory Bill making its way through the Houses of Parliament and containing proposals for the education of factory children between the ages of 8 and 13 in England, was opposed for being far too church controlled.)

At this point it is interesting to remember that Bishop William Ward (1827-38) was another man with a deep interest in the education of the Manx. He is chiefly remembered for the way in which he raised money in England for the erection of churches on the Island, he also collected £2,000 toward the foundation of King William's College, but, so far as this book is concerned, he should be remembered for the three combined church/school establishments he instigated at Baldwin, Dalby and Sulby. These villages were in quite remote rural areas and each of the buildings was constructed in such a way that the larger school portion was divisible from the rest of the church by sliding doors, only the sanctuary being consecrated. Bishop Ward had obtained £1,000 from the Government with which to build schools and it was his own idea to annexe a Chapel with sliding doors in this particular way.   [2]

An interesting thought here is that by so creating combined church and school premises, the Bishop was once again bringing these particular schools firmly under the control of the church, even though the clergy were no longer directly involved with the actual teaching therein.

If his successors had continued in this vein one wonders what the eventual outcome might have been with regard to secular education, especially as the Methodists and Roman Catholics were beginning to gain stronger voices in Island affairs ? There is a particular relevance when one considers that church schools were not always properly or ably controlled.

The National Society did not make onerous regulations about standards for building, inspection, or efficiency of instruction, save that the donating Society would undertake maintenance of the buildings, - in itself a huge step forward.

Among the earlier recipients of moneys on the Isle of Man from the National Society the highest grant was £150 for Dalby, then £100 for Sulby. Port St. Mary received £75 toward its school of 1837, Grenaby in Malew received £50, Laxey Glen £38 and Dhoon £44.

Mostly, the National Schools were built to a standard which was considered good for the time, but it should be remembered that when these new schools were proposed to be built, neither the National Society or the C of E provided the schools solely from the goodness of their hearts. More often than not the largest part of the initial funding for these schools came from local subscriptions, donations and other voluntary sources; in addition, no less than twenty-nine Manx schools received direct Imperial Parliamentary grants for building, enlargement, improvement, or fixtures during the years from 1832 to 1868, this was in addition to the grants allowed by the National Society.

*   *   *

The Inspector of Schools, Rev H.Moseley, in his report of 1847 stated that there were 52 elementary schools on the Isle of Man teaching 2752 scholars - one eighteenth part of the whole population.
In 31 of the schools reported upon, boys and girls were taught together by the same teacher who, in 23 cases, was a master and in the remainder a mistress.
The Inspector also found that the supply of slates and books was inadequate. In many schools the Holy Scriptures were had recourse to for the mechanical instruction of the children in reading because of the absence of books for secular instruction.   [M20]

By an Act dated 10/4/1851, measures became possible by which better provision could be made for Parochial and other schools, and for making further regulations for the better government of the Parochial schools and other schools in the Isle of Man.
By adopting the Act, a Parish could levy a rate to provide a commodious schoolhouse, a dwelling house for the Master, together with a garden, for the payment of a salary to the Teacher, to provide books and other apparatus for teaching, including other furniture for the schoolhouse - and for providing a retiring allowance for old and disabled teachers.
Previously it had been common law or tradition for a Parish to maintain just one school within the Parish. The new Act made it possible for a Parish to maintain several schools if it so wished.   [14]

Eventually, the Manx Government as 'Treasury Agents' for the British Government also became involved in the allocation of these grants of monies; sometimes they paid up to as much as half the construction costs.

The only religious denominations to build and control schools in the Isle of Man other than the Church of England were, the Roman Catholic, Wesleyan, Primitive Methodist and Methodist Churches, most of whom started their first schools around the 1830s.

The remaining denominations, whilst often highly critical of the performance of different schools, never made a start on the provision of schools of their own: it needs to be mentioned, however, that the persecuted Quakers did have a small school in Ramsey for a very short space of time during 1681.

*   *   *

Criticism of the performance of a local school board or authority was sometimes justified when that authority did not give much attention to its responsibilities and a good example of a seemingly grudging acceptance of the responsibility for education within its Parish was Lezayre, where the Vicar and Churchwardens did the least they possibly could to provide and maintain adequate or proper school premises.

Part of the sorry story is told in "The Annals of Kirk Christ, Lezayre", by R.D.Kermode. Procrastination is the best that can be said of their actions.

*   *   *

It was in 1872 that the Manx Government started to take some direct responsibility for education and, in June of that year, Tynwald chose the first five members of the Board of Education. There was critical comment in the same year when the Isle of Man schools received Imperial Grants amounting to £2200, money that was not from insular revenue.

There was a considerable difference between the way in which the Manx Government provided funding for schools and the system used in England. Under the Manx system the Treasury bore half the cost of new buildings whereas, in England, at this time, the whole sum was by then being borne by rates and local taxes.

In a report published about this time (the 1870's) the following schools all had Vicars who were either Trustees or who were responsible for the superintendence of religious instruction within their school :-

District	SCHOOLS	District	SCHOOLS
Patrick	Parish School	Braddan	New Parish School
	St. James, Dalby		Cronkbourne
	Foxdale		Baldwin
	New Parish School (?)		Oakhill
Lezayre	Lezayre	Malew	Castletown Girls.
	Sulby		Taubman Boys School
	Sulby Treen		Arbory Parish School
Maughold	New School	Rushen	Port St. Mary
	Dhoon Bridge	Girls School at Ballqueenes	
Lonan	New Parish School		
	Laxey Glen		
	Laxey Elementary	Conchan	Parish School

[M12l]

In the same report, the undenominational schools were recorded as being :-
Ballaugh Village Deeme (?) School founded 1797
Athol Street, Douglas. (Joseph Lancaster)
Dissenters:-
Wesleyan at Peel and Douglas.
Roman Catholic School   [M12n]

*   *   *

Once the Elementary Education Act of 1872 was passed, school inspections were carried out and it soon became apparent that many of the existing buildings were sub-standard. The various reports led to a surge of school building with the result that by 1881 there were :-

8 new schools - Ballaugh Board School. Maughold, the Dhoon.
Conchan Board. Braddan (East Baldwin). Lonan (South Cape).
Sulby. Lonan (Ballagawne). Rushen (Port St. Mary)

5 rebuilt - Rushen Parish (Girls). Cronk-y-Voddy. Bride.
Lezayre and Marown.

3 enlarged   - Michael Parish Church School. Andreas, and
Arbory District School.

The new Manx Board of Education took its remit very seriously indeed and was soon preparing further new plans.

PROGRESS

"When one dares not say what one thinks, one ends by not thinking what one says."
(Zeno)

Chapter four

The Ultimate ?

It was the Manx Board of Education which prepared plans for the first non-denominational Board School on the Isle of Man. It was to be situate in Douglas and it was a move bound to lead to considerable controversy.

The result was the Wellington Board School. Created at moderate cost within a suitably converted building, the school had sufficient capacity for 200 scholars and opened in 1873.

As could have been expected, there were protesters; they were led by churchmen, and the protests were allegedly due to the direct provision of a school being a charge on rates and being under the control of an independent Board.

One particular clergyman who had manoeuvred his way on to the leadership of the school committee concerned was the Rev Thomas Hobson, he took a a militant stand and, largely because of a resultant hostile publicity, it was not long before many parents removed their children from Wellington into other schools.

Toward the end of a bitter campaign there were just 60 pupils left in the Board School. The determination with which the church organisations, both Wesleyan and Established, tried to ward off the Board Schools can be judged by their action in offering to pay the fees of any remaining child in Wellington whose parents arranged a transfer of their child to one or other of the church controlled schools.

Fortunately, the School Board stuck to their guns; the Wellington Board School remained open and the Education Board soon prepared plans for a brand new purpose designed Board School which, in due course, became the Bucks Road School.

It is not surprising that those responsible for church controlled schools should feel a little aggrieved, they had, after all, been almost the sole providers of elementary education for a very long time and, from the mid 1800s, they had even received small grants from the Government which enabled them to provide a widespread network of Voluntary Schools. These schools seemed to be so well established that their managers viewed them as being a permanent part of the education system.

But such a situation did not seem right to Dissenters.

In fact, the Voluntary Schools were so well established, the Education Board could not possibly have closed them down all at once. To have attempted to do so would have created a resulting vacuum which would have been disastrous.

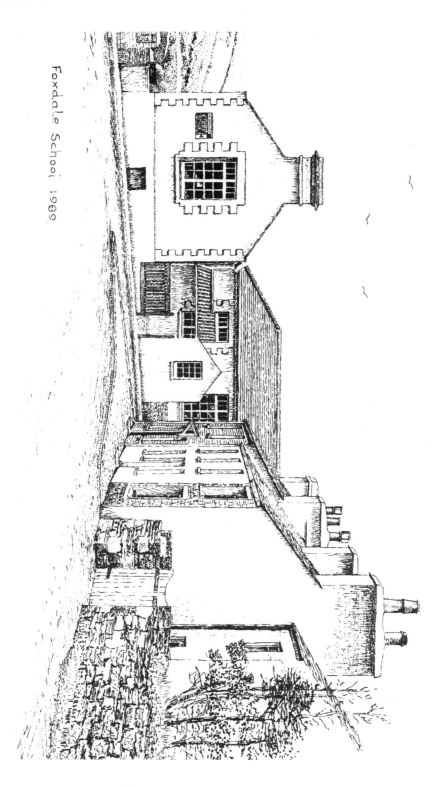

Foxdale School 1989

Foxdale School - Opened 1909. Drawn September 1989, as seen two years before closure.

A compromise was arrived at in 1870 by which church teaching was allowed to continue in all the Voluntary Schools, but it was made clear that the terms of the Act under which the new Board Schools were to be provided would prohibit the use in religious teaching, of catechism or formulary distinctive of any denomination.

This was a sensible compromise which allowed the Island to continue with an existing range of schools which did provide primary education. The schools could remain in use, an action which allowed the School Board to go ahead with the planning for new, improved and larger non-denomination schools which would eventually replace most of the National schools..

*   *   *

The New School Boards probably found that voluntary attendance at their schools continued to be a stumbling block. It was a matter of history repeating itself, the relative Act concerning compulsory attendance by children needed enforcement.

In 1878, the Manx Government passed an Act which made it clear that five, not seven, was the minimum age for school. The Act also made it an offence to employ a child under the age of ten; above that age, a child could only be employed if he or she had obtained his or her school leaving certificate.

On August 24th 1884, the Board of Education appointed Officers to enforce attendance at schools. These Officers were also required to implement the law concerning the employment of children.

The Attendance Officers' Districts were designated as :-

District No 1. Patrick. German. Peel. Michael and Ballaugh.
    "   No 2. Jurby. Andreas. Bride. Lezayre and Ramsey.
    "   No 3. Maughold and Lonan.
    "   No 4. Douglas and Conchan.
    "   No 5. Braddan and Marown.
    "   No 6. Santon. Malew. Castletown. Arbory.

District No 4 proved to be unwieldy and, in April 1896, a new District was created for Douglas alone.

A further Act, in 1888, made it clear that no employment was permitted during school hours for children under 13, whilst, in 1889, an Act provided that parents who falsified ages of children so that they could obtain work, could be fined.

By 1900, the Attendance Officers' districts had settled down as follows :-

District No 1.Patrick, German, Michael, Ballaugh, Peel.
    "   No 2. Jurby, Andreas, Bride, Lezayre.
    "   No 3. Maughold, Lonan.
    "   No 4. Douglas.
    "   No 5. Marown, Conchan, Braddan.
    "   No 6. Santon, Malew, Arbory, Rushen, Castletown.
    "   No 7. Ramsey.

It was on August 24th 1891, that the Lieutenant Governor, Sir J.W.Ridgeway, gave notice that it was his intention to extend free education to the Island.

Strangely enough this pronouncement did not receive the universal acclamation one would have expected. Malew School Committee, for example, was one of a few who actually objected and they were most vehement in their objections. Nevertheless, "Free" education returned to the Island in 1892, a wonderful achievement. Douglas School Committee being one of the first to take immediate advantage of the Act.   [M12r]

During 1893, the age of compulsory attendance was raised to 14 (subject to a few exceptions) and a few years later, in 1899, Manx schools became subject to a central school board known as the "Council of Education".

Every town and village was at once constituted a School District under a School Board and, by 1914, the School Boards were named as being :- Andreas. Arbory. Ballaugh. Braddan. Bride. Castletown. Douglas. German. Jurby. Lezayre. Lonan. Malew. Marown. Maughold. Michael. Onchan. Patrick. Peel. Rushen and Santon.

Douglas, which previously had a School Committee for several years, became a School Board in 1896.

Within a few years centralised control of elementary schools on the Island had proved most beneficial but there was one aspect of education on which the School Boards had a lot of leeway to make up and this was in the provision of Secondary Schools.

It was a sad fact that, no matter how great their ability, once the majority of Manx children had completed their elementary education there was no where further they could go, unless of course their parents were able to pay for private education elsewhere. The considerable fees required for such further private education usually prevented that happening.

From one observer's point of view it seemed as if there was a complete lack of interest in the provision of higher education both on the part of the Government and the Education Departments of the day. The observer was Samuel Norris, who, in 1903, when suggesting that there was a greater need for secondary education on the Island, noted that the amount contributed toward education on the Isle of Man was only 5/6d per head as against 8/6d in the UK.

Unfortunately, there was no likelihood of any major change being made under the Lt Governor of the time; he was Lord Raglan, Governor from 1902 to 1919, a man who believed in retaining the Status Quo. (*and to whom the Annual Reports of the Board of Education were presented....!*)   [M24] [16]

Interestingly, as from 1904, just one year after Mr Norris's comment, the direct comparison of costs between the schools of the Isle of Man and the rest of the United Kingdom, which had been a long standing item within the official Annual Reports of the Manx Council of Education, was dropped. This action suggests that pressure was brought to bear. The comparison has never re-appeared in the Annual Reports.

In truth, the Education Authority, even if they had wished to provide Secondary Schools, could not do much about it at that particular time because in 1900, the Law Courts had decided that ratepayers money could not be spent on any form of Secondary or Higher Education !

It was solely due to the actions of a constructive statesman that this divisive decision was abolished. He was Arthur James Balfour, who brought in the Education Act of 1902; even though it was fiercely attacked at the time, this act was to remain the basis of the English Educational system. A most important section gave power to Elected Councils and certain large Boroughs to provide for Education, both Primary and Secondary.

In the meantime the Manx Council for Education had done their best to overcome the problem without breaking the law in any way, by opening the first "Higher Education School" in Douglas during 1896. It was this school which eventually became the first Secondary School on the Island in 1904; the School was provided on an experimental basis within shared premises and, by 1910, there were 233 scholars on the roll. This became the Park Road Secondary School in 1919.   [B03]

Remembering those 233 'secondary' scholars on the roll in 1910, with numbers increasing in each successive year, the Council could hardly be accused of rushing to provide purpose built schools for Secondary Education following Balfour's Act, because the first practical steps taken by the Council of Education to provide purpose built Secondary Schools were not made until 1921, when the Council proposed conversion of Park Road School for the girls and a new school for boys at the Somerset Road site.

The Council of Education did, however, gradually add facilities for further education at various schools throughout the Island by the creation of Supplementary Classes and Evening Classes. During 1910, for example, there were nine schools in Douglas and five elsewhere taking part in the scheme.

The next step came during 1925/6 when Authority was given to provide Central School education for pupils up to the age of 16.

Raising of the school leaving age to fifteen was proposed in 1936 and came into operation during 1938.

In this particular instance the lengthy delay between proposal in 1936 and implementation was fortuitous because, by 1938, some of the new larger schools had been completed and were thus able to absorb the resulting expansion in pupil numbers.

Being able to absorb such an increase in the number of children attending and remaining at the schools might even have been put down to good planning but, in reality it was *just good fortune* because, around this time, the population of the Isle of Man was low. The reason being that by 1938 the number of people resident on the Isle of Man had not fully recovered from the severe fall in numbers experienced during the early 1930's.

Later, you will find seven chapters in which I have listed the names or locations of schools in alphabetical order; the listing is supplemented with fascinating and interesting detail.

I have not attempted to provide background information for every school because in some cases their progress or otherwise runs parallel to many others and repetition could make for tedious reading.

A few schools have been included within these chapters for which I have no background information whatsoever; sometimes this has been because I could not find anything about them in the time I had available but also because, confusingly, some of the school names are of a 'local' nature and I have not always been able to associate them with a particular building or location.

*   *   *

LEARNING DISABILITIES

Before closing this chapter I would like to mention that, although not part of the schools education system, the Island does take its role in helping those with learning disabilities very seriously. Small scale establishments have been provided throughout the Island, although most are in Douglas. These are carefully run places within which help is given, some are for the young but most are for adults.

It all comes back to something that one would have thought self-evident, namely, that education should be a preparation for a good life."
(R.F.Mackenzie)

*   *   *

Chapter five

Attendance and Lessons

This chapter precedes seven which outline the day to day working of teachers and children within several different rural schools on the Island, this is so that you can read about a few of the happenings, events, plans, successes and failures that occurred in schools throughout the Island before you start wading through the sentimental stuff !

The individual stories are not intended to be read as any sort of praise or criticism because, in their own way, I find most of them rather charming. *The items in Italics are my own comments.*

*   *   *

In the Manx Museum there is a battered school book once used by a Miss Ann Radcliffe's Uncle; unfortunately the original text has faded and is difficult to see; at a later date somebody even used the schoolbook as a notebook and wrote over the original text and the associated working out, which is a pity because the original entries were written in a beautifully formed copperplate.

The date of the book is 1848 and the format is one of "application", which is a <u>way</u> of describing the reason why something is to be done; this is followed by examples.

Within the book there is a great emphasis on bookkeeping but the period is beautifully illustrated by the content of some of the questions. One good example is this:- " A captain and 160 sailors took a prize worth £1360, of which the captain had one fifth of the whole and the rest was equally divided among the sailors. What was each man's share ?"   [M12a]

*   *   *

LOG BOOK INTERPRETATION

School log books were required by a new code of 1871. Where these have been preserved they are particularly useful for research purposes because the Principal Teacher was required to enter detail every week specifying progress of the school and teachers, together with dates of commencement of duty, cautions, illness, withdrawals (or resignations) etc....

The log book needed to be available for perusal by the School Inspectors and, where the books were completed in accord with the code, the information is very good —- but some teachers gave rather skimpy reports and oftentimes the information contained within has to be surmised rather than interpreted.

Let's be generous, in those cases where the entries in the log books were below par it may be that the teachers were tired at the end of the day ? *(If I had been in their shoes I would certainly have been mentally exhausted !)*   [M12g]

*   *   *

ALBERT ROAD ADVENTURES
(Excerpts from the Albert Road Infant School Log Book)

On Sept. 7th 1908, the Albert Road Infant School, Ramsey, re-opened after the summer holiday. Out of 145 children on the register there was an attendance of only 109.

Then, on Sept. 18th, there was a half holiday for the Oddfellows Treat,
Then yet another holiday !
    Sept. 25th.   Closed for one day for the races.
    Oct. 2nd   Half holiday - (Blackberry Holiday)
It wasn't all holidays however because, sadly, on Oct. 9th, a scholar died. This was W.Marnes.
On December 11th, the teacher was reporting a great number away because of colds and whooping cough.
On February 9th 1909, the school had 22 cases of measles. The Medical Officer then closed the school until March 1st.

Back to more holidays !
    May 14th.   Half holiday because one of the boys in the senior department
                        won a scholarship to Douglas Grammar School.
    May 21st.   Half holiday for Andreas sports.
    May 28th.   Holiday for Empire Day on Monday, followed on Thursday by
                        a holiday for the May Procession.
    Jun 26th.   Half holiday for St. Paul's treat.
    Jul 2nd.   Half holiday for the Mission School Treat.
    Jul 9th.   Tynwald Day Holiday.

There were 4 teachers on the staff and their scheme of lessons included :-
For the 1st and 2nd classes:-
                        Animals and birds. Nature studies. Plant life.
                        Common objects. Drawing.
                        Reading. Writing. Numbers. Repetition. Stories.

Albert Road
School, Ramsey

Albert Road School, Rasey. - Built on the outskirts of Ramsey in 1905 but now surrounded and bounded on two sides by busy roads. Drawn October 1995.

For the kindergarten:-

>Clay Modelling. Brushwork. Paper folding.
>Building bricks. Stick laying.

For the Babies:-

>Conversational lessons. Drawing in sand. Wool sorting.
>Bead threading.
>Reading - letters illustrated by drawings on the blackboard,
>easy sentences.
>Writing - small letters in sand.
>Numbers - to recognise numbers and figures.
>Repetition - nursery rhymes.

On Jan 28th 1910, only ten children went to the school because of heavy snow and the cold, yet the average for the week wasn't bad at 119.4 or 77.82 % of those on the register.

By May 13th there were 170 on the books with an average attendance of 136.8. Unfortunately the school finished 1910 on a bad note when, on Nov 22nd, the Medical Authority closed the school until December 5th because of mumps.

In 1911 the weather was awful and on May 2nd it was "Fearfully wet and stormy, only 67 attended and they were sent home." May 3rd was even worse with only 52 attending, they too were sent home.

The generosity of the school governors in granting all sorts of little holidays had continued during these years but, in 1914, **HM Inspector at last showed his displeasure and made a comment on the adverse effect of having excess holidays !**
[M15]

*   *   *

BALLASALLA BOTHERS.

On 25th July 1872, the Vicar and Wardens of Malew offered to transfer Ballasalla school to the new Malew School Committee. The transfer took place on March 14th 1873, but the following year, on Aug 27th 1874, **HM Inspector made a report following his examination of the school. In it, he was extremely critical of the poor attendance at Ballasalla, he also reported that :-**

"The offices for girls are in a disgusting condition quite unfit for service."

81 children had been 'presented' for the Examination and the results were as follows :-

>Reading   70 marks
>Writing   64 "
>Arithmetic   72 "
>   Total 206 = 85%

[M12r]

(Not too bad really.)

There was a need to provide additional classrooms for Ballasalla school and Mr John Callister, joiner, adapted the adjacent Teacher's house for this purpose; his bill came to £48.

As from 1901 the attendance records showed a steady decline. In 1895 the figure stood at 150, 152 in 1896, 111 by 1910, 86 in 1914, 71 in 1919, 72 in 1924, only 59 in 1927, 51 in 1929, 45 in 1935 and 42 in 1938.

It was anticipated that the decline would continue and a proposal was made that the school be closed in 1939. There was considerable local opposition which was fuelled by memories of mistakes that had been made in 1927 when the infant schools at Port St. Mary and Port Erin had been closed without any provision being made for transportation of the infants, who, as a result, faced very long walks to and from the Rushen School to which they had been transferred.

Previous HM Inspectors' reports had given good reasons for the closing of Ballasalla school, such as on 13/7/1922, :-

" The school was built on a cramped site and the playgrounds are so small as to preclude the full use of the Physical Training manual. Heating of the rooms is very unsatisfactory, during winter months temperatures often fall below 40 degrees and never above 54 on several days. Both natural and artificial lighting seem   inadequate."

On 17/6/1930, a similar report stated :-

"No training available in woodwork or domestic subjects, no school garden, playgrounds too small." and, on 3/6/38, :- "Problem of satisfactory grading not yet adequately solved."

Strong local opposition caused the school to remain open but you cannot help but wonder whether the parents had done the right thing because a visiting Elementary School Committee made the following comment on the 8th of July 1938, :-

" There is no doubt that Ballasalla is the worst conditioned school in the Isle of Man."

The Headmaster at the time of the report was Mr W.E.Stevenson and the certificated assistant was Miss Maddrell. Their work in running the school under such poor conditions was praised within the report.

The proposal to close the school led to a public enquiry even though evidence presented at a previous Council Enquiry on March 1st 1939, was such that closure seemed to be the only option.

In the report there were remarks which drew attention to some of the defects of the school such as :-

" Close proximity to other buildings, buildings so close that sunlight never penetrated; during many months artificial lighting was necessary throughout the day."

"Dark and depressing. Inadequate facilities for play or physical training owing to confined nature of the playground - in fact the majority of children played in the road."

If the proposal had been followed through at that time the intention was that most of the children were to be transferred to Castletown's Victoria Road School which would have been able to accommodate them with ease; special arrangements were going to be made for most of the children to travel to and from their new school by bus or train depending on where they lived. It was considered that the overall travelling time would be very little different to what the children had been used to.

In this particular case the threat of a forthcoming war became a blessing in disguise because the school did not close, the matter being deferred because of wartime conditions.

*   *   *

BALLAMODHA BEGINS

This school opened in May 1887, and in September 1888, HM Inspector made his first report in which he praised the teacher.

His next report, on July 26th 1889, must have horrified Malew Commissioners because he criticised their nearly new school by saying that cupboards and pictures were still needed, desks too, but he appreciated that the desks could wait until a new classroom was built !

(Maybe the Inspector had made a mistake ? One cannot help but wonder whether the Inspector had got his notes muddled up because a new school would hardly need an additional classroom within two years of opening ? There was no mention of such a shortcoming in subsequent HMI reports.)

The Inspector also complained about the school fire which was smoking within the class room and the poor ventilation in general.

The Inspector had every reason to be pleased with the teacher because, for a new school, the exam results were good. [M12r]

Average attendance.   Boys 19.1. Girls 27.3.
Average for grant 46.
Grants on average attendance :-

1	Fixed grant	4s 6d
2	Merit	2s 0d
4	Singing by ear	6d
5	Elementary subject	7s 10d
6	English	2s 0d
	total	16s 10d X 46
	Needlework grant	6s 9d

Presented for examination   45
Passes in reading   42
Passes in writing   43
Passes in arithmetic   42
                total   127 = 94.07%.

*   *   *

BARRAGARROW BEATEN

The Wesleyan School at Barragarrow, despite having been particularly successful in its early career was, by the 1870s, in a rather run down condition.

A newly appointed School Board had been made responsible for both Michael National School and Barragarrow and with this latter School they probably found that they had a problem on their hands. The Board took the Wesleyan School over in 1872 and let it continue in operation whilst they decided what to do.

Their mind was probably made up for them when, on October 24th 1874, the School Inspector had this to say :-

"The school is held in a wretched building quite unworthy in itself and provided with only one set of offices, quite improvided with desks, apparatus or furniture."

"It is Unfair to judge the Teacher who has been in charge such a short time. The children read fairly well and write and spell fairly but they are very backward in arithmetic. Very good in discipline and from what I hear of their previous work they reflect no small credit on Miss Wicksey."

In fact, Miss Agnes Wicksey was a teacher who had taken over the school on Tuesday November 11th 1873. She seems to have been shocked by what she found; there were no registers, no log book, no easel, not enough books, and she even had to tell the Commissioners to get a mat, fenders, dusters, towels and provide a clock.

A log book was provided for the school and it is from the few pages she completed that we can read the sorry story.

When she first went there she found that no one was appointed to clean the school or attend to the fires, instead these tasks were being done in a disorderly manner by the children at the opening of the school.

Miss Wicksey managed to get the Commissioners to employ a village girl, Anne Davis, to do those jobs.

On December 1st, a clock was supplied - but it didn't work ! After a little pestering it was cleaned and repaired; by Dec 26th the clock worked.

Miss Wicksey was pleased to note that since her appointment the number of pupils was slowly but steadily increasing, but, sadly, on Monday, 23rd February 1874, she had to report that one of the girls who had joined the school just a few weeks previously, a Hester Cameron (?), who had been absent the previous week collecting for the missionaries, had been out in severe weather. She caught a cold, and died on the Monday.

On the Thursday Miss Wicksey noted that several children were missing from class attending Hesters' funeral.

By early spring there seems to have been some sort of epidemic in the area because from March to July, all the children were suffering from coughs and sore throats, Miss Wicksey had to close the school for a couple of days because she, too, was badly affected; when she returned, she was still far from well.

The key to the school door broke in the lock on June 29th; this was because the lock itself was broken, it took until August 12th for the lock to be replaced !

Miss Wicksey left the school on August 14th. Her frustration came through in the carefully restrained comments she made as her last entries in the log book. They made me wonder what the Inspector must have thought, later, when he read her reports during his October visit ?

The new log book which Miss Wicksey had maintained so well and so conscientiously was neglected by those who followed her, only one astonishingly brief entry by an unnamed teacher in 1875; after Miss Wicksey's resignation the log book was certainly not maintained in a proper manner.

Within a couple of years Barragarrow school was closed.   [M12p]

*   *   *

BLUSHING BRIDE

The following excerpts are from the Log Book of Bride Parochial School which covers the twenty five years from 1873 to 1898. Previous to 1873 the school had been closed for an unspecified length of time.

The school re-opened with 35 pupils on Sept 24th 1873; by the second week the number had risen to 45 and :-
"Several new books, slates, pencils and pens were sold to the pupils from a supply provided by the Committee on the 25th."

By October there were 50 pupils, but with the school having been closed for a considerable period few were able to read, write, work simple addition, or subtract, many were entirely ignorant of their letters or figures and as a consequence organisation was rapidly affected.

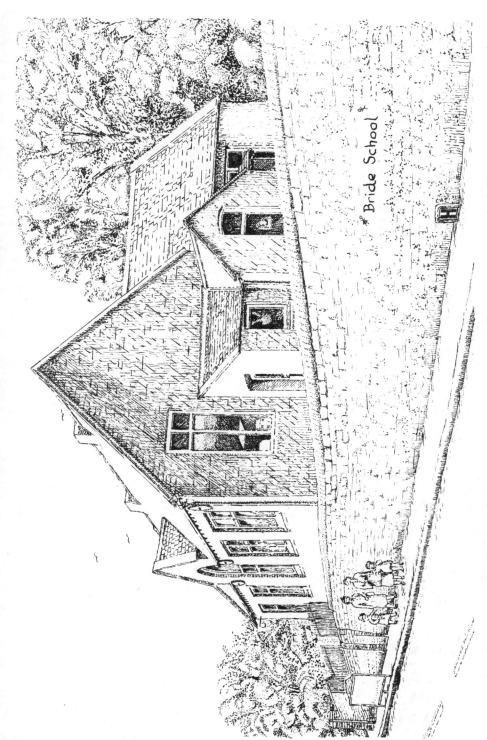

Bride School. - Opened 1876. Drawn October 1995 - before the installation of UPVC windows

1874
   Jan.(?)   77 on register, 40 present.
   Mar 23rd.   The fair of Ramsey taking place - very few present.
1875
   Jan. Inspector's report :-
"Attendance 23 boys 10 girls very small. The School Committee to be reminded that the Elementary School Act of 1872 required them to compel attendance between the ages of 7 and 13."
"A new school is urgently needed, present building totally unfit for purpose."

The school board must have taken the Inspector's recommendation very seriously because just one year later :-

1876
   Jan . Commenced duties in a temporary room in the Parish.
   May 15th 1876.Commenced duties in <u>new</u> school.
From then on the log contains almost continuous reference to poor attendance due to the agricultural requirements of the Parish, the children being required for work such as weeding, potato planting, threshing, potato picking, even ploughing matches.

   June 1878.   108 on register but average attendance only 58.
       1893. 108   "   "   "   " "   "   "   " 69.
   Jan 4th 1898. 38 present am, 44 pm.

                    *   *   *

Blushing Bride II.
EXCERPTS FROM THE 1898-1924 BRIDE LOG BOOK

This log book is as different as chalk from cheese to the previous one. The detail within its covers is remarkable and the few examples that follow have been chosen as tasters.
1898
At the front of the book there is a superb resume of the school syllabus for a year, the subjects were :-
   English - Reading, writing, copy writing, dictation, grammar.
   History. Geography. Map drawing. Arithmetic. Mental arithmetic.
   Drawing. Brushwork. Singing. Needlework.

   In addition, for the upper division, there was :-
   Reading, Recitation, Copy writing, Dictation and Composition.

   For Infants the subjects were :-
   Mat weaving, paper folding, paper cutting, drawing, singing, recitation, story lessons, reading, writing and numbers, also object lessons such as The Cat, The Sheep, The Hedgehog, The Frog, etc.

1901

The school Inspector seemed to be pleased :-

"The tone of this school is excellent, examination results show a great improvement over last year. Paperwork is particularly neat and well written. The least successful subject is mental arithmetic."

1902

Roll 75.

1911

January. School closed by the medical officer for one month due to a severe outbreak of mumps in the school and Parish.   [MM12h]

*   *   *

JUST JURBY

These items are from a minute book - <u>not</u> a school log book - relating to the Jurby School Committee's meetings from 1861 to 1879, it contains much of interest, as the following extracts show:-

"Feb 14th 1861. Jurby School Committee included W.Farrant. John Corlett. C.D.Caine. John Callister. The Chairman was the Vicar (Henry Hardy). On this day the Committee examined plans prepared by Mr J.H.Christian of London for a schoolhouse and a master's house."   (*Which they approved and adopted.)*

By May 1st, a Robert Kneale had joined the committee, on which date they accepted a grant in aid from the Council on Education of £228.06.00. Tenders were to be invited.

The accepted tender for the new school was £523, from W.Corlett of Ramsey.

On July 29th 1861, the Committee were making enquiries concerning the legality of selling The Old Parish School House and the land belonging thereunto, but it seems as if they settled on renting the property out because amounts arising as rent from the Old Schoolhouse and premises were soon being made as payments toward the schoolmaster's salary.

The School was renamed 'Jurby New Parochial School' on February 26th.1862.

At a meeting on Sept. 25th 1863, the committee drew up a schedule of school fees which were to be :-

Weekly payments :-	Children under 10	Over 10
Labourers and Journeymen:	1d	2d
Occupiers of 10 to 60 acres and over and }	2d	3d
proprietors of 5 to 20 acres }		
Others	4d	6d

A special Vestry meeting on Apr 21st 1865, called for a Parish Assessment sufficient to pay the architect his demands. As the School had been open for three years the architect must have been a very patient man !

The schedule of school fees agreed in 1863 probably proved to be unworkable, or uncollectable, because on August 21st 1867, they were revised to the more normal 'charging by standard' :-

Standard I	1d
Standard II	2d
Standard III	3d
Standards IV-VI	4d

The master was required to strictly enforce payments which were to be made weekly in advance.

Oct. 14th 1867. Proposals were put forward for a 'night school' which was to be held 3 times a week for 2 hours each time - fee for those attending, 2d a week.

May 11th 1868. Concern was expressed regarding the condition of the school well and, on June 1st, Mr W.T.Kaighin, of Ramsey, a plumber, was asked to do some work to the lead piping to the school pump.

On July 15th 1868, charges of drunkenness were made against the schoolmaster, John Wallace. The Lord Bishop approved a sentence of deposition and he was dismissed by July 30th.

An Assessment at the rate of 2/6d was requested at the Easter Vestry meeting in 1869, this was required so as to pay for hedging and enclosing a portion of the school grounds; by October this had risen to 4/- per Quarterland, with Mills, Intacks and Cottages in proportion. The Church Wardens were asked to collect these sums, but one of them, Mr David Kneale, refused. This refusal resulted in the Sumner of Jurby being required to give notice that the Vicar would :-

'Present him at the next Chapter Court to be held in Ramsey'.

Yet another Assessment was requested on Aug 22nd 1870, this time for 6/-. It was needed to cover the cost of cementing the walls of the master's residence following complaints about damp in the walls.

During these early years a number of masters came and went but we do know that on Dec 18th 1874, the current Master was due to receive £28 per annum, plus two thirds of the Government Grant, as well as the children's pence.

Apparently John Wallace (the sacked schoolmaster) had obtained a post at Ballaugh School after being sacked from Jurby. He was re-appointed to Jurby on April 14th 1875. Unfortunately there would seem to have been a dispute with the Vicar, Henry Hardy, because Mr Wallace smartly resigned on April 22nd.

This dispute and the resultant resignation caused all members of the committee of the Jurby Parochial School other than the Chairman to resign completely from school affairs.

By October 8th, a new Vicar had appeared, Rev F.J. Moore, but it would seem that he, too, was quickly at loggerheads with the new committee because at every   meeting from 26/11/1875 to 4/10/1876, he "declined to vote".!

School fees were revised again on Nov 9th 1876. The fees were now to be paid monthly.

(Even though the rates were quoted as quarterly !).

Standard I	2/- per quarter
" II	3/- " "
" III	4/- " "
" IV	5/- " "
" V & VI	6/- " "

A short time later this was amended to include :-

Infants under seven, 1/- per quarter.

It would seem as though the school committee were far from happy with the way in which the Vicar chose to take religious instruction; he was frequently causing some disruption to the school curriculum. In an effort to overcome the problem they tried to tie him down a bit by clarifying their own understanding of his   position! :-

"15/11/1876. Religious instruction to be superintended and defined by the Vicar who is to have use of the school for the whole of Saturday and Sunday as well as from 8.30am to 9.00am every Tuesday and Friday. At no other time without consent of the Committee."

The Committee also minuted the following:-

"Any scholar may be withdrawn by his parent from receiving such religious instruction without forfeiting any other benefit of the school.". At this the Vicar protested and said that it was 'Ultra Vires'. From then on he refused to vote at meetings for a while. (again !)

The fees as revised on Nov 9th, requiring them to be paid monthly, must have caused trouble at home because, on Dec 6th 1876, they reverted to being from 1d to 6d payable weekly in advance.

HM Inspector's report for 13/8/1877 included :-

"The children behaved well and acquitted themselves creditably. The scanty attendance is to be regretted, otherwise the school is doing well."

On the fourteenth of May 1878, the Parish Committee started proceedings to have the school transferred to the District Committee under the Elementary School Act of 1872; the reason being that they could not find funds for maintenance.

The Vicar by now was a Mr Wrigley, he was against the move and the Committee had to elect their own chairman !

By Sept 30th, Mr Wrigley had also moved on and Rev James Bellamy chaired the meetings from April 4th 1879, until transfer of the school to the District Committee was effected.   [M12c]

*   *   *

MARKING ST. MARK'S

When opened as a new school, St. Mark's had 88 pupils, the figure soon went up to 100 and in 1863 a new infant School was built.

Here is an excerpt from a report by HM Inspector twenty years later, on 30th July 1884, (By which time the number of scholars had fallen dramatically).

" The children are exceedingly well behaved and passed a good exam in the Elementary subjects and in English. Arithmetic in 3rd and 4th standard rather weak. Singing by ear very good, mental arithmetic moderate — the Master has charge of children in seven standards, plus a few infants, without any help."

Average attendance   Boys 17.8   Girls 15.4

Grants on average attendance :-

Fixed grant	4s 6d	
Merit	2s 0d	
Singing by ear	6d	
Elementary subject	7s 6d	
English	2s 0d	
33 boys and girls at 16s 6d		£27.04.6d
Needlework grant. 15 girls at 1/-		15.00d
	Total grant	£27.19.06

Presented for examination	34
Passes in reading	32
" " writing	32
" " arithmetic	28
Total 92 = 90.2%	

In 1894, there were 45 children and, in 1898, there would seem to have been an upset over religious education in this school as well, because the Chaplain formally asked Malew School Committee to record part of the original Trust Deed which included :-

" The Bible to be read daily by the children in the school, to be educated in the principles of the Christian Religion according to the doctrine and discipline of the United Churches of England and Ireland, such education to be under the direction of the Chaplain of St. Mark's Chapel."   [M12r]

*   *   *

MALEW SCHOOLBOARD MATTERS

The School Committee of Malew was formed on July 25th 1872. The importance the Committee attached to their appointment can be judged by the fact that one of their first actions was to have an engraved seal ordered.

After preliminary matters to do with organisation had been sorted out, their first real involvement with the schools came when the Vicar and Churchwardens of Malew offered to transfer to them the Ballasalla National School, to commence on March 14th 1873.

On May 28th 1873, the Committee decided that school fees for 22 poor children within their district should be paid for out of the school rate and that a copybook would be given gratis to these children.
The normal school fees were to be :-

Class I and II	Fourpence a week.
Class III	Threepence a week.
Class IV	Twopence halfpenny a week.
Infants	Twopence a week.

The following week they agreed to pay the fees for a further five children.

There were three ways in which money was raised to run schools; an amount from the school rates for the area, a grant which depended on results as determined by the Schools Inspector, and the childrens pence.

Her Majesty's Inspector in his report and schedule of grants for 1874 used the following figures for Ballasalla:-

On average attendance	72 @ 6/-	£21.12.0
On infants presented	16 @ 8/-	£ 6.08.0
Qualified for exams	45 pupils.	
Presented for exams	35.	
Passes in Reading	33	
Passes in Writing	18	
Passes in Arithmetic	19	
	Total 70 Passes @ 4/-	£14.00.0
	Total Grant	£42.00.0

(The poor results in writing & arithmetic adversely affect the grant)
In 1873, the Malew School Rate was set at a penny-halfpenny in the £ which brought in about £100, it remained at this rate for many years.

From HMI report for 1878 :-
"Owing to a smallpox epidemic opposite the school (which closed the school for four working weeks and two holiday weeks) an allowance has been made by the adoption of a lower standard than usual in judging spelling, arithmetic and grammar, a four week allowance has been granted."

Grenaby National School was transferred to the Malew Board during 1879, also St. Marks. St. Mark's average attendance was only 44.
The attendance figures at Ballasalla rose to over 105.7 in 1879, but there was a measles outbreak in Oct. and the figure fell dramatically to 63.3.
At Ballasalla in Sept. 1882, average attendance was only 77.2 against 151 on roll but by June 1883, the attendance officers had been out and about; their efforts caused the figures to improve and the average attendance became 101.5 against 141 on the roll.

*   *   *

PORT ST. MARY PLANNING

In July 1896, Mr M.J.Quilliam, the "Infant School" teacher, provided the following list of Object Lessons for use in the following year.
ANIMALS AND BIRDS.   Elephant. Camel. Cow. Sheep. Cat. Rabbit.
Sparrow. Blackbird.
PARTS OF BIRDS AND ANIMALS.
(1) Beaks of birds and their uses.
(2) Legs and feet.
(3) Paws and claws.
(4) Tongues and uses.
(5) Teeth and uses.
MISCELLANEOUS. Vegetables. Sugar. Tea. Coffee. Trees. Clay.
COMMON OBJECTS. Snow and rain. Leather. Wool. Matches.
Lighthouse. Farmyard. Sea-side.
MINERALS. Coal. Iron.
SEASONS. Spring. Summer. Autumn. Winter.

By contrast, Elizabeth Harris, the teacher who took over from Mr Quilliam in 1897, in presenting her list of Object Lessons for 1898 suggested the following :-

ANIMALS.   Horse. Sheep. Cow. Elephant. Duck. Cuckoo.
Codfish. Bee. Butterfly. Silkworm.
TRADES.   Fisherman. Policeman. Joiner. Blacksmith.
Shoemaker. Soldier.
VARIOUS.   Sponge. Coal. Milk. Bread. A Penny. Tea. Silk.
Ivory. Shells. Knives.

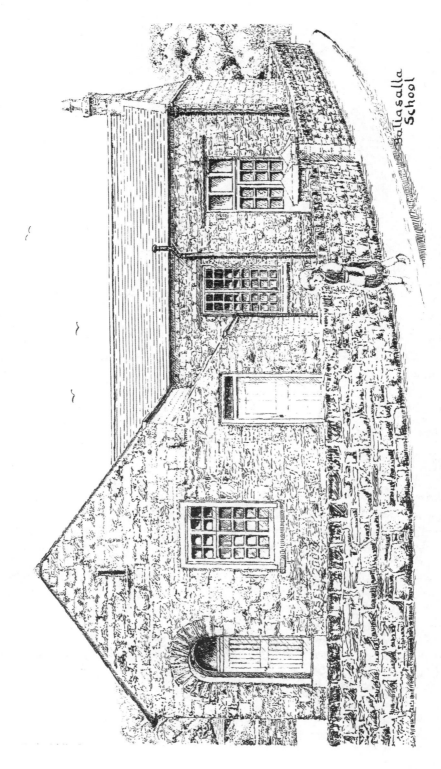

Elizabeth Ballasalla School - Opened 1845. Drawn June 2002

CONVERSATIONAL. The Seasons. A Post Office. A storm. The seashore. Farmyards. Wild Flowers. Rain and Snow. The Railway Station. Kindness to animals. Parts of the body.

*   *   *

ANALYSIS OF AN INFANT SCHOOL TIMETABLE
(Prepared by Miss Harris of Port St. Mary Infant School in 1903.)

Class I Subject	Minutes PW.	Class II Subject	Minutes PW
Writing	215	Writing	250
Reading	220	Reading	175
Arithmetic	145	Counting	120
Recitation	40	Recitation	45
Singing	50	Singing	50
Form & Colour	20	Form & Colour	40
Kindergarten	225	Kindergarten	225
Objects	60	Objects	85
Drill	40	Drill	45
Tables & Examples	135	Tables & Examples	125
Religious Inst	150	Religious Inst	150
Recreation	150	Recreation	150
Registers	50	Needle & Thimble Drill	25
TOTAL	1500	TOTAL	1500

*   *   *

WELL ROAD, Douglas. DAY SCHOOL SUBJECTS in 1841.

In this Wesleyan school the subjects taught in 1841 were :-
Reading, Writing, Arithmetic, English grammar, Knitting and Sewing.
The school hours being from 9am to Noon and 2pm to 5pm in summer or 4pm in winter.
There was a fortnight holiday during summer and a fortnight Christmas or winter holiday.
In 1843 there were 114 girls in the day school and 101 infants.

By 1854 the syllabus was much more ambitious with :-
Spelling, Reading, Writing, Arithmetic, Geography, Derivation of words, English Grammar, History, Book-Keeping, Mensuration, Algebra, Mechanics, Natural philosophy, Map drawing, Vocal music and Scripture lessons.

*   *   *

SCHOLARSHIPS

It was in the thirty-sixth (1907) Annual Report of the Council of Education that first mention was made of Scholarships.

The first fifteen were to King Williams College. Fourteen were open to Boys from Secondary Schools and one to a boy from an Elementary School. These were open for competition by pupils in the Isle of Man and were tenable as long as the holder remained at the College.

The Douglas School Board also awarded a number of Scholarships; these were for eight boys and eight girls tenable for two years but could be extended for a further two if conduct and progress had been satisfactory.

An additional eight Scholarships were set aside for children from the parishes of Lonan, Braddan, Santon, Marown and Conchan. Four were won by boys and four by girls.   [B03]

*   *   *

SCHOOL SAVINGS BANKS

Established during 1909/10 the first School Savings Banks were soon to be found working in the following Schools :-

Kewaigue. Rushen Parochial Boys. Peel, Derby Road. and in Douglas at Athol Street Boys, Demesne Road, Hanover Street, Murray's Road, Tynwald Street, St. Mary's and St. Thomas's.

During the first year the total sum deposited was nearly £700 and the number of depositors was 1,120.   [B03]

*   *   *

STAFF, STAFF ACTION AND SICKNESS - 1938

Here are a few of the log book entries prepared for the Derby Road Infant School, Peel, during 1938.

1938

Apr 1st.	Staff. E.Pollitt. E.A.Callister. A.C.Moughtin.
May 10th	Dr Soutar held a medical examination.
" 12th	School dentist called.
Jun 9th	School dentist called. Some of the children have gone to Belfast. Several are absent with chicken-pox.
Jun 21st	We have 31 cases of chicken-pox.
Sep 6th	Nurse Caine at school.
Sep 13th	Dr Soutar at school to weigh and measure the children.

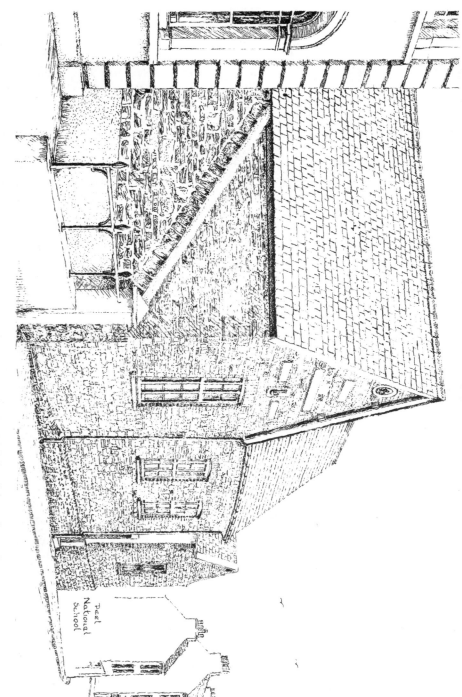

Peel National School - Was Known as Derby Road School for a long time.
Opened 1843, closed as a school in 1953. Drawn June 200.

Sep 23rd	Miss Pace - school dentist, inspected teeth of all the children present.
Sep 29th	Sent Jean Quirk home as she looked ill after having been knocked down by a bicycle on the way to school.
Sep 30th	Mr Lord called. I reported to him the damage done to the door of the 1st class at the Brownie meeting on Wednesday, also leakage in the roof.

Oct 3rd   Started giving children their milk today. Rain is pouring through a hole in the roof and the room is uninhabitable, the screen door has not been repaired and has to be left open, this causes a draught. We have moved into the 3rd class room. I have notified the attendance officer and the Director.

Oct 5th	Sent for Mr Jenkinson to see the damage caused by the storm to the roof and walls - men up today repairing roof.
Oct 7th	Dr Soutar held a medical examination today; most of the mothers came.
Oct 11th	Joiners are in class III today repairing the ceiling.
Nov 1st	Mr Blackie. HMI., called to inspect the school, he stayed from 10am to 3.45pm.
Nov 3rd	Miss Pollitt is absent this afternoon having received news of her brother's death.
Dec 8th	Miss Collister absent with severe chill.
Dec 13th	Miss Collister returned.
Dec 19th	Miss Collister absent and under doctor. Mr William Cubbon. MEA.,presented each child with an apple and a new penny.
Dec 21st	Childrens party this afternoon, tea was also given to the mothers.

The report made by HMI was as follows :-

Numbers have dropped to 72. Staff reduced to the Head Mistress, one certificated and one supplementary assistant. The three classes are for "under fives", "fives" and "sixes" respectively. There is a tendency to push the 4 year olds up into the 5's class, a measure that is not in the best interests of the children who should not make too early a start with formal work.

The premises are in many ways antiquated and it is understood that they will be replaced by a new school in due course.

A large room has been freed which is now used for PT when the weather is wet, for project work and as a sleeping room in the early afternoon for the babies.

The children receive a good start to their school life in the lowest class. They are sympathetically handled, well looked after and happily occupied.

In all essentials this is a good and happy school.

(Miss Collister passed away on March 1st 1939.)

ATTENDANCE AND LESSONS

"Let us reflect that the highest path is pointed out by
the pure ideal of those who look up to us, and who, if we
tread less loftily, may never look as high again."
(Hawthorne)

*   *   *

Chapter six

ANDREAS AND ST. JOHN'S
(two contrasting country schools.)

ANDREAS ANDANTE

In so far as the church was concerned, the Parish of Kirk Andreas was at one time
the richest parish by far, the reason for this lay in that the rectory, situated in rich
farmland, was entitled to the largest tithe assessment on the Isle of Man; because of
the importance and wealth of the Parish it was normal for the living to be held by
the Archdeacon.

It was probably the importance attached to Kirk Andreas that explains the early
commitment to education in the Parish as far back as about 1676.

When we take a look at the present church, we find a place which is frequently
haunted by visitors to the Island keen on viewing the early crosses on display
therein; for the rest of the time it is a lonely place, a church which is more often
empty than not during the week. The great days of Archdeacons and Curates have
faded into the mists; the congregation has dwindled to a faithful few, there are only
59 on the electoral roll and Andreas church is now in the care of a Rector who is also
responsible for Jurby.

Nowadays it is hard to imagine the tremendous busyness in the parish or to
appreciate the great importance of Kirk Andreas and its churchmen in the eyes of
the parish and local community during the 1800s.

For our purposes the story really starts in 1863, the year when a new Log Book
was started for Andreas School. The Master was Mr Arthur Davies but, as you will
see, the entries he made in the Log Book during the first few years suggest that the
local clergy held a firm grip on almost everything that went on in the school; not
only did the Curate or Vicar take religious instruction lessons two or three times a
week but the Venerable Archdeacon also popped in almost every week to see how
things were going on: In addition, there are many entries in the log book which give
the dates on which the school would troop off to the church for some service or the
other. One unstated justification for the school seemed to be its' ability to have
provided a handy choir for choral events !

This introduction has allowed me to give a general outline of the state of affairs which impacted on the school and for this reason I have omitted from the tale that follows most of the many, many entries, concerning the visitations of the clergy which continued for years on end, until a Master eventually rebelled; but more of that later !

My own observations are in italics throughout.

The first few pages of the 1863 Andreas Log Book are missing, this is the result of an act of vandalism, way back, for which the culprit was never discovered
Because of this damage we miss what might have been really interesting entries concerning the building itself and the early viewpoint of the Master, Mr Arthur Davies; instead, we have to open with critical remarks made by Her Majesty's Inspector.

1863. Apr 2nd Excerpt from HMI report:-
"In the general tone of the school there is wanting more of careful order, tidying up and exactness. The pupil teacher needs to be roused, no proper grappling with his work, rather a dull monotone."   *(Yes, we have all met that sort of teacher !)*

Apr 24th   Average attendance 76.7%.
              (Quite good for the time.)
May 1st   Many children absent - engaged in the fields.
(The Curate, Rev Edward William Kissack, was attending twice weekly to take the 1st class in religious studies, usually on Tuesdays and Fridays; the children probably loved him - he was only 26 years of age.)

Jun 11th   Cautioned the children not to play with timber of the house
              Mr Radcliffe is building near the school.
July 1st   The Lieutenant-Governor visited the school.
(This was Lord Loch, Henry Brougham Loch, who was Governor here until 1882, subsequently Governor of Victoria and then Governor of the Cape of Good Hope and High Commissioner of South Africa.)
Dec 11th   Holiday. Kirk Andreas annual fair.
1864.
Feb 16th   In an attempt to improve prompt attendance I have told the
              children that all latecomers are to have no play after this date.
              (Serious threat indeed !)
Mar 21st   Cautioned the children about going into the garden of
              Mrs Shimmin.
Apr 5th   Very wet day - very few scholars, only those from nearby.
Jun 8th   Many children weeding in the fields.

| Sep 19th | Small attendance due to scarlatina being prevalent. |

1865.

Jan 5th	Again, very small attendance due to scarlatina.
Feb 24th	Four boys played truant. Visited parents who promised to see after them !
Feb 25th	Three of the four boys came today and were publicly punished for their offence and promised not to run away again. Rev Kissack very conscientious with his scripture lessons.
Jun 6th	Great many away in the fields or fishing for sand-eels.

(There is a further gap in the log book at this point, pages 27 to 34 being missing.)

1866.

Mar 6th	Jane Kneen at home for the week, ill.
Mar 7th	A little boy hurt his eye badly in the playground, it was accidental.
Mar 22nd	One little girl, Elsie Radcliffe, suspended. She is at home waiting upon her Mother.
Apr 12th	Cautioned the children about playing ball in the yard on account of it flying over into the neighbouring gardens. My caution followed several complaints. (*Neighbours !*)
May 29th	One little girl sent home - there is supposed to be cattle plague at Ballaghane where her Father is working. Other parents have asked for her removal.
Jun 1st	One big boy in the 1st class is stopping at home, his Father having died suddenly.
Jun 14th	The cattle plague rumour proved false.

(A group known as the Isle of Man Cattle Plague Association had been formed on March 3rd 1866. Maybe this rumour had been caused by 'sympathetic' fears ?)

| Sep 24th | Damage to the log book has been discovered and disclosed to HMI. There is no reason for such an action and no clue as to the delinquents responsible.
School was attempted last week but so few came that it was abandoned.
It has been grievously wet and the unsettled harvest weather has set everything wrong. |

| Sep 24th | HMI report :- |

"This school is in a very creditable state of efficiency and order. Religious Instruction is particularly good."

| Oct 2nd | One boy absent - no shoes. |
| Oct 16th | One little girl hurt her hand in a mangle, she has been kept at home. |

Dec 15th	Venerable Archdeacon visited in the afternoon.

1867

Jan 17th	A window in the school got broken. I imposed a fine of a half penny upon all scholars, many paid at once. Any surplus after the repair will go toward a ball for the boys and a skipping rope for the girls - if enough.

(I wonder what the reaction to such a request would be today ?)

Feb 12th	One boy, (Callow) going to Australia.
Mar 22nd	A bitter cold snowy day - no children attended.
Apr 5th	School fairly attended. Went to church at eleven.
May 16th	Cautioned boys about using improper language, having heard a couple of cases.
May 21st	A few absent, bigger boys helping set potatoes and sow turnips.
May 30th	Holiday, Ascension day. Children met at three and marched to church to witness ceremony of laying a stone in the new tower.

(The foundation stone was laid by Mrs Francis Hall, widow of Archdeacon Hall. The tower being completed in August 1869)

(The Master's entries are usually brief, often saying no more than "the school goes on as usual." but, unusually, he makes his entries two or three times a week, sometimes daily, and amongst them there are just as many entries referring to the visits and lessons given by Rev E.W.Kissack and the visits of the resident Archdeacon.
The Archdeacon of Andreas from 1844 until his death in 1886 was Joseph Christian Moore, a highly respected man. One of his early acts in the Parish was to give £600 toward the £2000 cost of the new church, a tremendous sum of money for the time.)

Jun 28th	Mrs Davies has commenced as Seamstress.
	(This lady was the wife of the Master)
Jul 15th	Some children at home weeding, some herding.
Jul 31st	Half-holiday in the afternoon. Took whole school to the Point of Eyre in 13 carts provided by the farmers - a treat for good attendance on the day of the examinations.
Aug 8th	School attempted but hardly any children came because of the Agricultural Show at Ramsey.

1868

Jan 6th	Miss Davies taking infants during the morning - sewing.
	(Miss Davies was the Master's daughter.)
Jan 7th	Reclassified the school, made it into five classes.
Mar 26th	A good many little ones away - whooping cough.
Jul 22nd	Mrs Davies ill.

Jul 30th   Half-holiday. 13 carts to Primrose Hill, Sulby, and gave them
                  tea. The carts were provided by farmers and other costs by
                  subscriptions.
1869
   Feb 22nd   One big girl returned after a long absence. One girl dead from
                  scarlatina which is rather prevalent.
      *(Compared to the sort of entry made by other Masters and Mistresses when one of
their school-children died, the entry by Mr Davies seems rather cold and impersonal.)*
   Mar 17th   Several boys punished for misconduct on their way home -
                  stone throwing.
   July.   The Rev M.Gibson has been taking religious instruction.

          HMI. excerpt from report:-
**"I again found the school in good order and discipline. The attainment
generally speaking are very fair but the help of a pupil teacher is desirable. The
school might be better fitted up and its appearance made more neat. The
seamstress department seems to be going on fairly."**

   Oct 13th   The Rev James Moore is taking religious lessons.
1870
   Jan 12th   Rev W.T.Dinwoody is the curate taking lessons, the Archdeacon
                  continues his visitations.

   Jul 22nd   HMI report, excerpt :-
**" The school continues in a fairly creditable state. I would like to see better
fittings - the supply of books and slates was partially defective. Arithmetic needs
to be more accurate, there were 25 failures out of 91 scholars in the standards. The
people seem to have thrown every burden on the clergymen."**
   The number attending the examination was :-
   Under 6 years, 9.   Over 6 years, 85.

*(This report contains the first reference to the number of pupils attending the school, up to
this time Mr Davies had always recorded the attendance as being a percentage, but, of
course, at this distance in time we do not know what the percentage related to. It would seem
that the Inspector had a quiet word in the ear of Mr Davies concerning his daily entries in
the Log Book because from this time forward his entries were usually made weekly.)*

1871
   Aug 23rd   81 on register. Average attendance 26.
                  Presented for exams 60 - qualified for exams 63.
   Sep ?   74 on register plus 10 infants. Average attendance
                  26 children. *(Note the serious discrepancy between the numbers on
the register and the actual attendances.)*

1872
    HMI report extract :-
" **Ventilation in the school is not very satisfactory, I would suggest that two ventilators are placed in the apex of the roof. The staff comprise Mr A Davies. Master. (Certified.) Miss Elizabeth Davies, Sewing Mistress. William Teare, pupil teacher."**

    Sep 23rd   *On this day a normal report was made in the log book, but it was the last entry to be made by Mr Davies.*

(After having had good continuity amongst the teaching staff for many years, the school suddenly hit a rough patch. 1872 was the year in which the Andreas School Board was formed and I cannot help wondering if their immediate actions may have led to Mr Davies tendering his resignation. In Chapter 7 there is a brief record of the happenings under this Board.

    Nov 4th   Mr Pogson, seconded from Kirk Bride School.
    Nov 12th   Report by Charles Coppow :-
" **After the absence of a Master since the latter end of September, I found the attendance very low. Miss Davies and the pupil teacher are doing their best to keep the school together."**
1873
    Feb   There are repeated visits by the Archdeacon and Rev
                  Dinwoody.
(This remark suggests that Mr Pogson was less than enchanted by the visits of the clergy.)

    Jun 27th   Sent out the quarterly accounts. Numbers not so good.
    Aug 20th   *Mr Pogson suddenly died.*
    Sep 29th   John Wesley Bell took charge, there were 37
                  present, Miss Davies is continuing in post.
    Oct 20th   Thomas Mylrea appointed as Monitor at 1/- a week.
1874
    Jan 30th   Miss Davies left. Mrs Fell appointed in her place.
    Oct 30th   Average attendance this week 89, plus 5 infants.
    HMI report :-
" **New desks are required. The staff are Mr J.W.Bell. Master. Eleanor J.Lansbury. Elizabeth Lace."**

1875
    Apr 29th HMI report :-
" **New desks should be provided at once, the younger children have to sit at desks which are far too big for them. School walls are dirty, new maps are required. The offices for the children are insufficient."**
    Jun 16th   Mrs Fell, the sewing Mistress has died.

(The school was suffering from a lack of continuity which was not helped by the several deaths and resignations that had taken place amongst the staff within a few years.)

1876

The school was transferred to the Board of Education.

Sep 7th   Average attendance 74 plus 2 infants.

1877

Oct 27th   Mr Bell, the Master, finished.

Oct 29th   Mr James Little Phillips took over the school.

1878

Jun 28th   Yearly average attendance 100.9. Attendance for last quarter 123. *(Compare these figures with those for 1871)*

Sep 20th. HMI report :-

" None of the school committee attended on the day of the examination, the registers are not under proper supervision, the school portfolio is not properly kept. School room draughty, inadequately heated, no urinal for the boys, insufficient closets for the girls. Another blackboard and a set of reading books needed."

The effect of the school being transferred from Parish control to the Board of Education was at last being felt, the days of leaving the responsibility to others was over !

School Committees had specific responsibilities which included regular visits to the school to ensure that the school register was being properly maintained and that on the day of their visit the number of scholars present matched entries in the register; a member of the committee should have been on hand on the day of the school examinations to answer any questions the Inspector raised and to note his criticisms as well as having the school portfolio available for scrutiny.

1879

This year saw the first written entries in the Log Book by school committee members certifying their attendance, the people concerned were Joseph Moore and F.la Mothe; once started, their visitations were performed conscientiously.

1880   Scholars on roll 108. Average attendance 76.

1882

Jul 13th   *The first ever entry made concerning the Andreas School curriculum is within this Log Book - but it only dealt with geography.*

Oct 6th   Mr Phillips. Master, resigned.

Oct 16th   Edward Drew. Master. 70 scholars attended.

1883

Jun 26th   Very wet, only 29 present.

Aug 17th   Thin attendance. Children kept at home - in the fields.

1885

Jun 9th   I have given instruction that religious instruction will be dispensed with until the exams are over.

(Oh dear ! Mr Drew really put the cat among the pigeons with that instruction! It would seem that he was most annoyed at the way in which lessons were being disrupted by visiting clergy.

Whilst no names are given there would seem to have been some orchestration of the few protests that followed Mr Drew's action because these, in turn, were followed up by HM Inspector.)

1886 HMI in his annual report was critical of the decision made by the Master concerning dispensing of religious instruction and warned against any repetition.

1888

Mar 25th to April 17. School closed because of measles.

(Over the years there would seem to have been considerable friction building up between the school committee and the Master, Mr Drew, with the result that follows.)

1891

May 20th   The lock has been removed from the school door.
May 21st   A new lock has been fitted (on the instructions of the School Committee) and I am unable to open the school. I (Mr Drew) have removed the registers to my house for safe keeping.

Jun 12th   William Radcliffe. Master. I am having problems opening the school due to the previous Master having kept the record books etc.

1892

Mar 18th   Scarlet Fever outbreak.
Oct 19th   William Corlett (Branst), a lad in the 4th standard died rather suddenly, he was present all day last Friday in his usual health but taken ill on Saturday with Scarlet Fever, he died four days after the attack.
Nov 4th   Very stormy, only 25 present.
Nov 28th   82 present, largest number during present school year.
Dec 23rd   Numbers of children kept at home to pluck geese for the Xmas market.

1893

May 8th   Fresh cases of scarlet fever.
May 19th   A 7th standard girl, Edel Wynter, has died, she had been ill but suddenly became seriously ill and died within three hours. *(These entries should remind us of the frightening speed with which Scarlet Fever killed; just imagine the effect on the other children, the parents and the teachers ?)*

1894

April 9th to May 7th. School closed, scarlet fever.

Oct 8th   Whooping cough is prevalent.

Nov 5th   Attendance down to 51. There are at least 25 kept at home with whooping cough.

Nov 6th   School closed until Dec 3rd. Whooping cough.

1895

Feb 7th   School closed until Feb 17th - snow.

(*The result of the snowstorm/blizzard that swept the Island.*)

1896

Jul *(The Master prepared a long and very good list of object lessons for the smaller children.)*

1897

Pupils admitted from the Lhen school; it has been decided that all scholars over ten should attend Andreas instead of Lhen.

(The Lhen School continued thereafter as a junior and infant school, it was not closed until 1933, by which time the roll had fallen to 5)

Dec 9th to Jan 10th. School closed due to measles.

1898.

Mar 8th   Eliza Quayle, (Braust Cottage) in standard 2 has died from Erysipelas, she had been absent since Feb 23rd. *(Symptoms are an inflammation of the skin, it could be fatal, as in this case.)*

Dec 23   Last entry in the book.

And it was on such a sad note that this Log Book for Andreas School closed. One good piece of news was that Mr J.L.Phillips who left the school in October 1882, became the Head of Ellenboro Endowed School, Maryport., and became a member of the executive of the National Union of Teachers. [M 23]

*   *   *

SATISFACTION AT ST. JOHN'S

There is one particular Log Book for St. John's that I would like to explore in your company, it covers the years from 1889 to 1922, although, in fact, I will not be taking you beyond 1919.

The reason why I find this book so interesting is that for the whole of this period the school had only one Headmaster, Thomas Cain. He had started his Head Mastership at St. John's in 1875, and continued until his retirement in 1919, a remarkable length of time to be in charge of one school.

Most of the entries he made in the log book were in neat copperplate, clear and easy to read as well as being succinct.

As was usual with log books of the period there are many, many entries which are repetitious. (usually because everything was going well) Mr Cain's reports were made every two or three days and if I were to repeat them all they would become rather boring, so, as far as possible, I have chosen the entries which best illustrate the day to day happenings of the school.

Over the years Mr Cain had many different teachers and monitors to help him but I have only mentioned a few, just to show how their comings and goings were reported in the Log Book.

You will need to remember that during the first half of this story the school was being conducted in the little school which is now the St. John's Church Hall; this is especially important when you read of the number of children being taught there.

St. John's School would seem to have been a reasonably contented establishment, rarely is there any mention of a serious problem, but that does not stop Mr Cain from being critical at times and, generally speaking, I have used his own words.

1889.	Thomas Cain. 1st Class Master.
Jan 7th	J.E.Cashin appointed Asst. Master. Certified 1st Division Assistant.
Jan 11th	Average attendance 104.9.
Jan 29th	Miss Kate Robertson appointed Asst. Mistress.
Feb 1st	140 on roll - average attendance 107.6.
Feb 8th	Much troubled with smoke in the school - chimney needs cleaning.
Feb 11th	Thick snow, very few children - no attendance recorded.
Feb 15th	Attendance considerably down, caused by bad weather.
Feb 21st	We have not been able to have a fire in the classroom as the chimney does not draw.
Mar 1st	We suffer much from the cold - there is no fire.
Mar 5th	Chimney attended to - we have again been able to have a fire.
Mar 7th	Half holiday because yesterday was Ash Wednesday.
Mar 20th	Very wet and stormy, very few children - no attendance recorded.
Mar 29th	143 on register, average attendance 110.
Apr 18th to 23rd. Easter Vacation.	
Apr 26th	After Easter Vacation average attendance down to 93 children.
May 3rd	Asst. Mistress absent owing to serious illness and death of her Father. Best attendance for the quarter - 123.8
Jun 28th	Half holiday because of the St. John's Lodge of Oddfellows Procession.
Jul 4th	Broke up for week - Midsummer Fair.

Jul 11th	Class subjects for 1890.	
Recitation	Standard V & VI	Antony's Oration
"	" IV	Horatius
"	" III	The Inchcape Rock
"	" II	Compassion
"	" I	Fruitful September

Jul 26th   Two days holiday - Annual Outing of the Wesleyan Sunday School.

Aug 2nd   Mr Cain absent to attend a funeral.

(The Head Master seemed to attend funerals at least two or three times a year, I should imagine that he considered it to be a social necessity for a man in his position to show such courtesy; usually he recorded the name and age of the person who died, together with a very brief description of the person's standing or career.)

Aug 5th   Miss Robertson absent with neuralgia.

(Unfortunately for Mr Cain this Asst. Teacher was absent fairly frequently, neuralgia was frequently given as the reason for her absence. I have not recorded the large number of times that she was absent from the School.)

Aug 7th   Mr Cashin absent.

Aug 15th   Broke up for harvest vacation. Four weeks holiday.

Excerpt from HMI report dated 8/8/89 :-

" Discipline is well maintained and the school is taught with creditable zeal and success."

Sep 20th   School commenced with an attendance of 90, average for the week was 96.7.

Nov 1st   Fires in classroom, first for this season.

Nov 21st   Commence to teach drawing, to boys only, on Tuesday and Thursday afternoons from 1.30 to 3pm.

Dec 12th   School examined in scripture by Rev Mr Kneale of St. Judes.

(There are periodic reports of scripture examinations, sometimes by Mr Kneale and in later years by another clergyman who was an appointed examiner but these happenings took place at reasonable intervals, there does not seem to have been the sustained pressure concerning religious teaching that was maintained for so many of the earlier years at Andreas. Rev Thomas Redfern Kneale was a Diocesan Inspector of Religious Education in Schools)

Dec 20th   Broke up at noon - Christmas Vacation for a fortnight.

List of probable exceptions.

(Names of children Mr Cain considered to be unfit for presentation to HMI for the annual examination.)

Standard I			STANDARD II
Robert Fayle	Dull	William Crellin	Very dull
Walter McGee	Dull	F.Bridson	Dull
S.Kaneen	Very Dull	Jane Bridson	Dull
Louis Duke	Dull	Geo.L.Kennaugh	Dull
Philip Corlett.	Ill health	I.Moore	Ill health
S.Kaneen	Very dull	Ernest Corlett	Ill health
Violet Clague	Ill health		

STANDARD III

Eva J.Callister	Very dull	James Fayle	Very dull
Eleanor Quiggin	Dull	James Quirk	Dull
Emma E.Quayle	Ill health	G.Smith	Dull
May Caine	Under age	Caroline Clague	Dull
Eva Senogles	Under age	A.Schenck	Dull
Herbert Brew	Dull		

			STANDARD IV
	STANDARD V	S.A.Kelly	Very Dull
James Taubman	Dull	William Quirk	Dull

1890

Mar 3rd	Mr Cashin (Asst. Head) appointed Head Master at Patrick Parochial School w/e Apr 1st.
Mar 7th	Average down to 91.8 due to sickness.
Apr 15th	One day holiday because the paintwork done by contractors had not dried.
	Mr J.E.Caley appointed as Asst. Teacher.
May 8th	I was absent from school because of a very bad headache.
May 16th	Several of the younger children absent because of coughs.
May 23rd	I have had a bad cold in my head this week, consequently have had much difficulty in teaching.
	(Note, Mr Cain was a 'teaching' Headmaster.)
Jun 6th	Attendance not at all satisfactory - 76.4%
Jul 21st	Mr Caley (Asst. Teacher) absent at Liverpool.
Aug 14th	Arthur Foster aged 12 years, late a very promising pupil of this school, was buried this afternoon. Nearly all the children went part of the way and many the whole way with the funeral.
Aug 19th	Comment included within HMI report :-

"The number of children placed upon the exemption schedule as being dull is unusually large." *(Mr Cain being too truthful ?)*

Aug 22nd	As the corn is ripening fast we shall shortly have our Harvest Holidays.
Oct 10th	Several of the children have been absent through illness - scarlatina.
Oct 17th	Mr Caley appointed Headmaster of Dalby Board School, Patrick.
Oct 24th	Scarlatina is now very prevalent in this district and causes many absences.
Oct 31st	School closed by medical authority on account of scarlatina and measles.

1891

Jan 5th	School reopened. MrJ.Gawne appointed Asst. Master.
Jan 22nd	Rev J.Corlett called today.
Jan 26th	Rev J.Corlett visited today.

(Rev John Corlett was Chaplain of St. John's from 1865 until his death in 1909)

Feb 9th to 13th	Miss Robertson away with a cold.
Mar 6th	Scripture Examination by Rev Kneale.
Apr 2nd	Extremely wet - no attendance recorded.
Apr 24th	Without fires, first time this season.
Aug 7th	37 absent during the morning and 34 in the afternoon mostly for unsatisfactory reasons.
Oct 30th	Several children absent picking potatoes.
Nov 3rd	Mr Ferrier called. He strongly recommends my introducing musical drill saying it would improve behaviour or deportment of the children.
Dec 23rd	Mr Gawne has resigned.

1892

Jan 18th	Ground covered with snow to a great depth, there was no attendance.
Jan 29th	Many absent through sickness.
Feb 16th	Rather wet morning. 60 absent.
Feb 17th	Exceedingly cold with good deal of snow - no attendance.
Mar 10th	Very cold with a good deal of snow. No attendance.
Mar 18th	We are still working with insufficient staff which is unfair to teachers and the children.

(This sort of comment was not made because of any 'sour grapes' attitude, the log book was examined at frequent intervals by members of the school committee and the remarks were made as a reminder of the problem.)

Apr 25th	Mr Bramwell appointed Asst. Master.
Jun 16th	Rev Mr Kewley examined the boys in drawing.
	(Rev John Kewley was Vicar of Arbory)

Jun 7th	Rev J.Corlett examined the boys of Standards IV and VI in geography.
Jun 20th	Drew attention of enforcing officer to the case of Alice Corlett, absent for a quarter of the year with a sore foot.
Jun 24th	137 on register. Average attendance 113.3
Jul 15th	This afternoon the children went part of the way with the funeral of Amy Taubman - aged eight years - a scholar of this school.

Jul 29th	CLASS SUBJECTS FOR 1893 - Recitation.	
Recitation	Standard IV and VII	Wolsey and Cromwell.
"	" III	Alice Fell or Poverty.
"	" II	Compassion.
"	" I	The open window.

Aug 8th	Extremely wet - no attendance.
Aug 12th	Mr Bramwell absent all week without any reason being assigned. As we had a large attendance we were consequently under great difficulties.
Aug 24th	Excerpt from HMI report :-

"This school has made a decided advance and is now a very efficient one. Discipline is excellent."

Sept 1st	During the Harvest Vacation the school room is to be divided into two parts by a partition which will be a decided advantage.
Dec 5th	Several inches of snow - no attendance.

1893

Jan 13th	Average attendance 114.1 or 75% - fair for 1st week after the holidays.
Feb 10th	The children had a tea party this afternoon to encourage their attendance, hence we had a half holiday.
Feb 17th	Mr Bramwell absent all week, received a telegram from Peel stating that he was unwell.
Mar 24th	Potato planting, several absent.
Apr 14th	165 on register.
Jun 16th	Several absent - measles.
Jun 23rd	Many absences due to measles.
Jun 30th	Many absences due to measles.
Jul 6th	Holiday as the children had a treat in the form of a tea - a medal being presented to each child to celebrate the marriage of the Princess May and the Duke of York.
Jul 7th	Many absent - measles
Aug 2nd	Greeba Sunday School outing - many absentees.
Aug 9th	Lower Foxdale Sunday School treat - many absent, also several absent on account of harvest work.

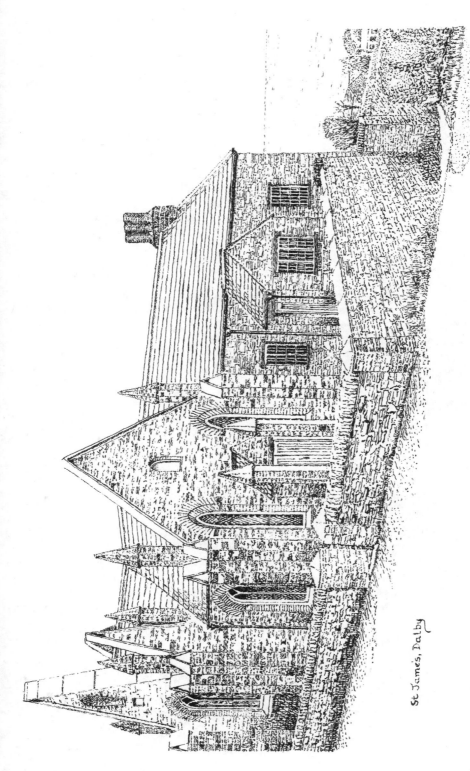

St James's, Dalby

St. James Dalby - Drawn August 1999. The church is within the spireletted front part of the building. The school occupied the rear portion nearest the sea.

Sep 17th   The room in which I teach is at present much overcrowded. Its' accommodation according to the minimum requirement is for only 49; the average this week is 53.8 and the total on the register due to use this room is 78. Efficient teaching and discipline under such circumstances is exceedingly difficult.

Sept 29   Number on register 165 - average 151.9.
(These are very high proportionate attendance figures for the 1890s')

Nov 10th   This afternoon the children went part of the way with the funeral of Caesar Albert Kelly aged 15 years - a booking clerk at St. John's Station and late a scholar of this school. He met with a fatal accident on the line on Tuesday evening last.

1894
Jan 25th   This morning Sir J.W.Ridgeway, our new Governor and Lady Ridgeway broke their journey to Peel at St. John's when a bou quet was presented to Lady Ridgeway by the children —after the ceremony on Tynwald Hill the children each received two oranges and a banana.
(The Governor was on the Island for less than two years, he was then posted out to be Governor of Ceylon in 1895.)
Feb 12th   Mr Bramwell absent for one week with no good reason.

Mar 9th to 16th Mr Bramwell absent without giving any good reason. It is reported that he has left his lodgings and the neighbourhood. The Committee will advertise for a new Asst. Teacher. *(I would suggest that Mr Cain was pleased to part with the unreliable Mr Bramwell.)*

Mar 22nd   Eleanor Bridson and Elizabeth Cain appointed temporary Monitors.
Apr 20th   We now have an overcrowded school and something must be done to provide further accommodation.
May 25th   Today I opened a parcel of slates and stationery for the school
Jun 15th   Attendance 164.1 or 89.6%, a very good attendance.
Jul 2nd   64 absent owing to the procession of the Peel Rechabite Club.
Jul 31   Many absent, the Foxdale miners children had a treat provided by Capt. Kitto.
Aug 17th   Sunday School outing to Glen Wyllin hence a half holiday.
Nov 9th   Several cases of whooping cough.

Nov 30th	Whooping cough prevalent, attendance suffering. Miss Robertson grievously complains of the overcrowded state of her classroom.
Dec 14th	188 on register. Average attendance 123.7 or 65.9%, this low figure is due to sickness.
Dec 20th	Miss Robertson has resigned.

1895

Jan 14th	Miss Christian appointed Asst. Mistress.
Feb 6th	Snowed very heavily. School closed.
Feb 15th	School closed. Roads in many places covered to a depth of from 9 to 12 feet.
Feb 18th	Very few came to school.
July 26th	SCHOOL PROJECTS FOR 1896 - GEOGRAPHY. Standards V-VII. United States. Australia. British possessions in Africa and India.
Sep 27th	Very warm in school, thermometer 75 degrees.

Present staff:- Thomas Cain. Master 1st Class.
George Bates. Asst. Master. ex PT.
E.J.Christian "   "   " ".
Elizabeth Cain. PT.End of 1st year.
Elizabeth E.Bridson. PT.

| Oct 18th | Yesterday afternoon the children had their photograph taken by Mr Shipside of Douglas. |

Dec *(For some unexplained reason the handwriting of Mr Cain, including his signature, suddenly deteriorated at this time. It remained legible but no longer retained its classic style.)*

1896

Jan 24th	Out of 15 on the infant register 8 are absent due to sickness.
Jan 27th	The children went into the church at 2 this afternoon to the funeral service of Ruby Chandler.
Jan 29th	The children again went to the church, this time to the funeral service of Ruby's brother, Arthur Chandler.
Mar 5th	At a Parish Meeting held in the schoolroom yesterday evening a resolution was passed authorising the school committee to proceed with the building of a new school as soon as possible.

Nov 6th   I was very unwell today and taught with much difficulty.
Nov 13th   Several children absent due to a measles epidemic.

(1896 had also been a bad year for Mr Cain in another way, there were frequent illnesses among his staff.)
1897
Jan 29th   Sickness bad with snow and rain making attendance very poor, only 98.3 and average of 69.2%.
Mar 5th   Miss Corlett commenced her duties as Asst. Mistress.

Jun 22nd   Holiday to celebrate the Diamond Jubilee of Queen Victoria. The children were treated to a tea and presented with a medal as a memento of the historic event.

Jul 29th   I was very ill today and absent from 9.45am.
Nov 10th   I was at Douglas today with Mr Anderson, architect of the new school.
1898
Jan 21st   The desks belonging to Standards II, III and IV were removed into the new school, in their place we have some very unsteady seats from the Wesleyan Hall on a temporary basis.

*   *   *

ST. JOHN'S (new) SCHOOL
1898
Feb 1st   Commenced work in our new school which is well adapted for teaching purposes.
(This is the school on the main road which continued to be in use until 2002.)

Feb 9th   Boys of the 1st class assisted the School Committee in planting a number of trees in the school grounds.
Jun 17th   Attendance is 91.3% for the older children and 81.6% for the infants.
Jul 1st   130 on roll, av 115.2.

Jul 22nd   Excerpt from HMI report :-
" **The elementary subjects are as a rule well taught and the class work creditable. The new premises are excellent. THE SEMI-OPAQUE GLASS IN THE WINDOWS SHOULD BE REMOVED AND CLEAR TRANSPARENT GLASS SUBSTITUTED."**
(My capitals. This remark by the Inspector must have come as a nasty shock to the School Committee, a fault being found so soon with their nice new school !)

Nov 4th	John Lewney has not been at school since the holidays, he has ringworm.

1900

Jun 1st	We gave this afternoon as a half holiday upon receipt of the news that the British Troops had entered Pretoria.

1901

Jan 30th	Today at 12, from the top of the Tynwald Mound, Prince Albert was proclaimed King under the title of Edward VII- the children were given a half holiday.
May 20th	Miss Howe has been sent to Cronk-y-Voddy school for a short while - Mr Kelly is seriously ill.
May 24th	Some children absent - whooping cough.
May 31st	14 absent with whooping cough
Jun 14th	Attendance greatly decreased to 75.4% due to whooping cough and colds.
Jul 12th	Whooping cough persists

1902

Mar 21st	About 51 children vaccinated.
Mar 24th	Many absent due to sore arms caused by the vaccination.
Jun 2nd	Half holiday in celebration of the Proclamation of Peace in South Africa.
June 13th	Several absent with chicken pox.

The staff are :-

Mr Thomas Cain.	Master 1st Class.
Wilfred E.Kelly.	Asst. Teacher ex PT
Annie J.Howe.	Asst. Teacher ex PT
Margaret Vick.	Probationer.
Evelyn Senogles.	Probationer.

Nov 14th	I took Standard III and IV children for a ramble during which I gave them an object lesson on 'Autumn'.

1903

May 22nd	Miss Cowin has been absent, she got hurt falling off her bicycle.
Jul 3rd	Many absent - thinning turnips.
Jul 10th	Many absent - thinning turnips.
Jul 17th	Miss Evelyn Senogles absent, suffering from quinsy.
Jul 24th	Miss Senogles still not well. Mr Kelly absent due to toothache.
Jul 27th	Miss Senogles' Mother wrote to say that her daughter, Miss Senogles, felt compelled to resign due to ill health.
Jul 31st	Many absent - still turnip thinning.

Sep 25th	Owing to the prolonged harvest through wet weather the average attendance is down to 81, an average of 66.3%.
Oct 30th.	Since the Harvest Holidays, attendances badly affected by the prolonged harvest, some of the corn being uncut even yet.
Nov 6th	Corkill family of four absent since the holidays with scarlet fever.
Nov (?)	Pembertons four children absent today with scarlet fever.

1904
May 10th	Motor car race trials - school closed
Nov 11th	The Leeces three children are absent with measles.
Dec 20th	School closed by the medical authority - measles.

1905
Jan 23rd	School re-opened but few present.
Feb 3rd	There are still several absent due to measles. Attendance 81.4%

Excerpt from HMI report:-
"Order good, work fairly good, all the paper work is most neat - a pleasing school. THE GROUND GLASS WHICH OBSCURES THE LIGHT IN THE WINDOWS SHOULD BE REMOVED; IT IS QUITE UNSUITABLE FOR A COUNTRY SCHOOL."

Nov 2nd. The first School Board Elections took place.

1906
Jan 12th	There seems to be an epidemic of mumps.
Jan 19th	Many absent due to mumps.
Feb 1st	Mumps has suddenly spread among the younger children, on medical advice the school is closed for one week.
Feb 5th	School closed by the medical authority.
Feb 20th	School re-opened.
Apr 18th	This am Fred Corris (Ballavagher) was trifling with a detonator when it suddenly went off and blew off two of his fingers.

Excerpt from HMI report:-
"THE OBSCURE WINDOWS ARE STILL IN POSITION. THE PRIMARY OBJECT IN HAVING WINDOWS IS TO ADMIT LIGHT TO THE CLASSROOMS."

1907
Jan 18th	Several children absent due to influenza.
Feb 1st	Attendance badly affected by influenza.
May 28th	Motor bicycle race - holiday.
May 30th	Motor car race - holiday.
Jun 9th	HMI surprise visit report:-

"I AM SORRY TO SEE THAT THE OPAQUE GLASS IS STILL IN POSITION."

Jul 11th	School closed at 3pm to permit the children to attend the funeral of Walter Pemberton, aged six.

Aug.   Annual report by HMI, excerpt:-

"I NOTE THAT THE OBSCURE WINDOWS HAVE NOT YET BEEN REMOVED. The old school building which is close at hand might with great advantage be utilised for the teaching of handicraft and cookery."

Oct 25th	Several absent due to effects of the weather. Owing to the wet, almost half the corn remains in the fields.
Oct 28	Many absent helping to put in the corn.

1908

Feb 8th	Visit by the newly appointed Bishop.*(Bishop Drury, a man of sin cere and fervent piety, kind and sympathetic to all.)*
Jul 16th	Attendance 125.

(It is noticeable that Mr Cain's handwriting started to improve from August onward, within a few months he was once again writing with a freely flowing copperplate - albeit a little shaky in places.)

1909

Jan 8th	Temperature only 42 degrees, cold all day.
Mar 2nd to 12th,	Continuous snow, attendances affected..

Jul 6th   Excerpt from HMI report:-

"Ventilation apparatus needs prompt overhaul, most swing windows are set fast with paint rendering the classrooms unwholesome."

Jul 23rd	There is an epidemic of whooping cough, the school is closed.
Sep 20th	School re-opened.
Dec 10th	On the instruction of the School Board I took the children into the old school room for drill. I found the air very damp and space so limited that exercise could not be performed.
Dec 13th	The girls, only, are away to the old school for drill.

(It seems rather strange that the School Board should have been encouraging the Head Master to make use of the old school, the attendances at the new school were not anywhere near as high as they had been before the new school was built.)

1910

Jan 17th	The School Board have provided us with a piano.
Feb 11th	The children of Mrs Cubbon (Ballaspet) and Mr Charlton (Ballachurry), attend irregularly.
Feb 18th	Clara and Ivy Callister (Upper Ballae) have been absent since Christmas.

Jul HMI report *(This is a particularly pertinent report and I have reproduced it in full as the first item in chapter 13.)*

1911

Jun 22nd.	The Coronation of King George V and Queen Mary. School holiday. Average attendances 92.1% .
Jul 21st	Children absent working on turnips.
Jul 28th	Many still absent - on turnips.

Excerpt from HMI report:-"THE OBSCURE PANES ARE TO BE REMOVED."

1912

Excerpt from HMI report:-

"Removal of the thick glass from the windows has greatly improved both the lighting and the cheeriness of the school."

(I expect that the Inspectorate cheered as well ! It had taken fourteen years of badgering to get this change made !!)

1913

Feb 18th	Attendance 91.6% - good.
Feb 28th	Infant attendance only 60% due to sickness.
Jul 4th	Dr. Stitt of Port St. Mary gave a medical examination to the children.

(This was the first such examination to be reported at St. John's School.)

1914

Feb 13th	Av attendance 93.9
Feb 20th	Av temp at 9am 47.8 degrees, at 11am, 52 degrees.
Oct 27th	The school bell fell today.

1915

Feb 5th	Temperatures 48 degrees and 50.7.
Feb 10th	Temperatures 44.8 and 47.2.
Jul 2nd	Several children absent -turnip thinning.

1916

Mar 15th	Children under 5 attend very irregularly.
May 22nd	We adopted the new 'Summer Time'.
Sep 25th	Small attendance due to the late harvest and the Great War. Adult labour is so very scarce and the services of the children have been utilized.

1917

	Miss Shimmin absent owing to the death of her brother Ralph, killed in action.

1918

Feb 15th	Absentees due to mumps.
Feb 22nd	Several children absent due to mumps.
Mar 1st and 8th	Many children absent due to mumps. Average attendance down to 70.5%.

Jun 7th	An outbreak of whooping cough.
Jun 14th	Many absent due to whooping cough.
Jun 19th	Whooping cough continuing.
Jul 4th	Children absent with whooping cough and working turnips. Av att 73.3%
Jul 12 and 19th.	Children still working on turnips and some with whooping cough. Av att 67.9.
Oct 24th	Owing to the illness of Mr Cain *(The Headmaster)* I have taken charge, Albert E.Corlett.
Oct 30th to Nov 20th.	School closed - influenza.
Dec 2nd	A letter has been received from Mr Cain in Nobles Hospital thanking the children for their flowers.
Dec 18th	The school attended the funeral of Alfred Kelly, aged 15 years.

1919

| Jan 13th to Feb 10 | School closed due to an outbreak of influenza |
| Feb 14th | Mr Thomas Cain has returned to take over the school. |

April 17th.   "Today, after a year of extended service I retire from my Head Mastership.
I commenced my duties at St. John's on April 5th 1875. I have always found the children all that a teacher could desire and I have had the willing support of the parents.
I wish my successor, Mr Ormerod, every success and happiness.

On that note we come to the end of this Head Master's remarkable career.
The log book continues without a break for a few more years and it may be that Mr Cain's successors were given inspiration in their work by looking back and reading of the many different problems he and his staff experienced over the years.
I find it interesting to see how the childrens' attendances in this country school were affected from start to finish by the need for them to 'help on the farm'. Similarly, how their absences due to illness changed over the years, especially with the seeming growth of contagious illnesses such as scarlet fever, whooping cough and,finally,influenza which caused the school to be closed on so many occasions.

ANDREAS AND ST. JOHN'S

It is when the gods hate a man with uncommon abhorence that
they drive him into the profession of a school-master.
(Seneca. c5 BC - Ad 65.)

*   *   *

Chapter seven

CONTROL - ANDREAS AND ST JUDE'S

You will have noticed that most of the Log Books and reports I have used as examples so far refer to the nineteenth century, this has been deliberate because the Isle of Man Schools of the time were struggling toward a better future against odds that would seem almost insuperable nowadays, no speedy transport, no phones, no computers, crude facilities, no artificial lighting and very little money. This chapter illustrates the difficulties still being faced toward the end of the nineteenth century, a time when the methods of control gradually altered and Schoolteachers were faced with the beginning of the twentieth century. We start off with Andreas again but this time it is from the viewpoint of the School Boards rather than the Headteacher.

A SCHOOL BOARD/COMMITTEE AND ITS' PROBLEMS - ANDREAS AGAIN !

The Andreas School Board Committee was formed in 1872 as part of the Manx Governments' Public Elementary Education Act, which, in effect, undertook direct responsibility for education.

Amongst the responsibilities of such committees were the following items :-
The provision of adequate schools within their jurisdiction.
The upkeep of such schools.
Ensuring the attendance of scholars.
Ensuring that schools were open to receive scholars.
Setting the local rate for education purposes.
Setting the rate of fees payable by scholars.
Ensuring collection of the rates and fees.
Ensuring that the teaching staff being employed were themselves educated to the required standards.
Negotiating and controlling the salaries of teaching staff.
Ensuring by personal visits the accuracy of the school registers and records compared with the actual number of
pupils attending school on the day of the visit.
Ensuring that all relevant papers, log books, and attendance
records were maintained and made available to Her Majesty's Inspectors.
Where applicable, to ensure that any legal requirements were
being met, with particular reference to the original deeds
and the requirements within those deeds concerning specific
restrictions especially with regard to religious matters.

The following excerpts are given as being representative examples of the entries within the Andreas School Committee minute book. They only cover the years from commencement in 1872 to 1891.

For the first year or two, the Andreas minute book is concerned with everyday matters such as, for example, elections, rather than school affairs, but, by 1875, the committee were really into the swing of things.

1875

Nov 5th,   Rev F.La Mothe attended a committee meeting to see if matters
                        could be so arranged that religious instruction in the School
                        (Andreas) could be carried out harmoniously between himself
                        and the Master, Mr Bell.?

The end result of this calm request was that on Dec 3rd, Mr Bell was given three months notice !.

Obviously someone then had second thoughts, because Mr Bell continued as Master until he resigned on Sept 15th 1877; but this was only a foretaste of things to come.

1877

Nov 7th   Mr J.L.Phillips took over Andreas School and the Committee
                        proposed that he be paid £60pa and the whole of the
                        Government grant, *(At first sight a very generous offer, but ...)* out
                        of which he would be required to pay the salary of the Pupil
                        Teacher and the Sewing Mistress, the cost of cleaning the school
                        and collecting the scholars fees.

(This proposal was submitted to the Board of Education as a recommendation for their approval, but the Board refused to approve and asked the Committee to think again.)

Nov 26th   Revised terms submitted - omitting the collection of school fees.
Dec 20th   *Once again, the Board of Education did not agree; they told the
                        Committee that the Master's Salary must be independent of the
                        salaries of the others and any cost connected with the school.*

1878

Jul 19th.   Essie Sansbury appointed as Pupil Teacher at the rate of £10 pa
                        for the first year, £12 for 2nd year, £14 for 3rd year.
Oct 4th.   Agreement was at last reached for the Master's salary, which
                        was to be £76 pa and one half of the Government Grant, the
                        Master collecting fees. (but not having them)

(This was only the start of a parsimonious attitude toward Masters' salaries. Andreas Committee fought tooth and nail to reduce the basic cost of teaching by almost every possible means.)

1879

Apr 4th Payment of half yearly salaries for Andreas School:-

Mr Phillips	£38.00
Elizabeth Lace. P.T.	£ 7.00
Eleanor Sansbury.P.T.	£ 7.00
Essie Sansbury. P.T.	£ 5.00
Annie Corkill. (Sewing Mistress)	£1.05.00

Fees collected by the Master £15.16.00 for q/e Dec 31st 1878.
"   "   "   "   "   £11.16.01   "   "   Mar 31st 1879.

Nov 7th.   The Committee advised Mr Phillips that they were reducing his salary from £76 pa to £60 pa.
(There was no justification for such a swingeing cut unless, perhaps, the Committee thought that Mr Phillips would have difficulty in finding another similar job ?)

Dec 19th.   Mr Phillips accepted the reduction - " but holds himself at liberty to accept any other situation at six weeks notice as, owing to the reduction of salary, to remove as soon as possible to another situation."

1880.Aug 13th   The Committee were offered a lease on the school at St Jude's, if the trustees were agreeable.

Oct 15th   Lease of ten years for St. Jude's School agreed at a rental of five shillings per annum, the committee to keep the building in repair.

Nov 15th   Owners of the old Smeale School sought transfer by lease to the Committee

1881

Jun 15th   Mr Phillips went to London for three days to sit for an exami nation to matriculate at King's College.

Nov 8th   HMI drew attention to insufficient accommodation at St. Jude's School.

1882

Mar 21st   The Smeale offer considered. No action taken.

Jul 7th   Question raised on the advisability of substituting for the schools formerly at Smeale and the Lhen by a new school near Ballawhale. (Ballawhane ?)

1883

Sep 1st   Notice of resignation by Mr Phillips.
(It had taken him three years, but he did as he intended.
The committee had not learnt from their past mistake however.)

Oct 10th   Mr Prew took over school, the Committee offered him as his salary the whole of the school pence and half of the Govt.
Grant.*(Maybe word had got around ! Mr Prew was not going to be caught out like this. He had applied for the appointment after seeing advertisements in the Manx Sun, Isle of Man Times and the Manx Herald offering £100 pa, no other method of devising the salary had been mentioned in those adverts.)*

Nov 3rd   Committee agreed to make up the difference !
1884
           The small school at Lhane offered for school purposes.
1885
May 6th   Consideration given to using the small school at Lhane for a
           'Dame" school.
Sep 4th   HMI reported that St. Judes was **"An efficient school."**
1886
Jan 25th   Miss Coormode Auduas appointed as teacher at Lhane School.
           Salary £26 pa.
1891
Feb 9th   After receiving a couple of horrendous reports from HMI con
           cerning a continuing drop in the standard of teaching at
           Andreas School, Mr Prew was given notice. The Committee said
           that a change of thought was desirable from a Head Teacher
           due to the school being in an inefficient condition.
           The post was then advertised at £80 pa with a house and garden !

                        *   *   *

*I have included the following excerpts from the Log Book of St. Jude's School because St.
Jude's had become the responsibility of the Andreas Committee.*

THE PROBLEMS OF ST. JUDE'S SCHOOLS

The first St. Jude's School was rather tiny. It was opened in April 1866, under Miss
Eliza Radcliffe; during those early years there was no need to keep a Log Book.
Miss Radcliffe opened St. Jude's first Log Book on April 10th 1874, she proudly
reported that she had attended a teachers' examination and had passed in Dec 1873.
Her first Log Book comments were only too relevant :-
"The neighbourhood of St. Jude's is a rural district. Most of the people are either
farmers or farm labourers on a farm. The farm labourers wives work on the fields
during the summer and autumn months and, notwithstanding the Compulsory
Education Act, it is very difficult to secure the attention of their children at school.
They are also withdrawn (many of them) before they have made but very little
progress. The average attendance during the last quarter was 29 whilst the number
who attended at all during the quarter was 51. A number of the absences are from
measles among the children, the state of the weather and the distance from school."
1874
May 1st   The clergy visited the school and heard the 1st
            and 2nd classes read.

May 15th	Two boys who have been in regular attendance have an impediment in their speech and are deaf, they are improving slowly in writing and arithmetic.
Jun 12	All very irregular in consequence of weeding season having commenced.
Jun 19th	Committed to his last resting place a beloved parent, consequently school doors closed this week.

Jul 23rd Annual average 15 boys and 16 girls.
Our vacations this year are to be :- Aug 9th to Sep 13th, Harvest. Dec 5th to Jan 5th, Christmas. (the usual is two weeks). Apr 2nd to Apr 12th - Easter.

| Jul 24th | Her Majesty's Inspector the Rev W.J.Kennedy, made his examination. Number present 49 |

Presented 25.   Passed in reading   24
Passed in writing   21
Passed in arithmetic   22

HMI report :- **This small village school is being diligently and usefully conducted by Miss Radcliffe, the sole teacher.**

| Nov 6th | A number absent for want of shoes and other articles of warm clothing. Weather cold and stormy. Got half a ton of coal for the school; price £1 per ton. |
| Dec 11th | Whooping Cough among children. |

1875.Jan 19th

Numbers on book		Average attendance
1872	47	27
1873	49	30
1874	49	31

Feb 27th   A new Girls Mixed School opened at Sandygate. A number of children from that district are withdrawn. (*I have not been able to trace any such school at Sandygate.*)

Mar 19th	A falling off this week, a few of the children are sick, others want shoes and warm clothing etc.
Apr 25th	Average 19.3 girls, 22.9 boys. Highest this year.
Jul 7th	Two boys who have been absent the last two weeks,kept to work in the fields, have done their work very badly.
Oct 18th	The school has been closed six weeks in consequence of the teacher being very ill.
Nov 12th	Average 14.4. Children taking up potato crop delayed by rain.

1876

Jan 21st	A number absent from colds and a few in want of shoes and other articles of warm clothing.
Mar 24th	Admitted girl age 14 years, negligible education.
Apr 2nd	Epidemic - 20 absent.

May 19th to June 2nd. Teacher very ill - obliged to employ a person to take charge of school.

Jun 30th   Miss Radcliffe resigned.

Aug 25th   Frances Elizabeth Deacon. Sole teacher.
(At this point no further entries are made in the Log Book for a long time. It would seem that the school was closed from 1876 until 1881 but whoever the teacher was when it reopened she failed to complete the book. It was not until 1884 that new entries commenced.)
1884
Jan 14th   E Garrett.Teacher. Started Jan 23rd 1881.
Mar 14th   46 on book, 43 present. *(A miracle ?)*
Jul 11th   Only 10 girls present out of 26. Attendance very irregular, consequently they make no progress.
Aug 7th   Agricultural Show Day. 10 in the morning, none in the afternoon.
Nov 4th   A very wet morning, only 11 present. Windows and roof let in rain.

1885
Mar 3rd   Francis Christian and Charles Edward Quayle playing truant - these boys are unmanageable.
Mar 23rd   Three children from one family absent,Mother sick.

Mar 25th   Same children absent, their mother died.

Apr 1st   A fair in the neighbourhood. 16 present.

June 8th   Two children absent. Death in the family.

(During the months of June, July, August and September hardly a day goes by without some reference being made to children being kept at home to help on the farms in one way or another. I have not entered many of them because they become repetitious but the number of incidents was unfortunate because the children did lose out on their education and the teacher became despondent.)
Jun 17th   Admitted one boy, parents will not give his age.
1886
Mar 1st   Heavy fall of snow and very stormy - not one child present.
(From Mar 2nd to Mar 7th the attendance was just one child.)
Mar 8th   26 present.
Apr 5th   Emily S.Keighin. Teacher. 29 present.
Jul 22nd   Opening of Ramsey Pier - a holiday.
1887
May 12th   43 children present out of 49.
Nov 11th   Mr Prew left after being in charge for two weeks.
                (This was before his disgrace at Andreas)
Nov 15th   Mr Daniel Gelling. Teacher.

1888

Feb 23rd	School closed owing to a ploughing match being held in the neighbourhood.
Mar 9th	Several children in the upper standard without copy books. I have told them they must have them by next Monday.
Mar 16th	School closed, heavy snow storm.
Apr 6th	Attendance low - measles, Easter holidays and Sulby Fair.
Jul 13th	Masons busy on repairing school ground.
Jul 19th	Masons still working on school ground.
	I have resigned. *(Mr Gelling)*

(There was no mention of a new teacher's name at this point.)

Aug 3rd	Average attendance low - Ramsey Friendly Society Parade. Holiday on Thursday - Agricultural show.
Aug 10th	Half holiday Monday afternoon, teacher not well enough to keep school open.

(The school then remained closed until October 1st due to the teacher being ill.)

Oct 1st	Re-open school, numbers small, harvest work going on
Oct 12th	Average 21.7. Most older children on harvest - which is still unfinished.
Oct 18th	Last day at school having resigned the mastership of this school. As I am still suffering from a severe cold I closed the school in the afternoon.
Oct 22nd	School taken charge of by Catherine Kennaugh. 44 on register, 19 present in the morning, 25 in the afternoon. Rev S.W.Hughes-Games visited the school. *(Arch Deacon of Andreas)*
Oct 23rd	The incumbent and Mrs Kneale visited school.
Nov 12th	The incumbent of St. Judes, Rev T.E.Kneale has taken the upper classes for scripture this morning during the timetabled period.
Nov 23rd	November being the time of year when farmers and farm labourers generally leave their places, a few families have removed from the district and consequently the children have left school. Average attendance 30.8.
Nov 27th	This afternoon being so wet and stormy the sewing mistress has not come so I have taken the subject instead. I noticed how well sewn some of the pieces were.

1889

Mar 8th	Two panes of glass put in windows.
Mar 11th	School porch re-tiled and roof repaired, new chimney pot fitted.
Mar 21st	Rev E.Clarj, Curate of Andreas visited the school.

(The teacher had the name wrong, actually, this was Rev Archibald Edward Clarke.)

May 10th	Joseph Callister in Standard 1 is so dull and backward in his learning and quite unable to do the work of his class.
May 24th	Boys attend rather badly - work in fields.
Jun 5th	A fair being held at Sulby, a few of the bigger boys kept from school - driving cattle to the fair.
Jun 20th	Only 27 out of 44 owing to a Parish club in Jurby having their annual festival.
Jul 22	William Kneale in Standard V came back to school today having been absent three weeks - in the fields.

Jul 29th SUBJECTS FOR RECITATION :-

Standards IV,V and VI.	The Lady of the Lake, or, The Building of a Ship.
Standard III	Meddlesome Matty.
Standard I & II	Naughty Pussy.

(This is the first time that part of the curriculum has been noted in this Log Book.)

School Examination today. Half holiday in the afternoon.

Jul 30th	One of the local Sunday School annual picnics; am obliged to give a holiday as the greater part of the children are going.
Aug 16th	Half holiday. St. Judes Sunday School annual picnic.

Oct 2nd. HMI report :-

In less than a year the new mistress has effected a great improvement in the state of the school. The children are well taught, pass credibly in all subjects but mental arithmetic, speak out and display satisfactory intelligence. Considering the circumstances of the place and the population the Good Merit Grant is well earned. The teacher deserves great credit for the work she has done.

Dec 13th	A few children kept home - scarlatina.
Dec 20th	A great number kept at home, some due to their parents fearing infection. Av 22.9.

1890

Jan 6th to 13th School closed - scarlatina.	
Jan 17th	School closed again, this time until Feb 3rd.
Feb 7th	School walls have been washed down and all doors and windows painted during the absence of the children.
July 4th	Harriett Galloway came back to school after a six week absence.
Oct 17th	Sent to the clerk the sum of £1.08.06 school fees.Commenced fires yesterday.
Oct 31st	Had two panes of glass put in windows.

1891
> Feb 13th   Sent to Committee £1.19.00 fees for Quarter ending Dec 31st

1890
> Mar 6th   Received two new desks as the old ones had got out of repair and were of no use, another still needed.
>
> Mar 9th   Forwarded £2.16.6 to Mr Clarke for quarter fees.
>
> Mar 22nd   Av 29.1. David Mylchreest has come back to School after an absence of nine weeks.
>
> Jun 19th   Have had locks put on the doors of offices. The pump has been attended to by making a drain to take the water instead of having it run over the playground.
>
> Oct 30th   The playground has had four cart loads of coarse gravel put on. It is now so rough and stony that it is almost impossible for the children to play in it.

1892
> Jun 17th   The Committee have given a Kindergarten desk for the infants as it is more suitable than the old style desks.
>
> Sep 30th   Attendance very bad owing to harvest and scarlatina in some homes.
>
> Nov 4th   None of the children who have been ill have yet returned.
>
> Dec 9th   A holiday as the children could not get to School owing to a snow storm which continued all day so that it was impossible for the children to come to School.

1893
> Apr 14th   John Kneale has been away for nine weeks through illness. Harriett Galloway having been away since August last through weak eyes. Av 44.
>
> Jul 21st   Children attending very well at present. Av 44.7.

1894
> Jul 27th   RECITATIONS FOR 1895
>
> Standard I   Selections from Poetry for the Young.
>
> Standard II & III.   Alice Fell, or, Poverty.
>
> Standard IV to VII.The Merchant of Venice
>
> Oct 22nd   Miss Catherine Lace has commenced duties here.

1895
> Feb 20th   Resigned my post as Mistress. Miss C. Lace.
>
> Feb 20th   James Derbyshire took charge as temporary Master.
>
> Mar 15th   Mr Derbyshire's charge terminated.
>
> May 18th   Took charge. Eliza Radcliffe. 22 girls, 27 boys present

You will recall that Miss Radcliffe had previously resigned in 1876 due to severe illness. Since her leaving, the school had been closed for eight years and then, from 1884 to 1894, had eight different teachers, a very demoralising state of affairs for the children because of the lack of continuity.

> Apr 4th   50 present

Jun 14th	Order is not yet what I would wish, some of the children come to School with very dirty faces and hands and a few with very ragged clothes. There does not seem to be any order in their homes.
Jul 20th	Anne Jane and Maria Mylrea age 9 and 7 have an impediment in their speech. Eliza Radcliffe of Standard IV has not attended over a few times during the last three months.
Oct 18th	James Ernest Radcliffe has bronchitis and is very ill, his brother William is dull and doesn't seem capable of improvement, attendance irregular.

1896

Jan 30th	Holiday. School in use for Bachelors Ball.
Feb 1st	On register, 35 over 7 years of age, 10 under. Av 34.5. Two boys and one girl live within half a mile of the School.
Feb 21st	Chairman of School Committee, J. Kneale, Esq. visited. Rev A Rolston held Bible lessons in the morning.

(One clergyman or another visited the school nearly every fortnight. Miss Radcliffe had the name wrong, this was Rev Adrian S. Rolleston who was Chaplain of St Judes from 1894 to Dec 1913, he was devoted to this chaplaincy and was respected for his habitual courtesy, kindly disposition and steadfast loyalty to friends.)

Mar 5th	A few of the children are very dull and do not seem to make progress. The others are doing fairly.
Mar 13th	Margaret Jane Sayle absent all week, has a sore eye. Mona Radcliffe has not attended, reason unknown. The two Mylreas, one attended 6 times the other 4. Margaret Jane Howland absent 5 out of 10 times.
Mar 20th	Mona Radcliffe is ill; ordered a change and rest from school for a few weeks. Mr Brew put in two window panes and supplied kindling through the winter. Rev Rolston came two mornings this week.

(The school either had delicate windows or boisterous children because there are numerous reports of panes being replaced.)

Apr 1st	A fair in the neighbourhood. Most of the children were absent so closed school in the afternoon.
Apr 10th	Lower classes being very weak in the 3rs and spelling, special attention has been given to these subjects.

(Unfortunately, Miss Radcliffe was not all that hot on spelling or the use of words either, for example, she frequently misused 'has' or 'have'.)

Apr 13th	Admitted William Henry Teare to infant class, Also John Robert, William Edward and Thomas Fell from Sulby School, also Eleanor Jane Fell, all very backward.

(Poor Miss Radcliffe, if only she had known the trouble the Fell family was to cause her; she frequently mentioned one or the other in a derogatory manner, their attendances were erratic and they could not do other than be a poor influence on the other children whose own education suffered because of the time needing to be expended by Miss Radcliffe when trying to eradicate the dullness that was soon evident.

It was from this time forward that the reports of HMI became rather critical of the childrens' achievements as a whole.)

Apr 27th	Admitted Eva Annie Howland, infant. Margaret Jane Howland and Margaret Jane Sayle attend badly; they are kept at home to attend to their little brother and sister while their mothers are at work in the fields.
May 14th	Ascension day, register not marked. The children usually go to church in the morning. A Club and Sports in the Parish in the afternoon so half holiday.
May 25th	Queen Victoria's birthday holiday.
May 27th	New lifeboat launched, the Volunteers in town, great excitement. Boys all gone to town after. Half holiday.
Jun 18th	Received 6 dozen penholders and 3 boxes of nibs by Bardsleys, Oldham. and one quart of black ink from Priestland, chemist, Ramsey.
June 24th	School door mended, also pump seen to by Harrison who is occupied on the new school on same day.

(This is the first mention of the new Board School being built on the other side of the road.)

OBJECT LESSONS FOR 1897 :-

(Metals, Minerals etc.)

1.Sovereign. 2.Crown. 3.Penny. 4.Horse shoe. 5.Earthenware plate. 6.Knife and fork. 7.Coal. 8.Salt. 9.Air. 10.Water.

(Vegetable)

1.Bracket (oak). 2.Chair (ash). 3.Apple. 4.Bread (Corn). 5.Carrot and potato (roots). 6.Linen collar. 7.Baby's frock. 8.Clogs.9.Silk handkerchief.

(Animal)

1. Horse. 2.Cow. 3.Dog. 4.Cat. 5. Goose. 6.Hen. 7.Lark. 8.Crow. 9.Swallow. 10.Herring. 11.Whale. 12. Frog.

(After having received a poor report from HMI, Miss Radcliffe attempted justification in the Log Book on Oct 23rd)

Oct 23rd	Weakness principally due to special efforts made on behalf of some very dull boys and a few girls who have been overlooked or pushed aside when younger - a few of them have been pushed out of other schools.

1897

Mar 12th	Av 44.2. 26 boys and 27 girls.
Mar 22nd	Mr Brew repaired the boys' offices and put in two panes of glass.
May 14th	There are a number of very dull children in school. They are too big for infants and too slow with the other class. They take up a good deal of time and make little progress. The work of the school is also hampered by the uncertainty of my position as Mistress during the last five or six months.
Jun 22nd	Diamond Jubilee Celebrations. A whole holiday, children entertained at Parochial School. *(Probably Andreas)*
Jun 23rd	Diamond Jubilee Festival at Sulby. Eight Sulby children missing as a consequence. School work being so interrupted the children are tired and inattentive.
Jul 23rd	Ann Jane Mylrea (11) very deaf. Maria Mylrea and Eleanor Mylrea (defective speech). All very backward. William Radcliffe and James Ernest Radcliffe (brother, with defective speech) both very backward.

Aug 2nd   School inspection 59 present. 26 girls and 19 boys presented.
Aug 12th 1897. Resigned my post as Mistress. E Radcliffe.

Miss Radcliffe had been with the school, on and off, since 1866 and it may be that the Andreas School Committee felt that it might be better to have a fresh Head Teacher for their new St. Jude's School; they may have intimated as such, especially after the last critical report made by HMI.

As a matter of interest, in addition to her many years of work at St. Jude's, Miss Radcliffe had also been the sole teacher at the new Lezayre Board School from Aug 14th 1876 to May 6th 1884; presumably she taught in another school from 1884 to 1895. I do not know if she went on to another school after leaving St. Jude's but, eventually, she was granted a superannuation pension of £7.16.00 pa.

(The summer holidays arrived and with them the end of an era, the closure of the original School and the departure of the Teacher who had been at the opening. When the children returned after their holidays it was to a new, much larger and brighter school)

*   *   *

ST. JUDES SCHOOL (II) The new school.
1897.

Sep 20th   Teacher John Martin commenced duties this morning.
                The New School of St. Jude's opened for the first time this
                morning. Poor attendance. Rev G.W.Gregson visited in the p.m.
(Despite the new School being a Board School the Reverend gentlemen intended their continuing presence ! This one was the Curate of Andreas.)

1898

Feb 8th.   Gave notice of leaving. John Martin.
(Oh dear ! Less than six months ! Hardly a good start for the new School. Perhaps the Fell family had been a sufficient depressant.)

May 2nd   Took charge of this School this morning. E. Smale.
Jun 6th   Av 55.2. Percentage attendance 80%.
Jul 20th   School examination by W.H.Jalland. 68 present.
Sep 29th   Excerpt from HMI report :-

"The new School is admirably lighted and ventilated and well equipped for its' purpose. The new Master has evidently been both diligent and successful and the School is now in a very efficient state in all respects."

Oct 31st   Jesse Cowin and Eleanor Kinrade absent all week, they are not
                yet 14 years of age.
Dec 12th   Thomas, William and Eleanor Fell still attend irregularly.
1899

Jun 28th   Very heavy thunderstorm only 4 children present am, the storm
                continued in the afternoon, only 3 present.
Nov 24th   William Fell has been absent for a very long period. His father
                refuses to send him although he has been fined repeatedly.
1900

May 25th   Received official circular drawing attention to the instruction
                that:-

" Instruction in Rural Schools must in future be suitable to the environment and pursuits of the district."

May 28th   In answer to my enquiry concerning the 'Instruction in Rural
                Schools' circular, I have received intimation from the Board of
                Education that the "Specimen schemes" are not yet issued !

And so the new school progressed,the state of the weather continued to cause poor attendances - especially rain; time and time again heavy rain is reported to be causing disruption. The high turnover of staff continued, Mr Smale resigned in 1904 to be succeeded by Isabella.A.Dodd, the assistant teachers up to 1907 were Miss C.J.Lace, Miss Hannah Lace, Miss Catherine Brew, Miss A. Harrison, Miss Sarah Ann Bannister and Miss Edith M.Morrison.

St. Jude's Parochial School - Mrs Eliza Radcliffe taught upto fifty children within this tiny place, in several grades and entirely by herself. Drawn August 1999.

The children started to receive praise from HMI, so it seems as if the "Dull" ones had worked their way through the system. A few continued to take time off to work on the fields, but with nothing like the frequency experienced by other Schools, and, of course, from the 1900s onward the school started to have its share of closures due to Scarlatina, whooping cough and measles.

Under Miss Morrison the school progressed admirably; this can easily be understood because this lady took tremendous care when compiling the curriculum for each succeeding year, the content taking up to four pages of careful writing in the log book, unfortunately, even this industrious teacher had left by 1911.

St. Jude's was a pleasing rural school, nothing remarkable about it, just a nicely situated place for the local children and a school which gained a good local reputation.

Closure eventually came in 1982 primarily because of the fall in numbers of the children attending.

Do you remember the changeover of pupils which had been such a feature of every November, when the farmers and farm hands removed to other locations ? Well, this movement had almost ceased and the number of true rural homes complete with young families and children who were resident in the area gradually became fewer and fewer until, nowadays, they have practically ceased to exist.

Teacher :- You should have been here at 9 o'clock.
Boy :- Why ? Did something happen ?

*   *   *

Chapter eight

A tiny rural school - The Lhane

This is the story of one of the smallest schools on the island, yet, surprisingly, it is a story of some tenacity because it remained open for a much longer period than could reasonably have been expected for a school with so few pupils.

The Lhane School served the few people who lived in that North-West part of the Island known as The Lhen; at one time it had an equally small school as a relatively near neighbour in the tiny hamlet of Smeale.
  Smeale School closed by about 1880, but I have not been able to discover its age or the true date of closure; neither have I determined when the Lhane School was first opened or when it was first closed.
  It was in 1884 that the small Lhane School building was offered to the Andreas School Board.

Our story commences when it was reopened as a school in 1886.

*   *   *

The Lhane School never had a large number of children in its' single, low ceilinged classroom, and, like all rural schools, it had even less when the children were needed at home or in the fields, but, apart from these occasions, the average attendance against the number of children on the register was surprisingly high.
  The real puzzle is this, however did it manage to remain open as long as it did ?
  The school had originally been opened at a much earlier date but, so far as this tale is concerned, the length of time is from 1886 to 1932 !
  In the nineteenth century the School sometimes had over thirty children on the books but for most of its existence during the early part of the twentieth century, the school hardly ever had more than a dozen or so on the register, sometimes as low as four, and yet during the 1920s, when schools were being 'concentrated' and the smaller schools were being closed right, left and centre, the Lhane School, with its solitary teacher, managed to escape the attention of the Council of Education almost completely.

Lhane School was under the oversight of the Andreas School Board and, in this instance, the Board were quite conscientious, they made sure that the registers were checked frequently and one of the Board was usually in attendance when the school was visited by HMI - although they did incur his wrath a few times by not turning up, maybe they couldn't find it ? !

In official circles there was one peculiarity that made this school special, it was classed as a 'Certified ' school and I wonder whether it was this slight difference that tended to create a vacuum in the Education board offices and made Lhane School seem to disappear from their closure programme ?

The reason I ask the question is that for many, many years, visits by School Inspectors were very few and far between; even in later years the Inspectors seemed to avoid the place from time to time, there was never that regularity which marked their attendance on other rural schools.

THIS WILL NOT BE A LONG STORY !

For a very good reason, because, whilst the Log Book was faithfully kept up to date and entries frequently made, the entries tended to follow a simple formula such as, 'attendance fair', 'attendance good',' attendance poor', rarely did the teachers mention how many of their children actually attended !

I do not doubt that the numbers were faithfully recorded in the School Register but for those of us who can only consult the Log Book, it is a bit frustrating.

If you are in a hurry and have to skip a bit of the story, do not, whatever else you do, miss the entry toward the end recording an outing to Ramsey, it is a little gem.
[M30]

1886
>   Apr 1st   Opened school. 4 children present. Mrs Teare.
>   May 14th   36 children present.

(The attendance officer, a Mr W.Caley, visited the school quite frequently, oftentimes weekly.)

1887
>   May 12th   One child withdrawn. (By death)

(HMI only visited on an irregular basis and on the first visit in 1890 had very little to say.)

1890
>   **Excerpt from HMI report :- "The walls of the room should be well cleaned and whitewashed."**

1894
>   Feb 1st   Commenced duties with Mrs Teare for instruction, E.Gale.

1894 cont.
> Feb 14th   Commenced by myself. E.I.Gale.

1895
> Aug 8th. Excerpts from HMI report :-

> **Present - Over seven   25**
> **Under seven   8**
> **Total   33. None absent.**

> **Averages attendances - Boys 12.8**
> **Girls 7.1**
> **19.9**

"The premises are in good condition but the ceiling is much too low.
BOOKS AND APPLIANCES :- Not a good supply. Infants require a ball frame and other instructive articles. New arithmetic cards are urgently needed.
DISCUSSION - Excellent
NEEDLEWORK & CUTTING OUT - Excellent.
SINGING - Good.   READING - Good.
WRITING - Very fair. The adoption of some definite marked style, say, the 'Royal' would make it good.
ARITHMETIC - Standard I to III Good.
> Standard IV & V Very variable and inaccurate.
Style and methods are good throughout. Infants very weak in addition and subtraction. The Mistress has taught the School well."
(Note the five 'Standards', all taught by the one teacher.)

1896
> Aug 3rd   Curriculum - recitation.

Standard I	Who made the sky ?	20 lines.
Standard II	The village Blacksmith.	40 lines.
Standard III	The May Queen	60 lines.
Standard IV	The May Queen	80 lines.
Standard V	The Merchant of Venice	100 lines.

(Choice approved by R.Garside. Board Inspector.)

Excerpt from the 1896 Inspector's report -

"Premises in Good condition but the room is too low."
"The general standard of education is considerably below that of the Elementary Board Schools under a certified teacher."
(Miss Gale was not a certified teacher)
"Almost half the children are too old to be attending a Certified School, such being intended only for young children in outlying areas where difficulties attend their travelling the three miles required by the Act."

"I consider that a small new school built at or near the Four Roads is required. A School in such a position would be available for all the children now attending the present School."

(The Inspector's suggestion was a good one, the position of such a school would have been a little nearer to Smeale but, in fact, nothing was ever done, no other school was built.)

1897

Aug 13th	Attendance good. there are 27 on the register, two being under seven.

1900

Aug 10th	**An Inspector's report was highly critical of the Local Board who, he said, had not provided the teacher with sufficient resources. He also said that :-**

"The want of a thoroughly equipped Board School is very manifest. On the whole, the teacher is deserving of praise under all the circumstances and she maintains good order."

The Inspector took drastic action, reducing the School grant by one third. Such an action would have shaken the Andreas Board.

1901

Mar 22	William Radcliffe, Master of Parochial School. In charge owing to illness of the teacher and closure of the Parochial School from an epidemic of the mumps.
Apr 1st	Teacher returns to duty.

1902

Aug 8th	*The merit award grant was reinstated.*

1903

All children over 10 years of age (have been)sent to the new Parochial School at Andreas. This leaves eleven children of whom four are under seven. The School is reduced to three classes, Infants and Standard I and II.
(But, of course, all being taught in one room by the sole teacher.)

1906

Mar 31st	Giving up duties in this School today, leaving the Island. E.I.Gale. *(After twelve years service)*
Apr 18th	Commenced duty. Annie Kelly.

1909

Nov 8th	Commenced duty. J.Cowle.

1911

Jun 12th	Mr Cowle left. H.Lancaster took over as temporary Mistress.

July 3rd   Began duties. A. Boardman.
Nov 6th   A. Boardman left.
Nov 7th   E. Teare commenced duties.

(About this time HM Inspector criticized the late age at which local children first attended school, often being about six years old. These were rather elderly toddlers for an infants school.)

1914
Feb 20th   The Council of Education made an unannounced visit. They found that all was satisfactory and that the correct number of children had been entered on the register.

(One can only but wonder at such a high powered group of people descending on this tiny rural school; can you imagine how the poor Mistress must have felt ?)

July   There is one deaf boy who is unable to work with the rest of the school in class. He is, however, deft both with his hands and intelligent, he would benefit by the instruction provided in a special school.

1915
Nov 1st.   Commenced duties. G.Teare.

1920
(The following report is exactly as recorded by the teacher.)

Thursday the 15th of July.

THE ROYAL VISIT

This was a great and memorable day for the children of the Lhane School.

They had been looking forward most eagerly to the King's visit and left the School at 8 o'clock in the morning with light hearts and beaming faces to walk to Andreas Village. *(Over two miles distant - remember, they were infants)*

Here they were joined by the Andreas children and were quickly and comfortably conveyed to Ramsey by motor char-a-banc.

At Ramsey, along with other schoolchildren they were marched under supervision to Parliament Square.

They had a very good sight of the King and Queen and Princess Mary as their Majesties, after inspecting the Soldiers and Sailors, spent a little time amongst the children.

Following on the departure of the Royal Party, the Lhane children, along with the Andreas and St. Judes children marched to the United Methodist Schoolroom for lunch and after enjoying an excellent tea they marched to the sports field at 1.30pm.

They enjoyed the sports very much and at 5 o'clock they had another good tea in the aforementioned building.

At 6pm they were taken to the Cosy Corner; here a happy hour was spent listening to the Pierrots.

After leaving the Cosy Corner the children marched back to the United Methodist Schoolroom where they enjoyed the buns provided and at 7.30pm the char-a-banc was again loaded and headed for Andreas. It carried back many thankful and happy hearts and on reaching Andreas Village the kiddies gave three cheers for the King and the School Board.

The Lhane children walked up to the Lhane from Andreas Village and, although they were rather tired when they reached home, they thoroughly enjoyed the whole day and without a doubt it will live long in the memory of each child.

*   *   *

1922.
JULY.   *The Andreas School Board relinquished its duties to the Central Education Authority in this month.*

1924
    May 5th   New dual desks and a piano provided.
1926   Average attendance 99.37%
1928   Average attendance 99.62%

1932   This School closed by order of the Education Authority.
                   Gertrude Teare   [M30]

(Miss Teare had been the sole teacher for 17 years but in her last year there were only 5 children on the register and a couple of these were due to be transferred to Andreas under the age rule. Another page of history was turned)

*   *   *

"This is the past, in process of being liquidated.
Sad, perhaps; but necessary. The past being cleared away."
(Malcolm Muggeridge)

*   *   *

Chapter Nine

CHARACTER OF A COUNTRY SCHOOL - CRONK-Y-VODDY
(Originally opened about 1842)
Based on the Cronk-y-Voddy Log Book

William Radcliffe described 'Cronk-y-Voddey' in 1925 as :-
" A hill village, with school and church, at the summit of the steep road from Glen Helen
to Kirk Michael. The church is the chapel-of-ease to the Parish of German - The district to
the east is barren moorland."
Our story starts on November 3rd 1873, when John Watterson, the Master, reported that
school commenced on that day; his phrasing suggests that the school had been closed for a
while; he had 16 girls and 15 boys in attendance, a total of 31, by Nov 11th the figure had
gone up to 43.
 His first disagreeable task of the week was the need to ask the children to bring 4d to school
as fire money for the winter.
 John Watterson entered his log book details frequently and factually, yet behind the very
neatly written words I believe that I discovered a real depth of feeling for 'his children'; there
was a compassion, but at the same time, whilst it is possible to sympathise with his
considerable frustration, there was humour as well.
 Within a few years other teachers came along, some stayed for quite a long time but
others just came and went. From the Log Book it is not possible to identify all the teachers
because their names were not entered as they should have been, neither their names or the
dates on which they started or ceased.
 The various changeovers between the teachers can only be discovered by a change in the
handwriting; with some it was confident and strong, others seemed rather hesitant, some
even wrote in a manner which suggested that their handwriting expertise was not much
better than that of the children they taught; blots were common.
 I have followed the story in date order and with the same brevity that was used in the
original log book; as far as possible I have used the teachers' actual words but you must
remember that these entries are only a tiny fraction of the actual number of reports,
nevertheless, I hope that I will have quoted enough to give you a good understanding of the
real problems faced by teachers - and the scholars - in such a remote area. My comments are
usually in italics.

1873

Feb 2nd	A few children missing - picking turnips.
Apr 1st	A great many children missing - picking turnips.
Apr 6th	Had singing for the first time with Rev J.H.Edmunds and Miss Eden assisting.

(Rev James H. Edmunds was Chaplain at Cronk-y-Voddy from 1865, he died aged 61 in 1875.)

Apr 27th	A great many children missing - setting potatoes and picking stones.
Apr 29th	I broke John Cowley's pop-gun for having shot Thomas Christian in the face.
May 1st	Many children missing - fair at St John's and others at mountain assisting in turf cutting.
May 14th	60 in school - taken to church - Ascension day.
Jun 19th/26th	Many children missing - having chin-cough.

(Chin-cough = whooping cough)

Jun 30th	Many children missing - employed in field work, haymaking and weeding.

1874

Jul 3rd	Rev J.Corlett, Chaplain of St. John's came with a new School Fees book which in my opinion would puzzle a Philadelphia lawyer to understand.

(Rev John Corlett was also Clerk to German Parish Commissioners)

Jul 29th — **Annual Inspection. 76 present of whom 36 were presented for examination. Passes 106, failures 2. The Inspector was highly pleased with discipline and demeanour.**

Oct 6th	Exceedingly wet and stormy, only 22 present.

(Note - Reports by teachers over several decades at this school all mention the effect of severe weather on school attendance; by all accounts Cronk-y-Voddy did experience tremendous downpours and heavy snowfalls.)

Oct 9th	Gave order to children to clean the school at noon today instead of stopping after school as the days are getting shorter.
Oct 15th	Gave John Christian, Charles Kissack and William Corlett 100 lines to write after lessons today for disobeying orders - shoving at reading - 100 extra to William for contempt - laughing.
Nov 20th	From H.M.Inspector's report :-

"The room is a very poor one and quite inadequate for its present purpose, it must be enlarged and remodelled, great attention must be paid to ventilation."

Dec 21	Mr Watterson had to tell the children that fees at the following rates were to be payable in advance :-

All fees to be made quarterly in advance.
1st and 2nd classes 3/3d - if at end of quarter 3/6d
3rd and 4th classes 2/2 - " "   "   "   "   2/6d

1875

May 7th   (*Mr Watterson made a normal everyday report in the log book* `
                   on this day, but, sadly, and to everyone's surprise, this was the
                   last entry ever to be made by him.)

May 24th
(Report following a surprise visit by an Inspector.)
" Register not marked. Log book not made up. Master away ill. Daughter in
charge of school. Committee should provide a clock."
(*Just as her father had been, Mr Watterson's daughter was devoted to the school, she*
stepped in and continued running the school during his illness, there is no   mention of any
break in the school routine or lessons. She made the required log book entries on and from
May 25th.)

May 29th.   Mr Watterson died. The school closed for one week.

Jul 20th.   School Inspection report :-" There were 56 children present and
             36 were presented for exams. There were 105 passes and only
             three failures."
(Mr Watterson would have been pleased, and the result, surely, was a creditable reflection
on the work as continued by his daughter. Unfortunately, Mr Watterson's daughter was not
an accredited teacher and the School Committee would not let her remain in charge. In
reality they had no choice, they had to replace her with an accredited teacher or lose the
school grant.
The next Master was William Callister.

Dec 29th   School Inspector's report :-
(This report was an extremely rare example of real compassion shown by one of
these officials whose visits to some schools were occasions to be feared. The report
included the following praise.)**"It has been represented to me that certain charges
of misconduct were recently proffered against the late Mr John Watterson which,
upon investigation proved to be either false or frivolous but which, nevertheless
so preyed upon his mind that they embittered the close of his life, if they did not
hasten his death. One of these charges was that Mr Watterson had neglected the
lower classes in his school and in justice to his memory I desire to state that no
school in the Isle of Man has done better in those very classes - I found excellent
order as well as attainments throughout the school."   A.P.Graves.**

1876
Jun 13th.   German School Committee brought Architect from Ramsey to
             consider the best site for a new school.
Aug 11th   76 present

1877

| | Nov 9th. | Dr. Higgins, the public vaccinator attended and 38 children were vaccinated. |
| | Nov 16th | Many children absent - parents blame vaccination. |

1878

	Feb 5th.	*Evacuated school - removed desks to Mr Cowley's barn.*
	Feb 6th.	*Commenced school in barn.*
	May 11th.	*Dismissed school half hour early today - Mr Cowley wanted to put stack of straw into other end of barn.*
	Jun 30th.	From HMI report:-

"The children have made very good progress considering the miserable premises, I am glad to think they will soon be in the new school."

*   *   *

1878.CRONK-Y-VODDY NEW SCHOOL

Nov 8/15th. Architect examined work of new school.

There is hardly any mention of illness among the children attending the school during this year.

It may be that the relative isolation of the school provided some sort of immunity from the more general childrens' diseases because, in 1878, there was an epidemic of small pox elsewhere on the Island which caused some 200 deaths.

Another reason may be much simpler, maybe the children had something especially good to interest them - the building of their new school ?

Presumably the new school was opened in this year but there is no indication in the log book of the event happening.

School room dimensions :- 38'6" x 17' x 15' high
Class room dimensions :- 15'6" X 12' x 12' high.

1879

| | Apr 18th. | Attendance very low - children employed spreading manure and setting potatoes - parents say they must keep the children away from school to get work done. |

1880

| | Jul 26th. | 66 on register - average attendance 30.75. |

1882

| | Jan 13th. | School Inspector's report :- |

"The floor and walls are very dirty in the school and class room, the walls are damp and the roof requires attention. Maps are being destroyed by damp."

(The Inspector was obviously very annoyed at what he found in this nearly new school, it was only three years old. Later in the report, he issued a direct threat to the school committee warning them that if matters were not rectified quickly he would take proceedings to have the school taken off HM Inspectors' list, which, in effect, would have closed the school. The work was done within a short time.)
1884.

A new teacher had been running the school for thirteen months and was getting more and more despondent, the teacher was obviously depressed by the weather, by the absences from school and a lack of support. It all started to surface when the following entry was made in the Log Book - the content of which was always noted by HM Inspectors.

Jun 17th.	Attendance is not so good as it ought to be. If I did not make special efforts myself and appeal to the parents by word of mouth and notes, our attendance record would be far from satisfactory. Our attendance officers are no better than two old women. The Michael officer has been here once in the thirteen months since I came and if our atten dance officer visits us once in every two months we think it a treat.
Jun 20th	64 on register, average 56.3 or 88%, better than usual.
Jun 30th	6 children live within half mile of the school, 41 within one mile, 11 within three miles and two over three miles.

1885

May 12th	I have been both surprised and grieved this morning on receiving the news of Ann Boydes death from inflammation of the lungs, she had only been absent from school one week and when I last saw her was a fine, healthy looking girl - age 8 years.

1886

Mar 1st	Such a snowstorm has not been known for 20 years. In this area the roads are quite impassable, in most places level with the hedges.
Mar 8th	The bye-roads are still impassable. 29 present.

1887

Jan 26th	As weddings are very unusual incidents in this neighbourhood I allowed the children to remain outside the school until 9.30 to witness the departure of one from the lane.
Feb 7th.	I had to punish Katie Cowley, one of my 6th standard girls for telling me a deliberate falsehood this morning.

Jun 17th	The Queen's Jubilee was celebrated here this afternoon. The children of the neighbourhood had tea in the school house after which they went into a field kindly lent by Mr Cowley and spent the evening playing games.
June.	Excerpt from H.M.Inspector's report :-

"This small and remote country school is taught with much care and creditable success - and praise must be accorded also to the discipline."

Nov 7th	Received a note from Mrs Kelly, Lherghydhoo, stating that Helen had chilblains and was unable to walk to school.
1888	
Jan 11th.	The Bishop and Mrs Bardsley visited the school and were greatly pleased.

(Bishop John W.Bardsley came to the island in 1887)

Feb 1st	Admitted James Kermeen. Age 8 next August, no previous education.
Feb 6th	The German School Committee have advised that fees at Cronk-y-Voddy are to be 2/- a quarter or 2d a week in all standards.
Jun 29th	There has been so much rain that only 19 attended. Three children are less than half a mile from school. Five are half to one mile. Twentyfive from one to two miles Sixteen over two miles.
1889	
Aug 12th.	School closed for fortnight - measles.
1891	
Jul 8th	School closed for one week - influenza. There are 46 on register, average attendance 32.9
1893	
Jan 9th	Very cold, 20 present.
Jan 13th	A stove which was formerly in use in St. Johns School was set up in this school on Tuesday last. By the by, it has a large crack in it, however it warms the room admirably.
Jan 24th	Several absent - Knocksharry Bazaar.
Feb 17th	Almost half have mumps. Here we are covered in snow whilst below Glen Helen none.
Feb 27th	Thick snow. Two children in the morning ten in the pm.
May 1st	Admitted George Mark Corlett,(Cronkdhoo) aged 10, has never been to school before and does not know the alphabet.
1894	
Mar 12th	Owing to the prevalence of wet and stormy weather during past months I have pasted a number of pictures on the walls to amuse and instruct the children at dinner time as the majority of them bring their dinner to school and it is seldom fit to go out to play after eating their frugal meals.

May 17th   Since the introduction of Free Education the number of infants has increased and I find it very difficult to instruct them properly and attend to the children in the standards at the same time.

Jun 30th   53 on register, 37 average.

1895

Feb 6th   School closed for 13 days, cut off by snow, on the highways it is 15 to 16 feet thick..

Feb 20th   25 present, 30 absent.

June   55 on register. Average attendance 40 or 72%.

Nov 8th   Admitted Joseph Edward Corlett aged nine. Has never been to a school before.

HMI report :-

The children are in excellent order and have again passed a very satisfactory exam considering the unfavourable circumstances of the district.

1896

Mar 17th   Yesterday was very stormy and the fires smoked fearfully, it being almost impossible to see the children at the other end of the room.

Jun 17th   Very wet morning, no children present. The reluctance of the children to attend is understandable, they arrive saturated and when they go home they arrive home in a similar condition.

Jun 30th.   14 live within one mile.
29 between one and two.
12 between two and three.
6 over three miles

1897

Mar 12th.   Weather for past six months extremely wet.

Aug 23rd.   Attendance return for 1896/7.

Attendances	School meetings	Average
20,060	414	48.45

It is noticeable that absences are now frequently blamed on weather or sickness - not quite so often on farming work, but there were the odd exceptions !

Oct 21st   Many of the children have been kept at home to help thresh corn and pick potatoes.

1900

Distances.   12 less than one mile.
17 between one and two miles.
13 between two and three.
3 over three miles
5 four miles.

Aug 15th.   Edith May Corlett admitted - over 8 years of age, does not know
              her letters. Another sister admitted sometime ago, aged 9, does
              not know her alphabet yet. They live over three miles from
              school and their attendance is irregular, moreover they are
              exceptionally dull and of weak intellect and they are a complete
              drag on the school.

1902
Jun 19th   The girls do their needlework very well. Oral work would be
              more satisfactory if the children were not so bashful, as they
              know much more than an outsider or stranger would imagine.
Jun 30th   Attendance suffered severely during 2nd and 3rd quarters
              owing to wet and cold weather. I never remember the weather
              being so cold in May. My daughter, Minnie E. Kelly, has been a
              most useful assistant to me, she has given most of the object
              lessons to the infant class.

Work schedule for 1902/3 :-
English, Geography, History, Arithmetic.
(Group I & II Board of Education Scheme 1 for small schools.)
The following items all as under former codes :-
              Singing, Drawing, Needlework, Physical Drill.
              Recitation. Group 1. The Two Crossing Sweepers.
                  "   "   Group 2. Selections from Shakespeare.

Jul 11th.   The attendance of the 1st Class boys is irregular, in fields,
              weeding turnips

HMI report for 1901/2 :-
**"The master and assistant have done their best under most trying conditions
caused by his continuing ill health. The school is doing as well as can be
expected but the higher grant is recommended with some hesitation. The
premises are in much better repair but the girls latrines smell badly and their
small playground is covered with loose big stones.**
School openings were 414, attendances were 17051 only 41.1% "
(The master was Sidney B.Kelly, assisted by his wife, Emily A.Kelly and his
daughter Minnie E.Kelly.)
*(Unfortunately the school was about to enter a phase during which the turnover of staff
was unexpectedly high, very unsettling for the youngsters)*
1903
Feb 4th   Master absent due to influenza and diabetes.
May 11th   Eleanor E. Bridson took over the school.
Oct 20th   One of the chief faults of the children is their lack of
              punctuality. Many are hindered at home attending to cattle etc.
Oct 30th   44 on register. Average attendance 36.2

| Nov 20th | Minnie has neuralgia and is unable to attend. I have had to teach all classes. |

(Mr Kelly died and his wife left the school but Minnie, who was only an assistant and quite unqualified, stayed on to help the new mistress, Miss Bridson; unfortunately, this lady was deeply affected by cold in the school, her Log Book entries repeatedly stress the cold - which was equally as bad in the school as in her schoolhouse.)

1904

Mar 30th	Because of the cold and damp I (Miss Bridson) have tendered my resignation.
May 20th	I have been told that the roof is to come off the house to try and cure the damp in the walls. Had to arrange urgent temporary lodgings.
Jun 6th	W.P.Holmes appointed temporary master.
Jul 4th	I have taken over the school. Anne Ashdown Porter.
Jul 20th	Minnie deserves great credit for plodding on under great disadvantages but she has no idea of a habit or a method of study - she is very anxious, willing and obedient.
Jul 23rd	Walter Corlett aged nine and a half and Daniel Corlett, nearly eight, from Cronk Dhoo, admitted. They do not know how to read or form letters.
Aug 25th	Farmers have asked me to defer the harvest holidays because the grain is still quite green.
Nov 7th	A perfect hurricane of wind and rain made it impossible for boys and girls even from less than half a mile away to struggle through, it was even worse in the afternoon. No registers marked.
Dec 16th	From October to April over 30 stay to eat their dinners in school. We provide them with hot cocoa and tea.

1905

| Jan 27 | Edwin Kinvig has ringworms also Alice Quairk. Schoolroom bitterly cold, children cannot write properly in their exercise books and slates are too cold for little ones to use. |
| Mar 10th | E.Kaighin has scalded her foot and cannot get her boots on. My rooms in the schoolhouse are so damp that both walls and furniture are mouldy. |

(Anne Porter, the teacher, was repeatedly ill from Jan 9th to May 9th.)

| Oct 23rd | Tom Looney was kicked in the face by a horse during the school holidays, he is still in bandages and unable to attend. |

(The local committee asked for a report from the Teacher because fuel consumption had risen at the school. In her reply Anne Porter stated that there were two fires in the school which failed to warm the rooms, and she had one fire in the schoolhouse to try and keep the walls dry.)

	Nov 22nd	Reprimanded and punished younger boys for making a urinal of the playground.

1906

	Jan 15th	Mistress ill with bronchitis and influenza.
	Jan 29th	Anne Porter resumed classes.
	June 14th	Anne Porter's daughter, Mrs G. Moore, took over the school temporarily.
	July 23rd	Mrs Anne Ashdown Porter has died.

(Mrs Porter had repeatedly complained about cold in the school as well as the cold and damp conditions in her schoolhouse. It is more than possible that these two factors contributed to her death.)

	Oct 8th	Mr H.Ormered took over the school. 48 on book, 24 present.

1907

Mr Ormerod prepared a thorough and comprehensive proposed curriculum for school work; it is not represented here because of its length, the proposal was the first to be written into the Log Book for a long, long time.

	Jun 28th	Many absent - on potato work.
	Jul 1st	Half day for Lambfell Sunday School treat.
	Jul 4th	Half day for Barregarrow Sunday School treat.
	Jul 5th	Tynwald Day holiday.
	Jul 8th	Mary Kermeen absent - minding cows.
	Jul 12th	Many boys absent - turnip thinning.
	Jul 26th	Many absent - Haymaking.

HMI report 1906/7 :-

"The warming arrangements in this school are quite unsuitable and wholly inadequate, the temperature is often down to 36/37 degrees. Unless steps are taken to make the heat satisfactory I may recommend a deduction from the grant and consider whether I can certify that the school premises are satisfactory."

(Mr Ormerod, the new teacher, obviously felt that the death of Mrs Porter was due to the cold and damp at Cronk-y-Voddy, he refused to live in the schoolhouse until such time as it was made habitable again.)

Aug 16th.   School Board members have inspected the house. The walls and floor are always wet, at times the floor has standing water, there is no waterproof course and I refuse to live in it. The Committee refuse to pay the rent of the house I occupy; this is the sort of encouragement I get.

1908
Apr 30th   The School Board have intimated that I will receive three months notice because I refuse to live in an unsanitary house.

(I should imagine that someone higher up in the school board must have had second thoughts concerning the three months notice; Mr Ormerod was an exceptionally capable teacher, nothing more was heard about it.)
1909
Mar 17th   The school has opened 81 times since Christmas, three children have attended less than 50%, six under 60%, four under 70%.
Jun 25th   School closed until July 26th - measles.

(Although she hasn't been mentioned lately, Miss Minnie Kelly was still assisting in the school.)
HMI 1908/9 report :-
"Miss Kelly is a useful helper and lays a sound foundation for the master's very good work. The well which is the only drinking water supply is but 10 feet from an earth closet - this should receive prompt consideration."

Nov 19th   The pump for our water supply has been out of order since November 3rd - we are without a water supply.
Dec 17th   School Board have arranged for a water analysis.
1910.
Jul 4th.   Average attendance 92.1.

HMI report:-
"Pump has been out of order from November to April inclusive, the school was without water for half a year."

July 13th.	Possible attendance	Absences
Amy Taggart	371	128
Jessie Taggart	371	90
Owen Williams	371	130
William James Caine	302	110
Reginald Lahmers	303	75
Ella Cannell	371	111

1911

Infants and Standard One have not missed one attendance during this week, I have allowed them to go home half an hour early as a reward.

Jul 28th   There were seventeen prizes for good attendance.

1913

Apr 9th   Expelled Harold Kinveg for bullying younger boys and misbehaviour.

HMI report for 1912/13 The report was full of praise for the school and the teachers but the Inspector again criticised the heating. -

"Heating most unsatisfactory, on 93 occasions the temperature was not above 50 and on 13 was below 45. This matter has been reported twice before, the school is not properly warmed."

1914

Jul 28th.   School closed until Aug 24th - whooping cough.

1915

Nov 15th.   Terrific storm on the 12th, only six from nearby came.

1916

Miss Minnie Kelly left and went to Ashton under Lyne.

Apr 17th   Mr Ormerod left the school.

Jun 2nd   New master, Richard E.Torr.

1920

Oct 29th.   47 on roll. Average 22.1. 89.5%

1925

Apr 1st   Mr W.E.Shimmin took over the school

Apr 22nd   Average 22.4. 89.5%

At some time a Miss E.M.Moore became an assistant teacher but she must have presented a pretty poor example to the children because the master was repeatedly recording her as being late or failing to attend. The strange thing is that this behaviour continued for years and she did not seem to improve at all, yet Mr Shimmin was happy to devolve responsibility on to her quite frequently; the following are a few of the relative reports.

1927

Miss E.M. Moore absent March 16th to 23rd, Apr 1st, Apr 7th to 25th, May 7th, June 29.

May 9th   Took on register Doris Mary Lace. Age four years nine months.

Jun 7th   Re-admitted Annie Elizabeth Lace (the Vaish), she has not attended for twenty-two months, is almost 10 years of age and is still doing schoolwork proper to infants.

Jun 15th   TT races on two days made work almost impossible.

(This was by now an almost regular complaint/comment)

Jun 17th   School closed for TT.

HMI report:-
**" Only 32 in attendance, continues to be effectively conducted, the needs of the
school are being met in a satisfactory way."**

Sept 5th   Mr Kissack of Crosby did repairs including :- Levelling of girls'
                  yard, cleaning and repair of lavatories. Installing new stove,
                  rebuilding wall at the rear of the boys' latrines.
Dec 22nd   33 on register. Average attendance 92.7%.
The children gave a concert/panto for the first time, there was full scenery,
dresses and songs, the presentation was "Red Riding Hood" and the school was
crowded. After expenses for the scenery and dresses the proceeds went to The
Childrens' Home, Douglas.

*(This was the forerunner of similar annual concerts but the proceeds from the later
concerts were used for the benefit of Cronk y Voddy schoolchildren.)*

1928.
The average attendance is only 68% and I believe that the children take advantage
of distance as an excuse, yet the boy who lives the farthest never misses, wet or fine.

May 8th   Mr Shimmin absent until May 14th
May 29th   Mr Shimmin in hospital. Mr G.W.Sayle in charge as acting
                  master.
Jun 21st   A stormy, wet morning and I was delayed by three punctures as
                  well as a dog bite for which I had to go and get treatment.
                  G.W.Sayle.
Jul 16   Mr Shimmin resumed.

*(Mr Shimmin was suitably impressed with the weather conditions affecting the Cronk y
Voddy area, he regularly took measurements of the rainfall, so much so that he came to be
considered a local expert.)*

October   Rainfall for the month was 10.65 inches.
1929.
Jan 22nd   Commenced sprinkling school each evening with a strong
                  solution of Jeyes Fluid as a precaution against the spread of flu.
Feb 11th   Blizzard. Closed the school at 2.30pm so that the children would
                  not be holed up for the night.
Feb 12th   Roads impassable, there were no children present.
Feb 13th   Ten children came.

Feb 18th	75% present but in the main room the temperature was 33 degrees and in the class room 34 degrees. It was too cold for written work.
Feb 19th	We are without coal despite my having ordered it. Temperatures 35 and 34.
Feb 20th	Without coal, Temperatures 33 and 35.
Jun 28th	31 on roll, average 28.

1930

Feb 11th	I have been ordered to Douglas Court House to give evidence regards rainfall in the case 'Gregson v Highways Board'.
Jun 11th	The three Kellys are absent with scarlet fever.
Jun 16th	Edith Ennett and Phylis Corlett sent home because I suspect that they, too, have scarlet fever.

1931   There were 58.55 inches of rain during 1930
1931

Jan	Only 22 on register.
Jan 30th	Rainfall during January 4.95 inches.
Mar 20th	Have been offered the Headship of Jurby School, am going to visit the school before deciding.
Apr 2nd	The last day with this school. W.E.Shimmin.
Apr 13th	Miss E.M. Moore asked to take over school for the summer term.
May 1st	Miss Johnstone appointed as uncertified assistant.
Sep 7th	Mr Peter Hyslop has taken over the school.
Dec 7th	Have admitted Kathleen aged 8 and Edith Killey,7, neither of whom has the slightest knowledge of reading, writing or arithmetic.
Dec 21st	Have received a letter from the Department of Education regarding a 10% cut in salary with effect from April 1st

1932.

1932

Feb 11th	Temperature at 9am, 35 degrees, there were 20 children in the morning and 23 in the afternoon.
Jun 17th	Four scholars sat for the recent scheduled examinations, three of whom have been successful, Charles R.Quirk, Leonard Atkinson and Margaret Corlett.
Jul 21st	Removing all desks, furniture and fittings to Douglas central store.
Jul 22nd	School closed - Sine die. Peter Hyslop.

The school was closed without any day or date being given for a possible re-opening, but the school never did re-open.

The closure was final, but the last short episode which I have listed above took place in 1932 and it epitomised Cronk-y-Voddy school, cold, as usual, and yet having scholars that did well.

Nowadays the old school and schoolhouse stand as one private property which is well maintained and painted by the owners: Standing facing the old chapel of ease, which is painted white and a landmark for miles around, the school seems to fit snugly under its wing and is hardly noticed by the hundreds of passers-by as they speed along in their cars or on their motor-cycles with their eyes glued to the road ahead.

I wonder if any drivers and passengers passing by in the comfort and warmth of present day cars, coaches and buses ever give a thought to the hundreds of children who made their way, by foot, day by day, through almost all weathers so as to get to this, their own little "mountain school", cold as it was.   [M16]

'Tis education forms the common mind.
Just as the twig is bent, the tree's inclined.
(Alexander Pope 1688-1744)

*   *   *

Chapter ten

PORT ST. MARY.
PROBLEMS AT AN INFANT SCHOOL
(Excerpts from the 1896-1927 Log Book)

Port St. Mary School was opened in 1880 for boys and infants. There was just the one well appointed building with a number of classrooms but the Boys School and the Infant School were taught as separate schools, each having their own teachers and Log Books.

The only time the teachers of the schools acted in concert was when, owing to sickness or bad weather, attendances were so low that they both agreed not to mark the registers, but this did not happen very often. Our tale relates to the infant school only.

1896
Jan 7th	Opened school with 60 scholars.
	Staff. M.J.Quilliam. CT. Nellie Kermode. Monitress.
Jan 20th	Kate Qualtrough has joined as Asst. Teacher.
Jan 23rd	73 infants present.
Feb 3rd	A very good attendance 80 present out of 84 on the roll. Dr. Rose visited during the morning.
Feb 20th	Very wet day, only about 20 present, the children were so wet that they were sent home as soon as it was fit to do so.
Mar 6th	The best attendance since the school opened. Average 86.
Mar 11th	117 on roll, 113 attended during the morning and 115 in the afternoon.
May 29th	Nellie Kermode. Monitress has left.
Jun 8th	Nessie Crebbin enrolled as Monitress.
Jul 2nd	HMI visited. 115 present. Half day holiday in the afternoon.

Sep 1st to 25th. Kate Qualtrough absent.

HMI report :-
"Infant class. There is every promise of this part of the school becoming thoroughly efficient. An excellent start has been made in the new room."
Nov 2nd   100 present out of 108.

(The attendance figures were quite surprising, to have risen from 60 to over 100 in such a short space of time suggests a great need in the area; they were rarely bettered in later years.)

Nov 5th   Mr M.J.Quilliam. Principal Teacher has resigned.
Mary Cowley is attending as substitute.

(This was only the start! The turnover of staff and the amount of sickness they experienced in the early years was remarkable.)

Nov 13th   Many children are absent because of colds.
Miss Qualtrough, Asst. Mistress, away all week with sore foot.
Dec 11th   Many children are absent with colds. The very wet weather making us unable to open school on Monday morning, all day on Wednesday and Thursday afternoon.

(I will not attempt to repeat the number of log book entries made concerning rainfall and wet weather generally. Sufficient to say that they continue throughout the Log Book, the heaviness of the rainfall being a direct cause of many absences by the children, especially those from remote areas such as The Howe.)

Dec 18th   Miss Qualtrough away Thursday and Friday because of her Father's death.
Dec 23rd   Mary Cowley, Teacher. Resigned
1897
Jan 12th   Elizabeth Harris appointed Teacher. Commenced duties today.
Jan 26th   Nessie Cubbin away with a severe cold.
Feb 5th   Miss Qualtrough absent all week
Mar 12 to 19. Miss Qualtrough absent all week due to sickness.
Jun 4th to 10th. Nessie Cubbin absent.

(Staffing of this infant school must have seemed to be an almost impossible problem, the number of resignations was bad enough but to have so much sick absence as well ?!)

Jun 22nd   Holiday in celebration of Queen Victoria's Diamond Jubilee.
June 25th to 29th Nessie Cubbin absent.
1898
Feb 22nd   Severe snowstorms have prevented children from attending. Registers not marked
Feb 25th   With this severe weather the average attendance is only 50.4, many are absent sick.

1899
> Feb 10th   Wet and stormy, many children away sick, some have whooping cough.
> Jun 27th   Holiday on account of the Club Procession.
> *(Presumably the Rechabite Club)*
> Jun 28th   Very stormy, only 9 attended in the morning and 27 in the after noon. Registers not marked.
> Jul 26th   Government Inspection. 86 present.
> Dec 14th   Holiday - War parade in Douglas.

1900
> Apr 18th   Nessie Cubbin absent.
> May 7th   Annie Crebbin has come in to assist because Nessie Cubbin is still absent.
> May 15th   Annie Crebbin has left. Gladys Jones has come in to take over.
> May 24th   Holiday to celebrate the Queen's birthday and the Relief of Mafeking.
> Jul 10th   Holiday given - Sunday School outing to Laxey.

1902

Excerpt from HMI report :-

"The infants are kindly handled by the Mistress and the work on the whole is creditable. A piano is needed to help singing and drill."

Staff. Miss E Harris Teacher. Nessie Cubbin. Probationer Teacher.

> Oct 6th   Average attendance for the June quarter 75.2
> Average attendance for the Aug quarter 77.2.
> Nov 21   21 children away ill with severe colds or whooping cough.
> Nov 27th   The attendance officer has confirmed that 18 children have whooping cough.
> Dec 9th   Average attendance for quarter ending Nov 30th, 43.6. The school has been closed until January 7th due to whooping cough and chicken pox.

1903
> Jan 7th   Only 24 present, many ill.
> Jan 20th   Nessie Cubbin sick all week.
> Jul 13th   Absence among children is now due to scarlatina.
> Sep 7th   Miss Crebbin has left again.
> Sep 23.   HMI report :-

" Order and instruction in the infant school are good. The room is not properly clean."

1904
> May 10th   School closed due to Motor Racing.

1905
> Feb 1st   Miss E. Harris has resigned. Miss H.A.Sansbury has commenced duties as Teacher in Charge of the Infant School.

Mar 7th	Miss Gladys Jones away for two days having a meeting with the authorities at the Training College, Sheffield.
Sep 1st	Holiday - Motor Races.
Sep 11th	Miss Jones has left, there is no successor.

1906

Jan 12th	Average attendance 43.4
Feb 12th	Attendance very poor, 20 in the morning and 35 in the afternoon.
Feb 13th	The school has been closed for a fortnight, mumps.
Sep 11th	Average attendance 58.2

1907

Mar 4th	Miss Amy Costain takes up duties as Assistant Teacher on Probation.
May 24th	Holiday for Empire Day.
Jun 20th	Attendance 80.7 !
Jul 5th	Holiday Tynwald day.
Jul 9th	Holiday - club excursion to Ramsey.
Jul 19th	Many away sick, very poor attendance due to measles.
Jul 26th	Average attendance 23.9.

1908

Oct 15th	Staff :-H.Sansbury. Certified Mistress.
	A.Costain. Supplementary Teacher.
	G.Crebbin. Monitress.
Nov 3rd	Miss Crebbin transferred to Port Erin Infant School. Nellie Roberts and Edith Carine employed as Monitors.

1909

Aug 30th	64 present out of 82 on the register.

1910

Apr 8th	25 children away all week with whooping cough.
Apr 29th	32 children away all week due to whooping cough. Average attendance 40.5.
May 20th	Holiday for the King's funeral.
Jun 21st	Holiday due to Sunday School excursion to Port Soderick.
Jun 23rd	Holiday for the Club procession.
Jun 30th	Children examined by the school medical officer Dr. Bromley.
Jul 5th	Holiday - Tynwald Day.
Jul 7th	Register cancelled today - very few children came in the afternoon because there were three picnics taking place this day.
Jul 12th	Holiday - excursion to Laxey.

This was not an exceptional year, one day and half day holidays were granted for all sorts of reasons, these were in addition to the Easter, Harvest and Christmas holidays; even an examination by HMI seemed to be a good enough reason to have a half holiday in the afternoon.

1911

Jun 16th to 22nd School closed for the Coronation holiday.

Sep 8th   During a medical examination of the school Dr. Bromley found one boy with a skin eruption on his hand. He was sent home with instruction not to return to school until it had healed or he had permission from a medical officer.

1912

Jan 26th   Very good attendance. Average 59.1 for the week.

Sept 8th   Opened school after summer holiday, 80 present, of whom 16 boys and 15 girls were transferred to the upper schools.

Nov 29th   There has been a very bad attendance this week owing to the stormy weather, only 16 present on Monday. Average for this week very low at 34.3.

1913

Jan 7th   Many absentees, several ill with chicken pox.

It would seem as if the medical officers had an inkling of an epidemic appearing in the area because one or other of the Doctors attended the school every few days for several weeks.

Jan 16th   Dr. Bromley examined the children.

Jan 24th   Dr. Bromley   "   "   "

Jan 30th   Dr. Taylor   "   "   "

Feb 14th   Dr. Taylor   "   "   "

Feb 21st   Dr. Taylor sent one boy home with measles.

Feb 24th   School closed for two weeks - measles epidemic.

In fact the school was to remain closed for six weeks but even that length of time was insufficient because when the school reopened, few attended, many children were still poorly.

May 16th   There are 61 children on the register. Average attendance 38.8 and most of those present are suffering from coughs and colds. 15 children have been absent all week, many others for several days. Two more children have measles.

Jun 20th   Most children are now back at school.

Jul 25th   Miss Amy Costain has resigned.

Sep 8th   Miss Annie Costain commenced duties as Uncertificated Teacher.

Sep 19th   During an examination of the children Dr. Bromley found one boy with eruptions on his skin. He has been sent home until he recovers.

Oct 3rd   12 children away all week with coughs and colds - all those who attended have very bad coughs, there have been several cases of whooping cough. Average attendance 37.5.

Oct 10th   Av 32.3. 18 children away all week with whooping cough.

Oct 14th   On the instruction of the Medical Officer the school is closed until further notice.

What a disastrous year, so much illness and such a turnover of staff ! There was the usual HMI examination during the year but the Inspector, appreciating that education within the school had suffered severely, made due allowance within his report.

1914

Jan 6th   School re-opened. Only thirty present, the remainder are absent due to coughs, colds and lingering whooping cough.

The low attendances continued to be reported almost daily until about Feb 20th.

May 8th   Many children absent because of influenza.

Jul 2nd   Half holiday on account of an aeroplane coming to Port Erin.

Nov 5th   Half holiday so that children can attend the Patriotic Concert.

Nov 24th   Dr. Bromley was able to report that the school was free from infant diseases.

1915

Apr 13th   Sent Charlie Corrin home - he has ringworm.

May 21st   Usual lessons suspended in the afternoon. Mr Kelly, a member of the school board spoke to the children on "The British Empire", after which the children sang Patriotic and National songs.

Dec 11th   Some children absent with chicken pox.

1916

Jan 10th   The school has been closed - a measles epidemic.

Feb 7th   School re-opened.

Mar 3rd   Low average attendance of 33.8 on account of measles.

Mar 17th   Average attendance 25.9, children away - measles.

Mar 31st   "   "   33.4   "   "   "

Apr 25th   59 on roll, 37 present.

Dec 1st   Dr. Freer made medical examination of the school. One boy sent home, he has diphtheria.

Dec 4th   School closed - diphtheria epidemic.

1917

Jan 22nd   School re-opened. 30 present out of 46.

Jan 26th   Violent storm. Register not marked. Av 29.1.

14 children have been absent all week, 8 of whom have diphtheria and are not allowed by the medical officer to attend school.

Mar 5th to 9th. Snow storms. Children unable to get to school, registers not marked.

Apr 11th   Severe snow storm, there were eight present during the morning and seventeen in the afternoon. Registers not marked.

May 11th   Average attendance 45.7. 2 absent with measles.

May 25th   "   "   . 29.9 on account of measles.

1918
> Jan 7th to Jan 11th. Snowstorms. Register not marked.
> Sep 20th   One child with whooping cough. Av 45.1
> Oct 11th   Average down to 28.8. Children ill with whooping cough.
> Oct 15th   School closed indefinitely on account of whooping cough.
> Nov 20th   School re-opened. 32 present.
> Nov 22nd   Twenty still away with whooping cough.
> Dec 18th   Miss Costain has resigned.

(I should imagine that Miss Costain was quite relieved when she left the school. The school had been plagued with illness almost from the time she had joined in Sept 1913.)

1919
> Jan 13th   The school has been closed for four weeks on the instruction of the Education Authority due to an influenza epidemic in Douglas.
> Feb 11th   School re-opened.
> Feb 17th   Mrs S Radcliff has taken up her duties as Assistant Mistress.
> Apr 28th   Three children ill with mumps.
> May 10th   Ten absent all week with mumps.
> May 16th   School closed on the instruction of Dr. Chambers
> Jun 16th   School re-opened. 53 present.
> Sep 29th   Miss Iris Bell commenced duties as Asst. Mistress.

1920
> Jan 16th   Good average attendance of 51.9
> Feb 13th   Many absent with chicken pox.

Similar reports were made on every entry until Mar 12 when the outbreak seems to have cleared up.

Jul 13th Excerpt from HMI report:-

"The Head Mistress occasionally takes groups of the children for walks on Saturdays - a very laudable effort on her part - but in such a neighbourhood this might well be done regularly and frequently in school time."

(The Inspector deserves praise for having discovered this little gem. From the following year onward the Infants were taken out on nature study lessons from time to time during school hours.)

> Sep 6th   63 present.

1921
> Jun 8th   Dr. Moore, accompanied by Police Sergeant Watterson, visited the school this afternoon and found seven children in a neglected condition. The matter will be reported.

Jun (?)	Dr. Moore returned and re-inspected the children who had been reported.

1922

Mar 3rd	Several children absent with influenza
Apr 21st	Seven children have been absent all week because of influenza. Average attendance 33.2. 75.5%
May 5th	Four children absent with ringworm.
Jun 7th	Two children sent home, they have whooping cough.

(There was a progressive impact on the school because of whooping cough and, on June 19th, the school was closed until July 17th. but on that day only eleven children attended, whooping cough was still prevalent. So, the school was closed again and did not re-open until after the summer holidays on SEPT 4th.)

Oct 20th A visit by Rev J.Cain and Canon Leece.
(This is the only reported visit by any of the clergy, quite remarkable when compared to other schools.)

Nov 10th	Eighteen of the children absent all week - there is a great deal of sickness among the children, especially those who suffered whooping cough earlier in the year. There are 43 on the register but average attendance is down to 21.6.

1923

Feb 6th	Acting on instructions, the name of Patricia Phillips has been removed from the register, she has only been attending part-time, receiving instruction at home in the afternoons.
Apr 26th	Holiday granted for the Duke of York's marriage.
Sep 14th	29 on register.

1924

Feb 22nd	Several children absent with influenza. 36 on register, average attendance 21.3 or 59.1%.
Feb 29th	Twenty children absent all week, ill with influenza.
Mar 5th	School closed on the instruction of the Director of Education because of the influenza epidemic.
Mar 24th	School re-opened.
May 13th	The first visit by a school dental officer. The parents were notified and several were in attendance.
May 23rd	Medical Inspection of the children. Parents had been advised and a number attended.
Oct 13th	One child absent all week with measles.

(This was the start of yet another epidemic with the number of children sick being added to every week until - eventually ! - on Nov 25th, the school was closed and remained so until Jan 5th.)

1925

Apr 20th	42 children present
Apr 21st	Holiday so that the children can attend the Childrens Music Festival.
May 21st	Half holiday - Rechabite Demonstration in Douglas.
May 29th	Attendance affected by Sunday School excursion.
Jun 10th	Two Sunday School excursions only 17 present.
Jun 12th	Two SS excursions. Average attendance 39.6.
Jun 12th	School closed for one week - Motor Races.
Jul 5th	Holiday - Tynwald day.
Jul 29th	Lessons suspended from 3 to 4pm. Parents invited to school to inspect the work of the children and attend a short entertainment by the children.
Sep 11th	6 on register, average attendance 34.
Oct 1st	Holiday for Harvest Festival.
Oct 21st	Medical Officer accompanied by School Nurse examined 18 children. Parents were not invited. One child with chicken pox was sent home.
Nov 2nd	One child sent home with chicken pox.
Nov 3rd	Ian Henderson was sent home, he has chicken pox.
Nov 12th	Holiday - Cruinnaght Festival in Douglas.
Nov 20th	Absences on account of whooping cough.
Dec 10th	One child absent with chicken pox.
Dec 11th	There seems to be an epidemic of chicken pox and influenza.

1926

Apr 9th	There are 46 on the register.
Apr 16th	A weeks holiday due to the Musical Guild in Douglas.
May 14th	There has been a re-appearance of mumps.
May 18th	One child absent with mumps
May 21st	Nellie Hildreth sent home with mumps.

(- and so it continued with more and more children being taken ill week by week. On June 7th there were only 34 children present out of 53 on the roll. The Attendance Officer confirmed that ten children were at home ill with mumps - and two more were reported on this day. The absences continued until the summer holidays but on this occasion the medical officer did not close the school.)

1927

Jan 10th	44 on the register, 34 present.
Jan 17th	Maurice Hodgson sent home with skin eruption on his hands.
Mar 30th	Average attendance 39.6. 46 on roll. 86.2%.

1927
>April 4th.   THIS SCHOOL WAS CLOSED TODAY, THE SCHOOL BEING
>TRANSFERRED TO THE NEW RUSHEN SCHOOL.
>H.A.SANSBURY. CERTIFIED TEACHER.
>M.E.MOORE. CERTIFIED SUPPLY TEACHER.

Miss Sansbury had been with the school since February 1st 1905, there are only a few references to her having taken time off for sickness or other reasons and the HMI reports on her school were invariably favourable. This lady must have been a fine example to all the infants who passed through her classes for over a quarter of a century.

"Childhood must be looked at self-indulgently, for the child still within, because it is both the soil and roots of what grows later."
(Monica Dickens)

*   *   *

Chapter eleven

A NORTHERN LIABILITY
Lezayre National School

The old Lezayre Parochial School had suffered because of the procrastination of local Vicars and their School Committees.

Thankfully, a new school was erected in 1876, and, after the extremely cramped and unhealthy conditions endured in the old school, this new building must have seemed to be a most spacious place to the scholars and teachers.

For a short time the new school remained nominally under the careless control of the same Parish Committee as before, but it wasn't long before that Committee fell foul of Her Majesty's Inspector and, within two or three years, the Committee were at last performing the regular tasks they should have been doing for decades past, relatively simple things such as checking the register, following through the requests and complaints made by the School Master or Mistress, taking an interest in examinations, actually getting things done.

Progress of the school - and its occasional failures - can easily be followed through because the various Masters and Mistresses did complete the school log book   fairly well over the years during which they served the school. Once again it is a story of triumph and tears for teachers and scholars alike.

The excerpts given here are but a small fraction of the number of entries within the Log Book but I have tried to illustrate the trials and tribulations fairly and you, too, will be able to read between the lines and appreciate the hardship of the time. You will also be able to see how education progressed in this school from the 1870s, when it opened, up to 1921, when the school closed.

In so far as it has been practicable I have used the Teachers' own words and their terse phrasing.

Excerpts from the Lezayre School Log Book.

(with added comment in italics.)

I am a certificated Mistress and my name is Eliza Radcliffe, I opened the school on August 14th 1876, with 2 boys and 10 girls.
(This was the same Eliza Radcliffe who had such a long association with St. Jude's School. In the first quarter at Lezayre there was an average of 5 boys and 11 girls, the preponderance of girls was to continue for quite a while.)
1877.

Re-opened school after Christmas with 11 boys and 15 girls.

Jan 29th	Two girls admitted - one, aged 12, can only read words of one syllable.
Feb 5th	Sold to the third class, Chambers Standard II Reading Books.
Dec 14th	Cold and wet, a few sick, a number in want of shoes and other articles of warm clothing.

1878

Jan 18th	For the quarter ended Dec 24th 1877, the school was open 116 times. Average attendance 8 boys and 13 girls. Children on the register attend very irregularly - there are some in the area who are never sent to school.
Feb 7th.	A few children have not paid for last quarter, two or three did not receive their bills.
Apr 5th	Total school pence for the year was £9.12.11.
Jul 17th	Held evening school for those not able to attend regularly to prepare them for the examinations. There is not much encouragement for teachers in this district.

(I feel sure that Miss Radcliffe was referring to the lack of support from the Lezayre School Committee.)

Aug 1st   A breakdown of the scholars in classes and grades.

	Boys	Girls	Total
Class I	-	7	7
" II	4	5	9
" II	7	6	13
" IV	2	5	7
Under sevens	3	1	4
Totals	16	24	40
Standard I	6	6	12
" II	4	5	9
" III		5	5
" IV		1	1
Totals	10	17	27

(Remember that the one teacher, Miss Radcliffe, taught the several classes and standards within one large classroom.)

Exam results.   Passes in reading   27
                "   " writing   26
                "   " arithmetic   23.

Excerpts from HM Inspector's report :-
"This small village school is well governed by Miss Radcliffe and the children have done creditably in reading, writing, grammar, arithmetic and geography. The school manager did not attend the examination - or even send the portfolio to it, ——— My Lords trust that the manager will more actually superintend."
(That was a nasty comment !)
1879

Feb 28th.   Average attendance 18 boys, 22 girls, highest number in the past year.

Apr 4th.   Average attendance 33. J. Kneale has been employed as a temporary monitor at 2/- a week.

(The teacher was ill from April 2nd to May 9th with bronchitis.)

1880

Jun 15th   A number of the children live about 2 miles distant and do not meet punctually at nine.

Jun 25th   A great falling off in attendance - weeding season in the fields. It cannot be avoided in this district, they are obliged to work. I do not expect to better the condition of this school here, I very seldom have a full class for a lesson and it is very hard work to prepare for the examination.

Nov 26th. Excerpt from the Inspector's report :-
"The proper portfolio should be provided by the manager. The Mistress has to contend with very irregular attendance and an entire want of interest in the school on the part of the manager."

1881.

Jan.   Chimney pots required, there has been trouble with smoke. Boys yard has been flooded. Ash wants removing. Fender needed for classroom, also poker and brushes.

Jul 1st.   Inspectors interim report:-
"Portfolio provided - after four years of requests."

Nov 3rd   The committee have ordered that the following fees are to be applied for every quarter:-

Class I   Children of labourers.   1/6d
" II   Children of Tradesmen and small farmers.   3/-
" III   Children of large farmers and others of similar circumstances.   4/6d

Dec. HMI noted that the monitor, J. Kneale, had been withdrawn.

1882

Mar 3rd	Needed: A clock for the school, a bell, and ash to be removed from the girls yard.
Mar 20th	Most children ill with mumps.
May 17th	Average attendance 22 boys, 22 girls. Highest in past year.
Oct 6th	Friction over the implementation of school fees, especially amongst small farmers; two families have withdrawn their children.
Nov 3rd	Only 13 boys and 16 girls attended at all during the week, the reasons why the others are missing include :-

    four - with measles.
    nine - picking potatoes.
    one - no shoes.
    four - reason unknown.

1883

Feb 23rd	Small attendance due to the prevalence of measles and whooping cough.
Apr 9th	John and Allen Corlett, Ballamanagh, withdrawn. Have not paid their fees for six months prior to December 1882, their attendance for the half year has been under 20 days each. Walter Cowell and John James Cain of Glenauldyn deserve to be dis missed, they only attend a few weeks in the year.

(Miss Radcliffe had been running the school single handedly since it opened in 1876, apart from the short time when J, Kneale was employed as a monitor because of Miss Radcliffe's illness,
 For some of those years she had little encouragement and the strain was beginning to tell on her. This was a shame because the numbers on the roll had progressively risen and the HMI reports had been good)

Jul	The Committee have informed me that my salary is to be £30 per annum plus half the Government Grant and half the childrens' school pence.

1884

Jan 19th	I have been given three months notice to terminate. Eliza Radcliffe.
May 7th	First day of new Master. Mr Richard Dandy.
May 9th	Average attendance this week. Boys 8. Girls 3.
May 16th	Average attendance " " " 22. " 12.
Jul 3rd	Miss Caroline Corlett will take sewing lessons.

1885

Nov 18th.	54 on register.

1886

Jan 29th	Very stormy in the morning. Fields flooded, only 14 present.
Mar 8th.	School closed last week due to severe weather.

(Flooding seemed to be a frequent problem for Lezayre School scholars, there are many entries in the Log Book which describe not only flooding in the fields but also of the school yards, a direct result of having been built on a hillside. The flooding of the fields was a serious problem for the children, they just could not get to school.)

July 14th
(The first mention in the log book of any sort of curriculum.)
The songs for exams will be :-

> 1. Be kind to your Father.
> 2. If I were a cobbler. (Round)
> 3. Hearts of oak.
> 4. Rosalie.
> 5. To the mountain.
> 6. A boat, a boat. (Round)
> 7. Blue Bells of Scotland.
> 8. The Minstrel Boy.

> Poetry will be :-
> For standard I. The child of the bird.
>   "   "   "   II. The child's first grief, and, The better land.
>   "   "   "   III. Bruce and the spider.
>   "   "   "   IV. Wreck of the Hesperus.
>   "   "   "   V. Lady of the Lake.
> Infants object lesson :- The cart horse.

1887
    Feb 14th   53 on register, 39 present.
Excerpt from HMI report:-
"The school is going on well under Mr Dandy."

(Unfortunately, it seems that three years was enough for Mr Dandy, he left later in the same year of 1887.)

Sept 12th. I have taken over this school. James Derbyshire. Master.
(This new teacher intended to display his efficiency from the start. His first self imposed task was to list the whole of the contents of the school.)
Inventory.

Master's desk	Nine desks with inkwells	One bell
Six short forms	One easel, two blackboards	One shovel
Two cupboards	One worktable	One clock
One bead frame	Two stools and one broken chair.	
Six wall maps	One bucket for drinking water.	

Two classroom regulations and one summary. Timetables.
28 pictures - large and small. Log book.

Mr Derbyshire followed up with a long list of text books and then made the following comment:-

School in very good condition except for bolt off door leading to boys playground; 31 hat pegs broken in Boys and Girls rooms. No keys to cupboards. Useless lock to Master's desk, key missing from desk drawer.

1887
HMI report:-
" The school is very good. The good merit grant is earned with great credit."

1888
Mar 2nd   Measles epidemic.
Mar 13th   Measles epidemic only four attended.
(The school then closed until March 26th on medical advice.)

1891
Aug 4th.   HMI report :-
"I recommend that a recently qualified Assistant Mistress be appointed to relieve the master in the instruction of the infants and lower standards and to teach needlework."
1892.
Jan 4th   A new Master. Robert Kelly.
Jan 22nd   A number absent due to mumps. Others cannot attend because they cannot get their boots on over their chilblains.
Feb 10th   54 on register - 41 attended.
Sep 19th   *(Another new Master)* John Edward Caley.

Dec 22nd   HMI report for 1892:-
"During a portion of the past year the school has been under the charge of a Master *(Robert Kelly)* who must have greatly neglected his duties (I give) formal warning that the school is inefficient and the grant may be withdrawn if the next report is similar."

1893.
HMI report :-
(The report for 1893 was quite unenthusiastic. Once again the Inspector suggested that a female ex pupil teacher be appointed, this time to assist Mr Caley, who was not a good infant teacher -nor for sewing ! HMI made a second examination during 1893 the report of which was recorded in 1894, in it the Inspector was able to say that the school was "Much improved.")

1894.   Miss C.J.CUBBON was appointed Asst. Mistress.
Nov 7th   Several scholars have been absent for weeks due to whooping cough. One scholar, Olive Goldsmith, has died.

1895.

Feb 7th to 21st. School closed owing to snow and blizzard conditions.
(This was the year when snowfall throughout the Island was the heaviest on record, most services were completely disrupted.)

Mar 22	John Caley has been absent for most of this year. A Doctor has certified that the boy is suffering from chilblains.
Nov 19th.	School closed for three weeks on the advice of the Medical Officer - measles.

1897.

HMI in his annual report recommended that the classroom be extended and that additional windows be provided.

Feb 1st   *(Over the previous couple of years the Master had spoken to the children from time to time about the dangers of playing on the road, of chasing after carts conveying tourists and asking for money, of stone throwing, and of climbing the hedges; during that time several of the school windows had been broken through one cause or another.)*

"Several panes of glass broken again; a boy named Kewley of Ballamanagh, was seen to break one with a catapult."

Oct 31st	Mr Caley returned following five weeks absence with a serious illness.
Nov 8th	The Assistant Mistress left the school, leaving a Pupil teacher, Gertrude Clarke, and a sewing Mistress, M. Teare.
1899	40 on roll - 20 attending.
1902	
Jan 24th	Fields are flooded and most children are absent.

HMI report for 1901 had been critical of the effort being made by the children in preparation for the exams, the teachers must have taken this to heart because the very next entry in the Log Book was a progress report on class work.

Jan 30th	Arithmetic	Sums right	Sums set
	Standard III	19	28
	" IV	13	20
	" V	4	12
	" VI	13	25
	Total	49	85
	Only	57%	

Feb 28th   Floods continuing. Many absent.

HMI report (excerpt) :-

" **Exterior of the school is unkempt and the coalhouse is not the place to store maps and other material. A piano or harmonium should be provided."**

Oct 24th   46 on register.

1904
> Feb 6th   School closed for two weeks by the Medical Officer. Measles.

1905.

Warned school of the dangerous practise of children running across the high road in front of any vehicle, cycle or motor-cars - especially during motor-car trials.

Mar 31st. HMI reported that a classroom extension had been provided. The actual school attendance figures were now the third highest on the Island at 91.9% and during the week ending Feb 23rd had even reached the record figure of 98.4%. There were 38 children on the roll.

1906

HMI delivered a scathing attack on the work of the school and included the words:-

"The teacher knows nothing of Kindergarten work."

1907
> Jan 24th   39 in class 45 on register.
> Feb 15.   Mr Caley left the school, ill.

I cannot do other than express some sympathy for Mr Caley, You will recall that he took over the school in 1892 from a Master who left it in a mess. While there had been the odd remark from HMI on occasion concerning moderate results in   examinations, there had not been any direct criticism during the fourteen years before the scathing 1906 report.

Mr Caley must have been respected as a teacher because there were no complaints made against him and he did seem to have a genuine concern for the wellbeing of the children; don't forget the high ratio of attenders, figures which would indicate that the scholars - and their parents - were pleased with the   schooling they were receiving at Lezayre. What is significant is the fact that he was able to maintain numbers on the register despite falling numbers within the rural population. Once Mr Caley left the school the number of scholars fell fairly   rapidly.

> Feb 25th   Miss Mary Bannister appointed as Teacher.
> Sep 9th   32 on register - 16 attending.

1908.

Miss Bannister quickly made her mark and, within the log book, she presented an excellent outline scheme of work for the year, very clear and a model that would be beneficial if used by any other teacher. She was a teacher who believed in the benefits of nature study and she frequently took the whole school out on little expeditions - up the steep hills at the back of the school, across to the fields, down to the riverside etc., she even extended the dinner hour so that the children could go down into a field and watch the motor-cycles going by on a race day.

1910

Excerpt from HMI report :-

"A flock of sheep was found grazing in the school yard which is still open to the public road - proper gates should be fitted."

1911

Mar 16th	School closed for three weeks - mumps.
Oct 20th	School closed for two weeks - measles.

1915

Dec 14th.	School closed for two weeks - influenza.

1916

Jun 12th	School closed three weeks - measles.

1918

Number on register 19. Average attendance 12.

Nov 1st	School closed for three weeks - influenza.

1919

Jan 14th	School closed for four weeks - influenza.

1920.

Oct 1st

In common with many other teachers on the Island, Miss Bannister submitted her resignation to take effect at the end of the correct period for notice from this date; her action was part of a general protest against the low rate of salaries on the Isle of Man. Whilst her protest was noted it did her no harm because on March 21st of the following year,1921, she was appointed Head Teacher at Sulby Board School.

1921

Mar 21st	Miss F.M.Mylra. took over from Miss Bannister.
May 21st	Number on register 11. Average attendance 5.

The last entry was made on July 20th, quite a mundane entry, nothing to suggest that the school was about to be closed, but it was.

Lezayre school closed that same month, never to re-open.

*   *   *

From your parents you learn love and laughter and how to put one foot before the other. But when books are opened you discover that you have wings.
(Helen Hayes)

Chapter twelve

MOUNTAIN MEDLEY

This is the tiniest chapter, but so was the school, a tiny chapter in the great big book of life.

This story tells us about the final days of the little school in Sulby Glen.

Sulby Glen was re-opened as a Board School on October 10th 1888, with Janet Smith as the Mistress and just twelve scholars. It needs to be remembered that the school was in a valley high up in the hills; the school itself was at the foot of a valley and the hills rose up sharply to the front and rear - especially at the rear.

*   *   *

The following items were chosen from the log book so as to give a word picture of the way the school was run and the problems that were faced by the scholars as much as by the school mistresses and masters. The log book itself contains much, much more but, as in the previous excerpts from log books, many of the entries are repetitious and would make the story long-winded if rewritten verbatim.

*   *   *

By October 26th, Miss Janet Smith had a fair idea of what her problems were going to be when she recorded the following :-
1888

Oct 26th   An attendance of 20. I find the children almost entirely ignorant of the very rudiments of education. Most of them never having attended school before.

1889

Jan 11th   Very dark in school owing to fog. had to stop work early in the forenoon although it cleared up partially during the afternoon.

Feb 22nd   19 on register, 19 attended.

1890

Jul 25th   Janet Smith (the teacher), left the school.

The remote location of the school, amidst the weather-beaten hills, was already having its effect. Time after time there were entries in the Log Book referring to heavy rains and snow which not only affected the light within the school but made the journey to and from school particularly arduous for the scholars, most of whom made their way to school by way of rough footpaths over the hills with absolutely no shelter from the elements.

      Aug 1st   Letitia Janet Smith. *(A new Teacher.)*
1891.
      Aug 7th to 14th. Very heavy rainfalls, very few attended school.
      Nov 27th   ditto
      Dec 4th   ditto
      Dec 11th   ditto
1892.
      Jan 25th   Snow, very few attended.
      Feb 19th   Snow,   ditto
      Mar 11th and 18th   Snow, ditto.

(The effect of snow must have been the last straw for Letitia because she was taken ill on Mar 20th. By extremely good fortune she had an accomplished sister who took her place immediately.)

      May 20th   Judith M.Kneale. Teacher.
      May 27th   20 on register - 20 attended.
      Jul 29th   27 on register - 25 attended.

Judith reviewed the measurements given for the schoolhouse, she recorded them as being :-

               Length   twenty-four feet, nine and a half inches.
               Breadth   fifteen feet, ten and a half inches.
               Height   seventeen feet, nine inches.

      Oct.   25 on register - 23 attended.
1893.
  Owing to bad behaviour and rebellion I have been obliged to expel William Albert Harris in order to maintain proper discipline and preserve my influence in this school.
      Jun 14th   William Douglas fell into the river at noon - was sent home.

Presumably Judith Kneale resigned or left the school, her departure is not recorded.

1894.
>   Sep 17th   Teacher, Elizabeth A. Kermish.

From Sept 17th to October 3rd virtually no children were attending school-almost all of them were out on the farms, required to work on the harvest.

Oct 24th to Nov 7th. Almost continuous heavy rain, poor attendance.
1895.
>   May 30th to June 28th. School plagued with whooping cough
>   Sep 2nd.   School closed from 18th July to September 2nd due to continuing sickness.

>   Nov 5th   Teacher Mary Fargher.
>   Dec 4th   Boys had to draw with slate pencils; in want of drawing materials.
1896.
>   May 13th   No boys present, all on the mountain cutting turf.
>   Sep 30   No children attended.
>   I have resigned. (Mary Fargher)

>   Oct 1st   Elizabeth Hutchinson. Teacher. 12 on register.

To the mistresses of this small and remote school, the place must have seemed to be at the back of beyond; it was out of sight, out of mind, and probably almost forgotten by the local school committee.

I hope that this little excerpt from the school Log Book has been sufficient to show the effect on the teachers.

Six school mistresses within eight years, such a rapid turnover tells its own story. Let us name them again in a sort of honours list :-

Janet Smith.   Letitia Janet Smith.   Judith M.Kneale.
Elizabeth A Kermish.   Mary Fargher.   Elizabeth Hutchinson.

The school closed with finality in 1907.

MOUNTAIN MEDLEY

"Dare to be true. Nothing can need a lie.
A fault, which needs it most, grows two thereby."

(George Herbert)

*   *   *

Chapter thirteen

NIGHTMARE TIME

This little collection contains items which would have caused school Masters or Mistresses many a sleepless night, the normal stress associated with running a school, coupled with the content of such reports could almost be guaranteed to give nightmares - especially when penalties were threatened !
The first relates to St. John's School.

1909

EXCERPT FROM HMI REPORT DATED AUGUST 24TH
St. John's School

"The school was closed for nine weeks owing to an epidemic of sickness, which has no doubt affected its educational progress. The instruction is taken as a whole very fairly satisfactory in the elementary subjects though the reading ought to be more bright, clear, expressive and intelligent in all standards above the fourth where it especially needs attention.

The class subjects are in the lower standards creditable but in the higher ones they are not well known and do not earn the higher grant in spite of making ample allowance for the difficulties arising out of sickness.

The manners of the children should be improved. Inattention, slovenly lounging and putting their finger in their mouths when answering are too prevalent. A gallery is needed for the infants."

*   *   *

NIGHTMARE TIME AT ST JOHN'S, 1910.

The second item in this little collection also relates to St. John's, it is the 1910 report by HMI. When reading it you should recall that the Headmaster had been running the school most successfully from 1875; several of his trainee teachers had ended up as Head Masters in their own right, and that hardly any of the previous annual reports on his school had been really critical.

St.John's nightmare cont.,

Some of the reports had pointed out minor faults to do with the structure, others criticised the assistant teachers, a few had strong words to say about the children, but this was a beauty !

I think that you will agree with me when I submit that a report like this, following on the equally unfavourable 1909 report, would be sufficient to cause sleepless nights, if not nightmares - especially for the caretaker.

ST. JOHN'S SCHOOL

REPORT OF HM INSPECTOR FOR 1910.

"The work seen varies a good deal, and the need of more supervision of the lower classes by the Headmaster is evident.

As he is occupied with Standards V, VI, and VII this necessary strengthening of his assistants is somewhat hard to accomplish.

More effective discipline is desirable in the second class; the teacher strives, but the boys especially, do not second his efforts with sufficient vigour.

The third class, Standard II, is very well taught, and the intelligence and interest shewn suggest what is possible in the school as a whole under favourable conditions.

The use of slates might be discontinued both for hygienic and educational reasons.

In the 4th class, which is otherwise satisfactorily taught, stumps of pencils and crooked fingers tend to develop habits that hinder progress; desk posture also needs care.

In the upper class the girls should cut out their own garments and do all that is possible for themselves.

A more careful oversight of the premises is desirable - the offices are wet, and the smell offensive. When in this state they are a distinct danger to health.

Ventilation is also neglected; some of the air inlets were closed and fast, and the mouths of others were filled with dirt and rubbish. In the playground, waste paper in considerable quantities has been allowed to accumulate.

The cleaning is unsatisfactory, the floor is ill-swept, the ledges and cupboard tops are dusty, the fire places are uncared for and unused, and dirty material is left in corners.

Three cells in the boys' offices were not clean; a pool of water stood by the front gate, and the overflow grate for the soft water tank was blocked.

The zeal and industry of the Headmaster are as evident as ever; but the difficulties referred to diminish the progress of the school."

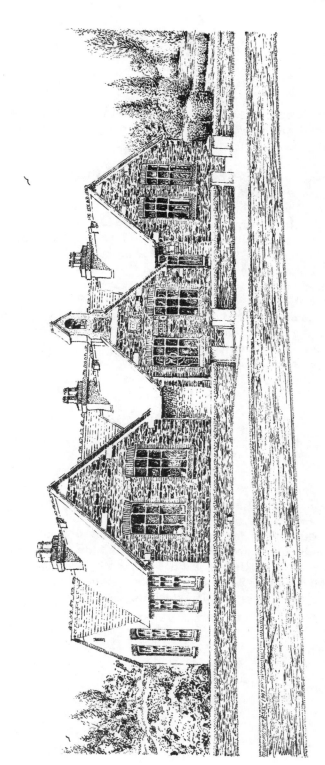

St John's School

St John's School - Opened February 1st 1898. Is in an enviable position as it faces the open space of Tynwald Hill with it's backdrop of the Arboretum. Drawn November 1997.

PORT ST. MARY INFANT SCHOOL

REPORT OF HM INSPECTOR. JULY 1907.

The role of the Inspector was to highlight faults and to make recommendations. This report makes recommendations in a kindly way, with especial regard for the youngest infants, but his remarks were positive on other matters.

" The Mistress has now the assistance of a supply teacher and the infants have made steady progress during the past year.

The children in the 1st Class are bright and well taught.

The school should be organised in two divisions and the management and instruction of the lower division should be more on Kindergarten lines with shorter lessons interspersed with games and such like.

The aim in Object Lesson teaching is that it should be not so much as to teach the children many facts as to awaken their interest and to develop their power of observation and concentration.

There are too many children over 7 years of age among the infants and no boy of eight should be retained other than under very exceptional circumstances.

There is no musical instrument in the school."

(The first two sentences are nice sweeteners, but the remainder would most certainly cause a few sleepless nights !)

*   *   *

The next report on Port St. Mary Infant School by HMI was made two years later; not a bad report really, but there is still enough within it to cause furrowed brows, especially the last sentence.

REPORT BY HM INSPECTOR FOR 1909

" The upper division of the Infant School is again doing well on the whole. It would do even better if the answers were under better control. As it is, although the instruction is on good lines it does not reach the whole class and the less bright children soon lose interest and become inattentive.

The teacher of the lower division, which includes the babies, is painstaking but lacks animation."

*   *   *

THE DREADED GRANT

The findings of HMI at the annual examination of a school and its pupils could indirectly affect the finances of the school because his recommendations were used to reduce or modify or restore the level of Grant earned by the school. For those Masters or Mistresses whose annual salary included a proportion of the grant this was a very serious matter.

The following resume was published by the Board of Education as a guide:-

The annual grant may be reduced by not more than half upon the Inspector's report for faults of discipline, instruction or registration on the part of the teacher, or for failure on the part of the managers to exercise due care in the supervision and verification of the registers or (after six months notice) to remedy any such defect in the premises as seriously interferes with the efficiency of the school or to provide proper furniture, books, maps and other apparatus of Elementary instruction.

If the Inspector at a visit without notice, not less than six months after the intimation has been given of the requirements of the Department reports that they have not been carried into effect a deduction may be made from the next grant to the school.

If any of the conditions of the annual grants set forth in this code .... are not fulfilled, the Department may reduce the grant under this article, if satisfied that the circumstances do not call for a refusal of the whole grant.

Article 9b (a)
The Department must be satisfied :- That the school premises are healthy, well lighted, warmed, drained, ventilated, properly furnished and supplied with suitable offices and contain sufficient accommodation for scholars attending school.
(At least 80 cubic feet of internal space and 8 square feet of internal area for each unit of average attendance.)

*   *   *

WHY INSPECTORS WERE NECESSARY

THE FOLLOWING REPORT REGARDING LAXEY GLEN NATIONAL SCHOOL WAS MADE IN 1901 AND SUGGESTS GROSS INCOMPETENCE ON THE PART OF THE LOCAL SCHOOL COMMITTEE.

LAXEY GLEN NATIONAL SCHOOL. 1901.

" Mixed schools :- The premises require thorough overhauling. There is a bad smell in the lower rooms; the wooden staircase outside the top rooms and leading to the girls' playground, is in a dilapidated and dangerous condition; the playgrounds are littered with paper and rubbish and the approaches to them are very steep and rugged.

The offices are in an unsanitary state, and the excrement from them is merely thrown over the wall of the playground on to waste ground on the other side, and there is still no water supply for the school, some new desks are required."

*   *   *

PATHETIC PATRICK (Parochial Board School)

This mixed and infants School really got a slating from HMI in 1906.
" Both the condition of the premises and the instruction leave a good deal to be desired. The management is perfunctory and the teaching seems to be affected by a similar want of zeal.

The cleaning is bad; dirty floors, dusty ledges, broken and blocked water pipes and gullies, a wet and dirty playground, worn out painting and ill kept offices.

In the School itself the Log Book, the Records, the term examinations and the general tidiness and arrangement of the rooms all need more care.

Spelling is moderate. Reading is barely fair. Oral arithmetic is slow and partial and the Music Tests were unusually weak."

*   *   *

THE SMALLNESS OF ST. JUDE'S

An impartial observer was necessary if the adequacy of a school was to be determined and this was one advantage of having independent Inspectors.

In this particular case an Inspector gave good advice to the Managers. It is very doubtful indeed if those managers (from Andreas) would have taken any action otherwise. In their opinion this remote little school had been soldiering on well enough before without any interference, thank you !

" The classroom is 13'6" x 8' x 7'6", is much below the minimum now required and to enquire whether the Managers see their way to enlarging it during the current School year, otherwise My Lords may have to discontinue its recognition for teaching purposes."

Surely enough to give the local Chairman another nightmare ?

" Higher education and great numbers - that is a contradiction in terms "
(F.Neitzsche 1856-1950)

*   *   *

Chapter fourteen

INSTRUCTIONS AND TABLES

(A wide range of subjects are included in this chapter, they make interesting reading because they illustrate so many different aspects of School management)

NUMBERS OF SCHOOLS AND ATTENDANCES in 1868

A summary of the number of Grammar and Public Schools in the Isle of Man, and the number of children attending them during year ended 31st day of December,1868. *(Of particular interest is the relationship between area and the number of children whose fees were being paid by the authorities.)*

	No of schools scholars	Scholars : boys/girls/total			Ages : max/min		No of free : scholars	No of schools which : which can hold more
PEEL	4	270	225	495	16	3	160	3
PATRICK	3	149	153	302	15	3+	158	2
GERMAN	2	87	77	164	16	4	16	2
MAROWN	1	24	22	46	15	5	3	-
MICHAEL	1	25	24	49	13	5	-	1
BALLAUGH	2	57	25	82	16	4	7	-
JURBY	1	17	17	34	16	5	-	1
ANDREAS	2	49	47	96	15	4	12	2
BRIDE	1	36	25	61	14	4	-	1
LEZAYRE	2	47	46	93	16	4	6	2
MAUGHOLD	3	41	39	80	15	6	13	3
RAMSEY	6	161	136	297	17	6	137	3 **

** There is a footnote :-

"25 of these boys at the Grammar School, but no return of its income given."

LONAN	3	189	131	320	16	4	54	2
CONCHAN	1	58	31	89	14	3	15	-
BRADDAN	4	88	87	175	15	3	-	2
DOUGLAS	7	895	821	1716	16	3	36	6
SANTON	1	28	22	50	13	6	5	1
MALEW	4	129	107	236	15	4	20	3
ARBORY	1	20	20	40	14	6	8	1
RUSHEN	3	152	84	236	16	6	50	2
CASTL/TN	4	182	113	295	17	4	27	2
	53	2704	2252	4956			627	32

[M12a]

(note that Castletown's minimum age was 2 and that five other schools accepted children at 3 years of age.)

INCOMES OF SCHOOLS - Year ended 31st day of December 1868.

	Govt. Grant:	Interest on investment:	Impropriate fund:	Subscriptions:	Average:
	£ s d	£ s d	£ s d	£ s d	£ s d
PEEL	189 00 08	nil	nil	131 02 01	111 14 00
PATRICK	182 03 06	-	-	137 00 00	112 15 06
GERMAN	69 19 08	nil	nil	26 10 00	75 00 00
MAROWN	nil	nil	5 10 00	2 00 00	22 16 00
MICHAEL	nil	nil	nil	nil	25 00 00
BALLAUGH	nil	nil	nil	nil	24 00 00
JURBY	14 15 10	nil	nil	nil	not stated
ANDREAS	40 16 04	nil	14 10 00	58.00 00	41 00 00
BRIDE	nil	nil	8 03 08	7 00 00	21 16 03
LEZAYRE	31 15 00	nil	nil	10 00 00	30 14 00
MAUGHOLD	nil	42 00 00	nil	nil	32 10 00
RAMSEY	57 04 08	nil	nil	71 00 00	27 05 00
LONAN	98 15 06	nil	5 10 00	58 00 00	107 00 00
CONCHAN	48 05 10	nil	nil	14 13 11	29 07 03
BRADDAN	32 11 08	nil	nil	62.14 07	47 10 02
DOUGLAS	572 11 09	nil	nil	185 00 08	372 12 05
SANTON	nil	nil	nil	nil	20 00 00
MALEW	61 16 04	2 00 00	13 10 00	31 00 00	58 05 04
ARBORY	nil	nil	12 18 05	nil	12 00 00
RUSHEN	127 03 08	4 13 10	nil	39 17 03	90 00 00
CASTL/TN	79 10 08	25 00 00	70 00 00	61 05 00	48 17 09

[M12o]

*   *   *

An example of fees paid at Castletown National School.

Year Boys	Free	1d	2d	total	Average attendance	School pence
1860	3	43	29	75	60	£17/06/5
1861	2	38	36	76	46	£13/15/6
1869	4	12	57	73	61	£19/02/5
Girls						
1860	2	70	49	121	86	£22/08/9
1861	9	68	47	124	84	£20/09/0
1869	2	23	40	65	51	£16/13/4
Infants						
1869	2	1	51	54	44	£16/12/5

[M20]

REPRESENTATIVE IOM GOVERNMENT GRANTS FROM 1867 TO 1882
(toward school building costs)

1867 June 13th.	Foxdale National School	£ 51/04/9
1868 Sept 21st.	St John's Parochial "	£ 28/02/6
1871 Jan 14th.	Rushen Girls Parochial	£ 18/10/0
1875 Mar 25th.	Arbory C of E School	£ 65/14/0
1876 Jun 7th.	Bride Parochial	£259/00/0
" Jun 7th.	Maughold	£118/12/0
" Sep 23rd.	Lezayre National	£113/16/0
" Nov 8th.	Onchan	£334/00/0
" Dec 9th.	Braddan	£282/04/0
" Dec 19th.	Andreas	£ 85/00/0
1877 Mar 1st.	Ballaugh	£386/16/0
1877 Dec 22nd.	Lonan	£188/12/0
" " "	Rushen Sch Committee	£326/09/9
1878 Aug 16th.	Marown " "	£220/10/0
1879 Jan 11th.	German " "	£168/02/0
1880	Michael Parochial	£ 48/00/0
1881	German Sch Committee	£ 46/00/0
"	Santon " "	£ 51/04/0
1882	Lezayre " "	£397/08/0
"	Rushen " "	£401/06/0
1883	German " "	£189/12/0
"	Arbory " "	£136/08/0
1885	Douglas " "	£1026/04/0
"	Douglas School of Art	£196/00/0
"	Jurby Sch Committee	£ 40/00/0
"	Ramsey National	£ 65/08/0
1886/7	Dhoor Board	£212/00/0

[M22]

*   *   *

POPULATION OF THE ISLE OF MAN

June	1921	60284	
April	1931	49308	
April	1939	52029	(estimated)
	1951	55253	
	1961	48133	
	1971	54581	
	1976	61723	
	1981	64697	
	1996	71714	

*   *   *

NOMENCLATURE
(Emphasising the important role played by the National Schools in the education of the Manx during the mid 1800s.)

Arbory (1872)	C of E
Ballasalla	National
Bride (1875)	Parochial
Castletown	National
Cronkbourne	C of E
Cronk-y-Voddy (1874)	
Ballaugh (1871)	Parochial
Dalby	National
Douglas, Athol St.	National
" St Mary's	Roman Catholic
" St Barnabas	National
" Thomas St	Wesleyan
Foxdale	National
Foxdale Girls (1873)	National
Jurby	C of E
Kirk Andreas	National
Kirk Braddan (1871)	National
Kirk German	Parochial
Kirk Onchan	National
Kirk Patrick	National
Laxey Glen	National
Maughold	National
Peel	National
Peel	Wesleyan
Port St Mary	National
Ramsey	National
Rushen Boys	National
Rushen Girls	National
St Judes (1874)	
St Marks	National
Santon	National
South Cape (1875)	
Sulby	National

[M22]

* * *

GRANTS

A comparison of the grants paid to schools in 1867 and 1889.

Annual grants were usually paid to most schools following a satisfactory report from Her Majesty's Inspector of Schools, but not all. An Inspector had the power to recommend a lesser sum if the performance of the school was not up to an acceptable standard or if the school building, toilet facilities, equipment or, in later years, heating, were not, in his opinion, satisfactory.

The grants were based on the number of children presented for examination together with the number and grade of passes. Most of the money paid out in grants went toward the teacher's salary.

	1867		1889
	£ s d		£ s d
		Arbory.	56/19/0
		Baldwin	30/06/5
		Ballagawne	75/15/6
Ballasalla	36/15/2	Ballasalla	91/05/0
		Ballamodha	10/04/0
		Ballaugh	87/10/0
		Braddan	71/07/0
		Bride	60/01/5
Castletown	63/18/0	Castletown	234/10/0
		Cronk	41/09/0
Cronkbourne	33/17/2	Cronkbourne	30/11/0
Dalby	31/14/6	Dalby	41/09/7
		Dhooar	36/05/0
		Dhoon	1/12/10
Douglas :-			
Athol St	178/16/4	Athol St	421/15/0
Roman Catholic	55/18/10	Roman Catholic	184/12/6
St Barnabas	194/12/2	St Barnabas	37/14/10
		St Thomas	103/05/0
Thomas St	90/05/8	Thomas St	313/17/6
		Doug Board School	426/06/8
Well Rd	24/13/10		
Foxdale	141/11/7	Foxdale	155/01/6
Jurby	10/09/4	Jurby	40/10/0
Kirk Andreas	40/03/4	Andreas	58/07/0
Kirk Conchan	43/10/6	Conchan	109/07/6
Kirk German	62/18/10	German	93/16/4
Kirk Patrick	44/12/5		
Laxey Glen	69/14/10	Laxey Glen	300/02/6
		South Cape	104/02/6
		Lezayre	29/19/2
		Lhane/Lhen	10/19/0
		Marown	66/13/8

A comparison of grants, continued.

		Maughold	43/16/2
		Michael	73/03/1
		Oak Hill	25/05/6
		Peel	475/02/6
Peel Wesleyan	47/07/8	Peel	103/03/3
Pt St Mary	29/15/6	Pt St Mary	78/15/0
Ramsey	32/10/4	Ramsey	249/13/9
		Ramsey	114/19/2
Rushen Boys	39/11/8	Rushen Boys	77/12/6
Rushen Girls	28/09/2	Rushen Girls	116/07/6
		St Judes	18/01/8
St Marks	20/06/4	St Marks	30/02/6
Sulby	21/18/2	Sulby	58/08/0

[M22]

*   *   *

INCOME AND EXPENDITURE OF NON-BOARD SCHOOLS y/e 31 Mar 1888

	Income £ s d		Expenditure £ s d
Grants	2704 15 01	Salaries	4213 09 08
Endowments	159 09 00	Books	249 07 02
Subscriptions	318 11 07	Fuel and Light	192 01 06
Collections in-Churches & Chapels	94 12 03	Repairs	- - -
School Fees	1294 04 02	Replacements	267 11 11
Books sold to-Children	34 15 10	Rents	51 18 05
Science & Art-Annual grants	74 13 06	Rates/Taxes	26 04 09
Other sources	71 04 07	Other	120 06 10

[B01]

*   *   *

THE EDUCATION VOTE FOR THE YEAR COMMENCING Apr 1st 1889.

(Approximate estimate of the amount required for the purposes of education.)

Expenditure	£ s d	
Annual Grant	5600 00 00	
Inspections under Education Dept	289 00 00	
Pensions	37 10 00	
Audit & Inspections	40 00 00	
Secretary's salary	200 00 00	
Printing and advertising	36 00 00	
Architects' fees	5 00 00	
Industrial school/boarding out	50 00 00	
Attendance Officers	140 00 00	
Building grants	1382 10 06	Total £7815 00 06

(This vote resulted in the following resolution.)

RESOLUTION OF TYNWALD COURT

At a Tynwald held on the 5th day of April 1889.

Resolved :- That a sum not exceeding £7815 00 06 be applied, from the Customs and Revenue of this island for the purposes of Public Education, for one year from the 1st day of April 1889.   [B01]

*   *   *

SCHOOLS AND AVERAGE ATTENDANCE BETWEEN 1871 AND 1890

Year	No of schools	Av attendance
1871	25	3279
1872	28	3600
1873	29	3678
1874	32	4090
1875	34	4097
1876	35	4208
1877	38	4296
1879	40	4453
1880	41	4954
1884	42	5429
1886	44	6069
1888	45	6103
1889	46	6291
1890	48	6397

1889 :- 35 Board Schools and 11 Denominational.   [B01]

DISINFECTION

(An instruction issued by the Board of Education in 1901 to all school authorities.)

This circular is urging the necessity for the proper disinfection of all school premises on the outbreak of an epidemic due to the average attendances having suffered considerably from this cause.

School buildings should remain closed and not used for meetings of any kind - especially Sunday School purposes - and only re-open on the authority of a medical certificate.

*   *   *

DEATH RATES OF THE CHILDREN OF SCHOOL AGE ON THE ISLAND AND THE NUMBER LEAVING THE ISLAND (from 1898 to 1909).

Years	Death Rate per 1,000	Left island
1898/9	33	305
1899/0	29	261
1900/1	28	338
1901/2	35	295
1902/3	33	393
1903/4	26	239
1904/5	38	251
1905/6	29	255
1906/7	27	278
1907/8	24	273
1908/9	22	242

[B02 & 3]

*   *   *

MEDICAL EXAMINATIONS.

The first general examination of schoolchildren by medical officers was made at the instigation of the Council of Education during the months of April, May and June, 1913.

1,519 children were examined and the first shock was the very large number found to have defective teeth, no less than 83%.

The following table names the various diseases or defects found, the number of children affected and the percentage to the whole.

DISEASE OR DEFECT	NUMBER	%
Cleanliness-		
(a) Head - Nits	61	4.01
(b) Body - Bites	48	3.16
Clothing - Insufficient	56	3.68
Footgear - Defective	25	1.64

DISEASE OR DEFECT	NUMBER	% (Continued)
External Eye Disease-		
Strabismus	44	2.89
Blepharitis	33	2.17
Conjunctivitis	8	0.52
Other disease or defect	6	0.39
Vision-		
Slightly defective	104	6.84
Defective	153	10.07
Wearing Glasses	42	2.76
Nutrition-		
Teeth- 1 to 3 bad	509	33.50
4 and upward bad	765	50.36
Nose-	15	0.98
Throat-		
Mouth breathers	338	22.25
Inflamed	59	3.88
Tonsils-		
Slightly enlarged	392	25.80
Enlarged	226	14.87
Much enlarged	63	4.14
Adenoids-		
Slight	162	10.66
Marked	74	4.87
Glands-		
Sub-maxillary	240	15.80
Cervical	119	7.83
Ears-		
Disease	9	0.59
Hearing	15	0.98
Speech-		
Stammer	9	0.59
Lisp	4	0.26
Thick	14	0.92
Mental condition-		
Backward	12	0.79
Dull	15	0.98
Defective	6	0.39
Heart and circulation-		
Organic disease	17	1.11
Anaemia (functional)	164	10.79
Lungs-		
Bronchial	122	8.03
Dull	109	7.17
Tubercular	32	2.10

DISEASE OR DEFECT(continued)	NUMBER	%
Nervous system-		
Chorea	3	0.19
Epilepsy	1	0.06
Paralysis	4	0.26
Other diseases	8	0.52
Tuberculosis-		
Pulmonary	32	2.10
Glandular	20	1.31
Other (hip) disease	1	0.06
Rickets-		
Head	7	0.45
Body	10	0.65
limbs	5	0.32
Deformities-		
Spinal disease etc	4	0.26

In addition there were 37 children with miscellaneous diseases or defects but as these were within 21 different categories there is no need to record them here.

[B04]

*   *   *

"The recent school of novel writers forget in their insistence on life, and nothing but life, in a plain slice, that a story must be worth the telling, that a good deal of life is not worth any such thing, and that they must not occupy the reader's time with what he can get at first hand anywhere around him."

(Thomas Hardy)

*   *   *

Chapter fifteen
Structural problems.
Just a few examples of the many problems faced by the Educational Authorities.

School Halls
(From a report during 1935)
"The provision of school halls in Douglas, and consequently the activities which a hall makes possible, are below the normal standard. Demesne Road has a good hall.
Tynwald Street has two, but they are both very small and the use of the upper one *shakes the building; while the hall at Murray's Road Mixed, though large, is said to be unsafe for Physical Training and Dancing,* and is therefore useless except as a spare class space and for assembly. Of the other large schools on the Island, the new schools at Laxey and Rushen and the school at Albert Road Ramsey, have admirable halls, but that at Peel has none."   [B07]

*   *   *

Welfare

"It is worthy of mention that in many of the schools, staff rooms and sanitary accommodation for the staff, especially the women teachers, are either lacking entirely or are much inferior to what is now usually provided. This is so even in such a good building as that at Murray's Road, Douglas.
While no new expenditure on this item can presumably be expected at present, the point might well receive attention whenever a suitable opportunity arises at a particular school."   (from a 1931 report)   [B07]

*   *   *

Peel problem

"Attention is drawn to the inadequate ventilation at Peel and to the unsatisfactory state of its floor." (Inspectors report 1934)   [B07]

Safety of buildings

On account of accessibility the building Inspector reported in 1934 that Douglas Tynwald Street Girls' School and Ramsey Albert Road School should not, unless there were no other convenient premises, be let for public meetings.

Murray's Road School in Douglas was also to be excepted.

*   *   *

Physical training
(A 1937 report)

"The Building Programme of the Authority should make adequate provision for indoor lessons so that physical training may be conducted regularly throughout the year.

The elementary school playing fields are not at present adequately maintained and it is hoped that, as soon as convenient, a scheme might be devised which will ensure that field games are carried out under suitable conditions."   [B07]

*   *   *

Water supplies

It was not until 1956, that a piped water supply was made available to Marown School; the water main had to be laid from the Crosby Railway Crossing and the cost was shared equally between the Water Board and the Education Authority. A scheme for water borne sanitation was put in hand at about the same time.

Similar action was due to take place, in 1957, for Dhoon and Kewaigue.

(In fact it was several years before Kewaigue was attended to, mainly because of an argument concerning who should pay for the necessary sewerage disposal pipework.)
[B08]

*   *   *

School clinic

The inconvenient premises in Tynwald Street, Douglas, used as a School Clinic for many years was reported as being in need of replacement in 1957. Tynwald voted £10.000 in 1958, for the erection of a new school clinic in Murray's Road, Douglas.
[B08]

*   *   *

Rot

During the years leading up to 1964, proposals had been put forward for thorough modernisation of Murray's Road School. The options considered in the planning stages received considerable support because, in relative terms, the main structure was not all that old, completion had been during 1899, and the school had for many years been the virtual 'Flagship' among schools.

A firm of specialists was called in to make preliminary investigations and their examination of the building showed that both wet and dry rot were so extensive in the roof timbers and other parts of the building that, together with other serious shortcomings, the advisability of modernisation was called into question.

The report, as you can imagine, caused many furrowed brows and an urgent need to reconsider what should be done.

With the substantial amount of repair work shown to be necessary it was obvious that the combined cost of repairs and modernisation would be so high, in relation to the cost of new premises, that the only economically sound solution likely to provide a satisfactory answer to the various problems would be to demolish and then erect a new building.

Such an unexpected finding was a frightful blow to the Finance Board, they had prepared adequate budget figures for nothing more than a modernisation scheme.
Due to the heavy demands being made on the building industry at that time the Finance Board had already been asked to curtail public building works and they were not willing to support the proposal.
(for the outcome, see Murrays Road School, Douglas. Chapter 19)   [B08]

*   *   *

Toilets

During 1966/7 a start was due to be made on the provision of indoor toilet facilities in the older schools, the first two schools to be dealt with were Foxdale and Michael.

*   *   *

STRUCTURAL PROBLEMS

It must be good to think the common thought,
To learn with learners, teach with teachers. (T.E.Brown)

Chapter sixteen

Compassion

Almost all of the items in this chapter are taken from reports made to the Council of Education or Board of Education and have been chosen to show that not all decisions were based on cost; even though most were !.

The first two have a special relevance because they were made at a time when the Isle of Man was suffering from a serious depression. Just the same as in England, unemployment was high and among those continuing in work, wage and salary cuts were widespread.

There had been a boom in employment after the 1914/19 war but on the Island this had been tempered by closure of the mines in 1919/20. When the boom subsided, the lack of mining opportunities helped emphasise an unpalatable fact - there were insufficient jobs available for boys and girls to go into when they left school.

*   *   *

"Closure of Small Country Schools". (1932)

"Proposals have been put forward for closing several schools which, owing to their remoteness and to steadily decreasing numbers, have proved unduly expensive to maintain and not capable of providing so stimulating an education as is possible in schools with more children and more teachers."

"Provided that the numbers do not drop too low, and provided that teachers with the special gifts required can be found, there is much to be said for these small country schools. They become small families with a life of their own, and the teacher's contact with the children is so individual and intimate that they can exert a remarkable influence for good on their pupils.

Still there will be cases where circumstances render closure not only inevitable but desirable, and this is true of the present proposals."

"At the same time, closure will throw on the local Education Authority a much bigger responsibility, it will not be a question merely of arranging for the safe transport of the children from home to school and back again."

Closure of small country schools cont.

"The Authority will become responsible for these children for the whole day, and will need to concern themselves with the drying of their clothes and shoes where necessary, with ensuring that they have hot food and drink in the winter, and that they are properly occupied and looked after during the whole of the interval between morning and afternoon school." [B07]

Unfortunately, good intentions were not enough; in the following year it was announced that Baldwin, Lhane, Cronk-y-Voddy and Dalby schools had been closed at an overall annual saving of £1440. [B07]

*   *   *

Deaf and Dumb Children

Approval was given in 1931 for the establishment of a day class in Douglas for the education of deaf and dumb children.

"A day class may not be able to give the all round training obtained in a residential institution, but many parents will no doubt be glad to keep their children at home rather than send them to England. The scheme is to operate for three years in the first instance."

"The establishment of the class will take some time and in the meantime the Authority have provided £720 in their estimates for 1932/3 for the maintenance of children in the Liverpool School for the Deaf and Dumb (nine children at £80 each)."

"In addition to an initial charge of £50 for furniture, the Authority estimate the cost of providing for ten children in a day class as follows :-

Five from Douglas and neighbourhood.
Five from remote areas.

Teacher in charge	£225
Boarding expenses	130
Travelling expenses	25
Books, stationery,etc.	17
	£397 ."

(see also, Raphael Rd. Douglas.) [BO7]

*   *   *

Education of Unemployed Youths

(The early 1930's were bad years for working people, unemployment figures were unusually high and children leaving school had the greatest of difficulty in obtaining work of any sort. This was particularly true in the Isle of Man where, for a considerable time, large numbers of children had been leaving school only to become immediately unemployed. In an attempt to ease the problem and, at the same time, provide some sort of industrial training, the Education Department started a special scheme to assist unemployed youths.)

In 1933/4 there was an estimated expenditure of £1,200 in connection with a centre for the education of unemployed youths made up as follows:-

Teaching Staff :-

Teacher in Charge	£300
Two Pt Time Teachers	160
Maintenance allowances. (50 boys for 30 weeks)	375
Travelling	70
School materials, books,timber,etc.	150
Fuel, light and cleaning	80
Furniture	75
	£1,200

The first experimental class started on Monday, Oct 1st 1934, when 37 boys presented themselves for enrolment and during the year of 1934/5 there was an average of 45 youths between 15 and 18 years of age who attended.

Each boy received a grant of 6d per attendance but no payment was made in the respect of any week during which the attendance was less than 80%.

Out of a total of 8,738 possible attendances, the actual attendances were 8,305 or 95%, a surprisingly high figure which suggests that the classes were appreciated.

There was an average of 26 lads who took a mid-day meal at school.

During 1938/9 boys leaving the classes found work as follows :-
Apprenticeships :- Engineering (2), Painter, Motor mechanic, Chemist, French Polisher, Boot & Shoe trade.

Labourers :- Woollen Mills (3), Farm, Gardener, Coal boat.
Shop boy. Electrician. Fisherman, Baker, Navy, Van boys (3), Buffet boy, Message boys (3).

The scheme was wound up in 1940 by which time there were no further applicants.

Milk for School Children

In November 1933, the Authority adopted the report of a Committee which recommended that they should undertake the supply of half a pint of milk daily to under-nourished children during the winter months. It was suggested that, where the home circumstances necessitated it, the milk should be supplied free of charge, but that milk should also be available for other children whose parents were prepared to pay for it. From the information laid before the Committee, it appeared that about 800 children should have the additional nourishment, and the approximate quantity of milk required would be 5,250 gallons.

Before proceeding with the scheme, the Authority invited tenders to ascertain the cost and enquired into the steps necessary to ensure that the milk would be pure and free from harmful bacteria.   [B07]

*   *   *

Retarded and Mentally Deficient Children

"The problem of the education of mentally defective children is one which lies on the border line between medical care and education. It is probable that this matter will need consideration in the near future. The total number of such children on the Island is too small and the population too scattered to justify the establishment of a Special School.

In the case of the higher grade mentally defective child the question of educational provision should be regarded as a part of the whole problem of provision for retarded children rather than as a separate entity." (1935)   [B07]

*   *   *

War time precautions

Attendances in the afternoon were to be from 1.15 to 3.00pm from November to the end of February, and 1.15 to 3.30pm for the rest of the year.

It was arranged that immediately an air raid warning was sounded or the presence of enemy aircraft or vessels were apparent, all children within eight minutes' walk of home were to be sent home. All other children to be taken to a place of safety.

In each case the Head Teacher would act with the discretion appropriate to the circumstances, especially if circumstances arose in which it was not desirable to carry out the procedure in its entirety when it might be advisable to retain all children in the school or to take them to selected places of greater safety. (1940)[B07]

Low Flying Aircraft

In 1943/4 parents in the Jurby district refused to permit their children to use the coast road from Jurby Church to Jurby School and the Ballavarran Road owing to the danger from low flying aircraft.

The Council came to the conclusion that the parents were justified in regarding the roads mentioned as dangerous.

The Authority agreed to arrange that the School Bus should make a detour to avoid any possibility of an accident that might involve young children.

*   *   *

School closure - Dhooar.
This article illustrates the care taken on investigation before the closure of a school could be permitted in 1965.

During April 1965, the Education Authority gave public notice concerning proposed closure of Dhooar School at the end of the Autumn term, September the 13th.

In April there were 10 infants and 14 juniors attending but it was anticipated that by the autumn these figures would fall to 7 infants and 13 juniors.

Detailed information was obtained about the addresses of all pupils and it was found that 20 of those likely to attend were from Ramsey, 1 from Jurby, 1 from Bride, 8 from Lezayre, and of those from Lezayre, 4 were as near to Ramsey as the Dhooar.

After full consideration of objections the proposal to close was approved, it being understood that transport would be arranged to Andreas School for those children who could be properly regarded as resident in the Dhooar area.

*   *   *

THE FUTURE
A Tynwald motion carried on March 21st, 1967.
"In view of the proposed raising of the school-leaving age, the development of the Island's educational system and the impact that the recommendations of the reports made by the education experts could have upon the Manx educational programme.

Tynwald respectfully requests the Isle of Man Board of Education to make recommendations during this session as to the Island's future policy toward education so as to achieve the maximum benefits for Manx children and to make the best use of our resources and personnel."

....and a fitting conclusion too.

Dhoar School, Lezayre.

Dhooar School - Opened 1885. Drawn July 1999. Preferred by many Ramsey parents to their local schools.

"Far from being in any way a backwater, the Island
stands in the forefront of educational progress."
(Archdeacon Stenning)

*   *   *

Chapter seventeen

Within the next seven chapters you will find the Manx schools listed in an
alphabetical order. I have tried to provide a little background information
concerning the schools themselves as well as giving a brief indication of their
location, where the schools are, or were, to be found.

*   *   *

THE SCHOOLS.

FROM ALLAGAGH TO DHOOAR.

ALLAGAGH - see Maughold - The Lhaggan.

ANAGH COAR PRIMARY SCHOOL - see Douglas

ANDREAS. (1)
A rural school was founded here in 1676, probably a Petty school within the
church.
The experience of Andreas Church was given as an example when demonstrating
the problems associated with children attending school within a church. At a
visitation of the church in 1757 it was said to be in need of repairs to roof and doors,
the insertion of panes of glass, and cleaning and white-washing of the chancel,
mainly due to wear and tear caused by children attending school.
In 1787 a school was gifted by Philip Radcliffe of Ballaradcliffe; it was provided on
land at an estate known as Gatt-na-Nain or Gat-ny-Nain, this was followed by a gift
from Emmanuel Moore which went toward the provision of a house for the master.
Subsequently, another new school was built on part of the Archbishop's glebe;
construction was helped by the provision of a Treasury Grant of £72, the old school
being offered for sale in 1836. (In 1848 the school was known locally as :- "Mr
Cannall's School - opposite Ohio Cottage, Andreas.")

ANDREAS PAROCHIAL SCHOOL (2)
The school was extended during 1875/6 at a cost of £203 01 07d, the money being
raised as follows :-

Donation from the Archdeacon	£11 10 2d
From the rate	£106 11 5d
School Board Grant	£ 85 00 0d

In 1876 this 'new' Andreas Parochial School was transferred to the Andreas School Board under the direction of the Board of Education.

ANDREAS PAROCHIAL BOARD SCHOOL.(3) (Andreas District)
The present school was built in 1902/3 with accommodation for 80 mixed older scholars and 44 infants but within four years it had fallen foul of HMI :-
"It is a pity to find signs of dilapidation and neglect in such fine new buildings. The walls begin to look discoloured, the fences are unkempt and broken down, the seats in the Boys' Offices have been misused, all the offices want emptying, and the cement floor in the Girls' Cloak-room is wearing into holes, there is also a broken window and many broken gates."

*   *   *

Since that time the school has been considerably extended and in 2002, had 7 classrooms and an undivided hall 16m x 12m for the 81 boys and 86 girls who attended.
There were 9 teachers including the Head Teacher as well as 2 NNEB and 3 lunch time assistants.
The childrens' ages ranged from 4 to 11.
There are no plans for further permanent extensions in the near future but it may be necessary to have a mobile classroom soon.

The school is in the centre of the Village with it's main entrance on Bride Road, the A17.   (See also, chapters six and seven)   [M12j] [M27] [B03]

*   *   *

ARBORY CHURCH OF ENGLAND SCHOOL.(1) (Arbory District)
Arbory probably had a schoolhouse separate from the church by 1705.
In 1833, the Parish School was definitely being held within a house until a new school was provided in 1835.
The new school was built on land at Ballaclague previously conveyed to the Vicar and Churchwardens in 1834, the cost was defrayed with the help of a Treasury Grant of £50 and money from the National Society. When built, the dimensions were 30'x18' and there was a small house for the Master.
In 1872 there were 70 on the register at Arbory and during 1873 the school was extended at a cost of £165; by 1877 there were 100 on the roll. Further land was acquired in 1879 and by 1881 the school was provided with its first playground.
[M12m]
The school was transferred to the Board of Education in 1875.

ARBORY SCHOOL.Ballabeg.(2) (Arbory District)

A further classroom was added in 1882 and by 1895, there was a Headmaster with two assistants for the 135 pupils.

The School Inspector was not happy when he visited in 1919, he criticised the **"cramped accommodation, which was inadequate for proper organisation, unsuitable windows, offices (toilets) that were unsatisfactory and floors which needed repair."**

The Inspector recommended a new building on a more open site, but nothing was ever done about the provision of a new school.

In 1925, the school was wired for electricity and, by 1938, piped water had been supplied; previously all water had been obtained from the school well by hand pump.

There was a revision of school accommodation during 1937, when 24 scholars over 11 years of age were transferred to Douglas or the Rushen School. Arbory was then redesignated as:-

ARBORY JUNIOR AND INFANT SCHOOL.(3)

By 1940 the roll had fallen to 40 but by the 1950s it had recovered and was up to 82.

New toilet facilities were provided in 1952, a long awaited improvement because up to this late date there were only dry closets with ash pit disposal.

After falling to 45 in 1963, numbers on the roll steadily rose until, by 1974, a mobile classroom was required.

A new building was provided within the same overall site in May 1976, and during the following year the old part of the school was renovated, the whole continuing in use today.   [M12m]

From the road the school looks deceptively small, yet it now houses 7 classrooms and possesses a 15m X 11m undivided hall.

There are 8.5 teachers including the Head, another teacher for the Special Unit, 1 N.N.E.B for the school and two more for the Special Unit. There are also 5 mid-day helpers.

The childrens' ages range from 4 to 11, there are 89 boys and 90 girls; included within these figures are 70 infants.

Rather surprisingly, the 'temporary' mobile classroom provided in 1974, continued in use despite the new building that was opened in 1976; it is still in regular use. Rather naturally, the Head Teacher would like to see a further extension built so as to provide two proper classrooms in place of the mobile but so far as I am aware no financial commitment has been made to do so. Arbory School is on the Main Ballabeg to Colby Road, the A5, just South of Ballabeg.

ASHLEY HILL - see Onchan

AULDYN -see Ramsey

BALDWIN. ST. LUKE'S SCHOOL. (Braddan District)

St. Luke's combined church and school was built in 1836, with the Chaplain superintending teaching. This National school remained in use until the East Baldwin Board School was built in 1877.

Known as 'The Church on the Hill' and situate on a by road between the East and West Baldwin roads, the building is well maintained and continues in use today as part of the church.

BALDWIN BOARD SCHOOL. (Braddan District)

In 1911 there were 22 infants and 42 boys and girls.
" 1920   "   "   18   "   "   35 "   "   "

BALDWIN PAROCHIAL SCHOOL. (Braddan District)

In 1911 there were 26 infants and 80 boys and girls attending.
" 1920   "   "   14   "   "   69 "   "   "   "

BALLACLOANE -see Douglas

BALLADOOLE SCHOOL. ARBORY

At an unknown date, possibly 1833, this was known as 'William Paddy's School' after the Master Mr W.P.Cannell. The school was kept in a house which was also a Sunday School. 12 boys and 12 girls were taught in one room.

BALLAGAWNE SCHOOL - see Lonan.

BALLAKINNISH SCHOOL, Braddan. Opened 1815

BALLAKISSACK (Santon). (Santon District)

The old school was sold around 1849 for £101, this sum was used toward a new school which had received funding from several sources - Parliamentary grant £100, National Society £30, Parish donations £148 and £40 from elsewhere. Total cost was £419.

The school was on a side road off the A5 between Santon and Fairy Bridge.

BALLAMOHDA. Ballamoda or Ballamoddy.

This school was closed on 31st December 1940. During August 1939 there were only 10 children on the register and by December only six remained, the others having voluntarily transferred to St. Mark's School. Letters of protest had been made but, as adequate transport arrangements had been proposed, the Council approved closure.

Ballamodha School was just off the A4 Foxdale Road

BALLAQUAYLE - see Douglas

BALLASALLA PAROCHIAL SCHOOL (1)
The location is uncertain as are the dates of opening and closure.

BALLASALLA SCHOOL. (2) (Malew District)
Built from 1843 to 1845 with £30 from the National Society and a Parliamentary grant of £88. The original building still stands near the corner of the little bye road leading to the ford.

BALLASALLA PRIMARY SCHOOL.(3) (Malew)
In 1952 tenders were invited for the construction of a four classroomed school at an estimated cost of £18,500.
The new school was provided in 1954, the final cost being £18,438. the opening date was Nov 12th 1954.
This school is just off the A5, to the left, when leaving Ballasalla for Douglas.

BALLAQUINNEY - Marown.

BALLAUGH SCHOOL.(1) (Ballaugh District)
In 1669 it was reported that Ballaugh was 'keeping school' for itself as well as for those who cared to come from Kirk Michael and Lezayre. A school was also reported as in being during 1676.
The Rector of Ballaugh, Thomas Walker, (1679-1729), left money in his will to build a new Parochial School and, in 1721 he gave four acres for the use of the Parish schoolmaster in perpetuity and to build a new house for him.
By 1730 a school and schoolmaster's house had been provided and by 1797 there was a Village School for Girls.
In 1822 it was reported that the Girls School had 40 pupils and the mistress received a free house; the Parochial School had an attendance which varied from 80 to 90.
The Parochial School lasted until 1872 and a village school then came into existence for one year only as an interim measure until the National School opened in 1873, this new school was handed over to a local school committee backed by the Board of Education during year ending 31st March 1875.
The old School and School house were sold by public auction in 1931 for £195.

BALLAUGH BOARD SCHOOL.(2) (Ballaugh District)
In 1905 there was a poor HMI report on the building which included :-
"The School is very dark; in winter it is only by a painful effort that one can read at all. This is caused by the use of ground glass, which, in towns is sometimes justifiable, but in a country village is an unmixed evil."

Ballaugh Scholl - Drawn October 1997 before its extension.

Ballaugh Board School HMI report cont.,
"Clear glass should be substituted. More cupboards are wanted to hold the books and maps, which make the room most disorderly."

The present school has four teachers and one ancillary, was extended during 1996 and is situate on the Station Road which leads from Ballaugh Village to Ballaugh old church. There are four classrooms and an undivided hall. At present there are 61 children attending, all between 4 to 11 years of age.

BALLELBY

BALLURE - see Ramsey

BARREGARROW (1) (Michael).
A National School was provided in 1842; during 1873 it was handed over to a local committee backed by the Board of Education.

BARREGARROW WESLEYAN SCHOOL.(2) (Michael District)
This school grew from a thriving Sunday school which was started in 1820; by 1848, Barregarrow Wesleyan had 50 scholars and by the 1850's it had become a Wesleyan Day School which it continued to be until taken over for a few months during 1872 by the newly established School Board.
The school was then allowed to carry on but it soon received some rather damning HMI reports and by about 1875, the scholars were transferred to other schools including Cronk-y-Voddy.
The original school building is now used by a metal worker, it is situate on the other side of the road from Barregarrow Methodist Church, just off the road between Kirk Michael and Glen Helen.   (see also Chapter twelve)

BISHOPSCOURT.
The reconstruction of 1891 was mentioned in a sermon by Rev H.T.Adamson who reminded others of some aspects of the ministerial life. An "Academic" Theological College was in existence here from April 1891 until closure in 1947.
Situate on the A3 road between Ballaugh and Kirk Michael.

BOOINANE

BRADDAN (1)(GERMAN) SCHOOL.
Reported as being ruinous and out of repair in 1718, the school was repaired that summer but by 1730 the school was being held in the clerks dwelling house in Braddan. In 1757 the school was being held in the church.

BRADDAN PARISH SCHOOL.(2) Ballakennish.
Opened in 1815.

BRADDAN - OAKHILL SCHOOL.(3) (Braddan District)
The Vicar of Braddan raised money for the 1860 Braddan School together with a Parliamentary grant of £344 and a parish effort held on the evening of May 23rd 1860; by about 1880 the school had been handed over to a local school committee backed by the Board of Education and in 1890 was classed as an efficient school, nevertheless, the School was closed by 1891.

BRADDAN PRIMARY SCHOOL.(4) (Braddan District)
Presumably a new school opened in 1891 because in 1894 a building grant of £360 was allowed for Braddan School House and Teacher's residence. The school is entered from the Braddan Road.
During 1967/8 Tynwald agreed to the funding of a modernisation and extension scheme which included the provision of two modern classrooms. The anticipated cost was £46,000.
The school has nine classrooms and an undivided hall for the four to eleven year old children who are taught there. At present there are 106 boys and 97 girls of whom 81 are infants.
There are ten teachers, including the head, and there is one classroom assistant as well as a part time assistant for special needs. There are also 5 dinner ancillaries.
A further extension is being considered for about 2006, this time the cost will not be nearly so modest, £280,000. and the plan may be shelved.

BRADDAN SCOILL VALLAVEELT (5)
This new school was opened in September 1992. No permanent extensions have been constructed but it has been necessary to make use of mobiles. There are 17 class rooms at present, this includes a computer room, music room, special needs room and the mobiles. The teaching staff, including the Head Teacher, is 16 plus 2 NNEB.
The school has been provided with two halls: The Sports Hall is undivided but part of the Assembly Hall is used as a dining area.
The childrens' ages range from 4 to 11, there are 152 boys and 146 girls of whom 124 are infants.
An extension was planned for 2004 at an estimated cost of £1,023,000.
The School is off Meadow Crescent, Braddan.

BRIDE RURAL SCHOOL.(1)
It was reported that Bride had a rural school in 1676, probably held in the original church. Land for a school was provided in 1775, and the present school stands on the same site.

BRIDE PAROCHIAL SCHOOL.(2)
Was re-opened on Sept 29th 1873 with 35 pupils, by 1874 there were 74 on the register.

BRIDE PAROCHIAL SCHOOL.(3) (Bride District)
A new school opened on May 15th 1876, the dimensions of the school rooms were :-
Principal room 51'6" x 20'4" x 14' to beam.
Class room   18'0" x 15'3" x 14' to beam.
The school was handed over to a local school committee backed by the Board of Education during year ending March 31st, 1876. Alteration and improvement was made in 1902/3 when the capacity was reduced to 100 mixed older scholars and 30 infants.

The alteration and improvement did not impress HMI in 1906 when he reported :-
"The buildings are not satisfactory, and are not well kept; the ventilation is insufficient, there is no drinking water, the offices are badly kept. Imperfect lighting in consequence of semi-opaque glass."

*   *   *

BRIDE SCHOOL.(4)
With an even plainer name this is the same school, still situate on the Cranstal Road, the A 16 from Bride Village to the Point of Ayre.
There was a scheme put forward in 1948 which proposed closure; fortunately this did not happen, but by 1951, the school attendance age was altered so that Bride could only teach children under eight. The age was further reduced to seven in 1976. The school continues in use.
There is one large classroom but no hall and, at present, there are 15 boys and 5 girls within the age range from 4 to 7.
There are 1.5 teachers, one full time nursery nurse and a part time ancillary.
In recent years there have been alterations to the kitchen, boiler house and cloakroom and there is the possibility of a new toilet block but the school does not feature in any other proposal for capital commitments.

*   *   *

CASTLETOWN - see chapter eighteen
*   *   *

COOILL.
A school for the district was provided within the original Cooill Methodist Chapel built in the 1790s.

CREGNEISH CHURCH SCHOOL.
The church was opened in 1838 at a cost of £150; at first only the Sanctuary was consecrated, the rest of the building being used as a school, but the school only remained on the premises for a short period of time.

CRONKBOURNE C of E SCHOOL. (Braddan District)
Opened in 1862. William Fine Moore conveyed the land so that the poor of Cronkbourne and Tromode might be educated in the principles of the Established Church.

The school remained open until 1874 and was re-opened from 1880 to 1892; on average there were about 45 scholars. In 1888 HMI reported as follows :-

"The mistress works the school single handed. A pupil teacher should be provided at once as well for the childrens' sake as hers."

CRONK y VODDY.(1) (German District)
Locally this was thought of as being 'The Mountain School" because of its extremely remote position on the highlands of the Parish of German. The Committee of the (privy) Council for Education gave £48/10/00 to supplement donations of £81 toward a new school in 1842.

For a few years there was an unusual reversal of roles here because in this case the school was used for church services during the years up to 1851 when the adjacent chapel of ease was built. The Master from 1851 to 1853 was Mr J Bolton.

CRONK y VODDY. (2)
A new school was provided in 1879 following strong criticism by HM Inspectors and it remained in use until 1932. In 1893 the Board of Education recommended special grants, backdated, of £10 for 1889/90 and £20 for 1890/1 because the school was in a thinly populated area.

The school building still stands although it is now known as "The Old School House"; it has been converted into a private house - a fate also reserved for the nearby Chapel of Ease.

I have chosen this school for a chapter to itself because the log books reveal such tremendous character and characters.

(See chapter nine.)

DALBY, ST. JAMES CHURCH AND SCHOOL.
Built as the result of Bishop William Ward's initiative in 1839 to the same basic design as St.Stephen's, Sulby and St. Luke's, Baldwin, whereby the chancel and transepts were separated from the nave by folding doors so that the nave could be used as a school. Surprisingly, for such a remote place, the school had 84 scholars in 1873. Like Cronk-y-Voddy, this school was given special grants because it was in a thinly populated area. £10 in 1889/90 and £10 for 1890/91.

Dalby School cont.,
Dalby school continued in use until 1932 by which time the number of pupils had fallen to an unacceptably low level. The few remaining pupils were transferred to Patrick School.
The church stands on the road from South Barrule to Glen Maye.

DHOOAR SCHOOL (1)
Situate in the Parish of Lezayre, although some four miles distant from the Parish church of Kirk Christ. Different spellings for the place name include Dhoor and Dour.
Land for the original Dhooar or 'Kneales' school, on the right hand side of the road from Ramsey to Andreas, was bequeathed in the will of John Kneale during 1813.
There were several money bequests but it seems that the school was not built immediately, nevertheless, it was reported that 40 boys were attending there in November 1827..

DHOOAR NATIONAL SCHOOL.(2) (Lezayre District)
In 1884, land on which a school should be erected and which was forming part of the estate of Ballakerbery, on the left hand side of the road from Ramsey, was conveyed to the Lezayre School Board. A school was built with the help of the Board of Education which gave a grant of £212, it became a National School and opened in 1885.
The School was improved in 1905 by enlargement of the infants' room and cloak rooms, the erection of lavatories, heating by boiler and erection of new outdoor offices. There were 78 mixed boys and girls and 30 infants.
For many years there were between forty and sixty scholars who walked from and to Ramsey every day so as to attend Dhooar School, this was because Dhooar was a "Free" school whereas all Ramsey schools required fees to be paid. Closure came in 1965.

The school remained empty for many years after its closure until, in the 1990s',it was used by a builder for storage purposes, The building and the playgrounds still look much as they did when in regular use as a school and it has not yet been converted for any residential purpose.

DHOON BRIDGE SCHOOL see Maughold.

DHOON SCHOOL. (Maughold District)
In February 1875, the Maughold School Commissioners bought land for a new school at a cost of £60. The school was intended as a replacement for the old Dhoon Bridge School and the Lhaggan School.

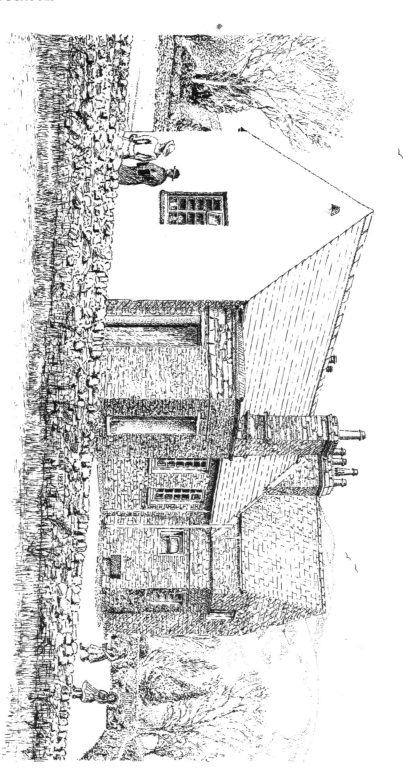

Maughold Central School - Open from 1852 to 1922. Drawn October 1997.

Dhoon School cont.,

Opened on January 10th 1876, with 30 on the roll; by 1889, there were 84 children at Maughold Central and a similar number at Dhoon.

The 1908 report on Dhoon school by HMI must have been particularly pleasing:-

"There is much to praise in this school; the discipline is so kindly and yet so strong that whether the master is there or not the children work away with quiet industry, and his guidance is all that is needed. Arithmetic and Composition, Reading and Writing - the higher and more Mechanical Subjects - are alike well advanced, and the school is in many respects a model of what a country School should be."

In 1976, the number was down to 46 but in recent years the numbers have risen steadily. A new toilet block was added during the 1990s as well as mobile classrooms.

At present the school has three classrooms, this includes two mobile classrooms, but there is no hall. The teaching staff number 3.5.

The children, who are between the ages of 4 and 7, number 30 boys and 33 girls, a total of 63 of whom 33 are infants.

An extension with permanent classrooms is now under way; included are the provision of enlarged playing fields, completion should be during 2003, total cost, including fees will be £1.903m.

This attractive country school is on the A2 road from Laxey to Ramsey and is on the left hand side of the road just past Glen Mona.

THE SCHOOLS

"The most striking peculiarity of Castletown is its intense respectability."
(from a guide book)

*   *   *

Chapter eighteen

CASTLETOWN SCHOOLS

CASTLETOWN.
Capital of the Island until 1869

CASTLETOWN PETTY SCHOOL.(1)
It has been suggested that the Earl of Derby maintained four free schools on the island at some time before 1651, one of these was at Castletown and it is possible that this became the town's first Petty School

The CASTLETOWN PETTY (or English) SCHOOL.(2)
Originally in a house on the Parade, the school was transferred to the old Chapel in 1698, when all three schools, the Petty School, the Academic School and the Grammar School, were kept in the chapel for a period until, in 1708, the Petty School was moved back to its original premises. The school seems to have faded away by 1838.

THE CASTLETOWN FREE GRAMMAR SCHOOL
The Grammar School was endowed in 1666, and its first home was in a house in the Market Place, it was then moved by Bishop Barrow to the old St. Mary's Church in 1698.
In the meantime the Petty School seems to have been closed and the building was sold; the Petty School could, possibly, have been moved into the ancient Chapel of St. Mary because in 1708, the old Petty School was re-purchased by Bishop Wilson and re-established thus allowing him to move the Grammar School into the Chapel.
The Chapel also housed the Academy or Academic School intended for the training of youngsters for the Manx Church or other public service.

At the 1714 Presentments:-
"Voluntary contributions toward the work (of repairs) have not extended to discharge the expenses of it (the Chapel) .... the Church Wardens are ordered to collect the assessment from inhabitants in and bordering on the town. Voluntary contributors to be exempt. Church Wardens to be allowed 1/- apiece for their trouble."   [M12f]

The Castletown Free Grammar School cont.,

The schools were separated after 1830 when the endowments of the Academic School were transferred to King William's College. The Grammar school remained where it was until closure on December 31st,1931.

From this date Bishop Barrow's Trustees had no further use for the old school and so, in July 1932, Castletown Commissioners borrowed £200 to purchase premises in School Lane, which included the old Grammar School; they intended to demolish all the buildings, including the school, the reason given being that the area included old or unhealthy buildings. The cleared land would have been used to enlarge a car park

Fortunately, there was public protest and the old Grammar School was given over for use as a scout hall, remaining in such use from 1932 to 1950. The school has since been restored and the building is now open as a museum complete with a Victorian period schoolroom.   [12f]

CASTLETOWN PUBLIC LIBRARY. THE ACADEMIC STUDIES.

Castletown Library was built in 1707 and stands almost opposite the Castle entrance. The lower floor of the library accommodated the House of Keys until 1869.

Attempts were made with academic studies on the first floor but the place never attained Academic status although the few students did progress well.

The same could be said about the academic studies which were pursued at Bishopscourt in later years; neither place was ever to qualify as being an Academy.

By 1781 the hopes for a separate academy at Castletown had been abandoned and the unique collection of manuscripts and books from the library were placed with the Grammar School; eventually, these valuable and historic items were all transferred into the care of King William's College, but, unfortunately, the whole of this rare Manx collection was lost when the college was burnt out in 1844.

BOWLING STREET ACADEMY.

Joseph Stowell opened an 'Academy" in Bowling Street during 1795 but he died in 1801, and the school was closed.

THE TAUBMANN SCHOOL.

Erected in 1799, this was an endowed school for boys, created by the will of John and Esther Taubmann. The couple left land at Ballahot in Malew, the earnings from which was expected to provide an income aimed at supporting a free school in Castletown and for the education of "twenty five poor boys."

CASTLETOWN NATIONAL SCHOOL.(1) HOPE STREET

Opened on August 26th,1822. The school was in a converted warehouse and had 80 pupils. By 1828 there were 106 boys and 90 girls. The girls of the school were transferred to Victoria Road School on the 18th of October 1909, the infants being transferred to the same school on the 20th of March 1911.

Hope Street School was then closed.   [B04]

CASTLETOWN NATIONAL SCHOOL BY THE LAKE.(2)

The location of this school came about as a result of the granting of a site by the Crown on July 18th, 1836.

Construction was helped by a £90 grant from the National Society, the remainder was covered by voluntary contributions.

The school opened on Queen Victoria's coronation day, 28th June 1838, and by 1839 there were 270 children attending.

A further grant from the Government of £82.06.0 and another £30 from the National Society helped provide the teacher's residence which was built at a cost of £315.04.9.

Almost seventy years later, in 1907, HMI was complaining that :-

" **The continued use of these inconvenient and unsanitary premises cannot longer be maintained."**

The school closed about 1907 and the building now houses the church of St. Mary's on the Harbour.

DERBYHAVEN.

The Rev Gilmour Harvey sold a house for use as a Church School in 1859.

KING WILLIAM'S COLLEGE.

Colonel Cornelius Smelt laid the foundation stone of the college on June 23rd 1830, almost his last public duty.

The College opened in 1833 and was named after King William IV, but it derived no benefit from the monarch. (He was pleading poverty at the time.)

The College was gutted by fire in 1844 but, by good fortune, the main stone structure survived more or less intact and, within a relatively short space of time it was rebuilt and re-opened. Since then there have been many extensions.

As from April 1st 1933, the College was recognised by the Education Council for grant purposes. The initial grant was for £1.278 18 06d and an additional grant of £400 was given for an advanced course leading to the First and Second Medical examinations. A further grant of £51 14 8d was paid, equal to half of the employers' superannuation contributions.

There were twelve Governors, eight appointed by the Trustees of Bishop Barrow's Charity and four by the Education Council.   [B07]

King William's College cont.,

In 1935 the fees per annum were from £28 to £32 15s for Tuition and £102 to £128 5s for Board and Tuition. In that year there were 12 free places for scholars from the Island's Secondary School and a further 24 boys received bursaries valued at not less than the Tuition fee. The examinations taken were from Oxford and Cambridge.   [B07]

At present the College has 32 classrooms and a fine undivided hall that is 11m wide by 25m in length. There are 36 teachers and 40 ancillaries for the 156 boys and 119 girls. The age range being from 11 to 18.

The college does have a long term development plan.

The main entrance to the College is from the Douglas Road, Castletown. (the A8)

THE BUCHAN SCHOOL. A HIGH SCHOOL FOR GIRLS.

It is possible that the school was started in 1875 but it is known for certain that there was an opening ceremony within rented premises opposite the Castle during 1879.

The school then moved to Bay View House in 1888, to the Promenade in 1897, and to No 16 The Green.,in 1899.

The school was then moved into the Bowling Green Street premises.

It was during 1922 that the School was recognised by the Council of Education.

In 1929, fees were from £13.10s to £24. Boarders paid from £72 to £82, including tuition. In the same year the School was teaching 11 boys and 42 girls, of whom 22 were boarders.

From April 1st 1929, the school was recognised as being a Secondary School and awarded a Grant of £350 per annum by the Council of Education. The Grant carried certain conditions; free places were to be offered to 10% of admissions and no religious instruction was to be given during school hours.

An inspection made about 1939 pointed out that the school building consisted of four houses (joined by internal passageways) which were not only unattractive and lacking in amenities but in several respects were below the standard of modern secondary schools. It was considered that, ultimately, the school would have to be rehoused because in those premises it was inadvisable to allow any considerable increase in the number of pupils.

In turn, the restrictions imposed by these buildings meant that the very high ratio of teachers to pupils could not be reduced; at the time, the ratio stood at 7 pupils to one teacher, whereas, for example, in Ramsey Grammar School the figure was 19.5 to 1.

The Buchan School cont.,
The Managers purchased Westhill, a property to the West of Castletown, for its boarders in October 1939, a Tynwald committee having voted £250 toward the purchase price and £1,750 toward the estimated cost of extensions and adaptations.

[B07]

Phase one of a new Buchan School opened in 1977, and the Bowling Green site was then vacated, but it seems more than likely that the money expended and owing on the new school far exceeded any possible income and, in December 1989, it was announced that the school would be 'fused' with King William's College.
The merger took place during December 1991.
The Buchan School is now at Westhill, Castletown, and the main entrance is from Arbory Road. Surprisingly large, there are 20 classrooms and an undivided sports hall for the 260 scholars; there are 120 boys, 100 girls and 40 infants in the Kindergarten. The age range extends from 3 to 11.
No further extensions are being considered at present.

CASTLE RUSHEN HIGH SCHOOL.(1)

The school lies on the left of the road from Castletown to Port St. Mary and, despite originally having been formed within an unique set of unusual school buildings, it has become one of the leading schools on the Island.

Initially, the school was housed within converted huts and other wartime buildings on what had been the former Fleet Air Arm training camp at Scarlett. The whole site, 17 acres in extent, cost £4,950 and a further £5,000 was paid to the Admiralty for the buildings thereon.
Tynwald passed a vote of £24,000 to upgrade the buildings but a further £21,000 was also needed to pay for equipment, furniture, asphalting etc. Many of the wartime buildings were demolished and it was the really clever planning of the remainder by the architects that resulted in a practical working school

Opened on September 14th 1948; the school started with a roll of 147 boys and 116 girls, taught by a staff of 18 which included the Head. These original pupils and the staff should be very proud of their involvement and subsequent achievements because this school was a pioneer in the development of Comprehensive Education within the British Isles.
A large hall/gymnasium with changing rooms and showers was provided during the spring of 1949.
By 1955 there were 415 pupils and in 1958 it seemed that there was a distinct possibility of overcrowding within a few years. It was at this time, not before, that the Board of Education first discussed the need for a brand new building.

CASTLE RUSHEN HIGH SCHOOL. (2)

As the result of the deliberations of the Board of Education, a new, replacement, school was completed in 1962, at a cost of £175,000, plus £5,000 for fittings; the first occupancy was on September 10th. All the old buildings were demolished during the summer holidays and an official opening ceremony took place on November the 8th, 1962.

There have been successive extensions - the first in February 1969, another in 1971/2, and by 1979 there were 950 pupils.

In 1984/5 a new sports hall was built and by 1998, there were 990 pupils with 70 staff.

A "Post 16" accommodation has been completed. Overall cost was £914,000. Preliminary thoughts are being given to a school extension starting about 2007, fees are estimated at £234,000, construction costs £2.687m.

CASTLETOWN, VICTORIA ROAD PRIMARY SCHOOL.

A handsome stone faced building very near Castletown Railway Station, access being from Victoria Road.

Built in 1895, the school was originally intended for boys but, in October 1909, girls from the National School were removed here and from then on it was a Mixed and Infants School for many years. In 1921, for example, there were 35 infant boys and 28 infant girls, 74 boys between 7 and 15 years of age and 67 girls of a similar age group.

In October 1967, Tynwald was asked to approve funding for an extension which was to include two modern classes as well as indoor sanitation, the overall costing was estimated at £24,460. There are ten classrooms as well as an 18m x 8m undivided hall with a stage.

The school now has pupils from 4 to 11 years of age, 250 in total made up of 122 boys and 128 girls of whom 101 are infants.

There are 11.5 teachers as well as 1.5 NNEB.

A further extension is anticipated for 2006, this will provide a sports hall, 2 extra classrooms and a separate nursery. The present estimate of cost for these extensions is £943,000.

CATHERINE HALSALL GIRLS SCHOOL. Hope St ?

In 1758 the will of Catharine Halsall appointed four of the clergy as Trustees for the "erecting, building and endowing a Free School ... for teaching Girls only to read, sew, knit and spin." A salary was specified for the Mistress and there was also £2 per annum toward repairs. The school may have been on Hope St.

In 1829 there were 40 scholars.

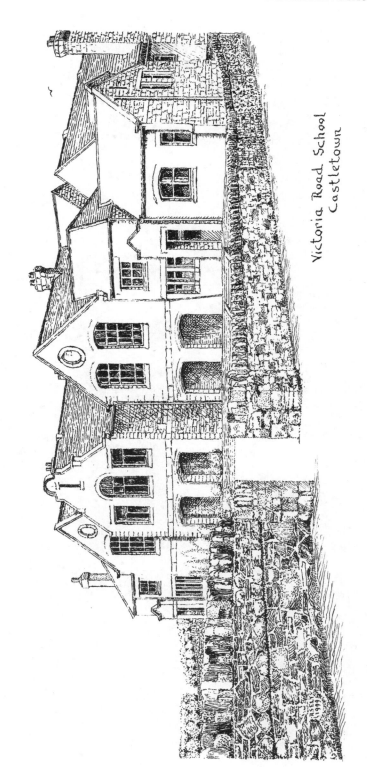

Victoria Road School
Castletown

Victoria Road School, Castletown - A stone faced building started in 1895. Drawn September 1999.

"Education is what survives, when what has been learnt has been forgotten."
(Education in 1984)

*   *   *

Chapter nineteen

THE SCHOOLS OF DOUGLAS
CAPITAL OF THE ISLE OF MAN SINCE 1869

ABBEYFIELDS WESLEYAN SCHOOL
A small school to the North of Douglas. Closed 1898.

ANAGH COAR PRIMARY SCHOOL
Funding for the purchase of a site for this school was provided in 1967. The land was owned by Douglas Corporation who were willing to sell to the Education Department for £15,000, this sum including provision for roads and sewerage but, at the time, this was not agreed upon.
The school was eventually opened on Darragh Way, Anagh Coar, during 1976. It has since been extended.
During the year 2000 there were 51 infants, 67 junior boys and 66 girls. The teaching staff numbered 7, including the Head. There are only two classrooms but there are also 4 teaching bays and an undivided hall measuring approximately 20m X 12m.

ASHLEY HILL PRIMARY SCHOOL - See Onchan.

ATHOL STREET SCHOOL - See Douglas Lancastrian School.

BALLACOTTIER SCHOOL
This new school opened in 1998 and is situate in Clybane Road, Farmhill, Douglas. The school has 14 classrooms and a clear hall measuring 52' X 72'.
During the year 2000 the school taught 103 boys and 105 girls aged from 3 to 11 years of age. A Special Needs unit forms part of the school and has 2 teachers and 3 NNEB. The main school has 9 mainstream teachers, a Head teacher and 2 NNEB.

BALLACLOAN INFANT SCHOOL. Demesne Road.
Originally a boys school it was converted and reopened in 1974. There are three double sized classrooms as well as a teaching area comprising the library and computer suite. The undivided hall measures 49' X 25'
There are eight teachers, including the Head, two NNEBs' and one part-time classroom assistant for the 63 boys and 84 girls, all of whom are infants. The school is entered from Demesne Road.

BALLAKERMEEN HIGH SCHOOL
In 1936 a plot of land, 2 roods and 21 perches in extent was purchased by the Education Dept. and during 1937 it was proposed to build two schools on the site, one for boys and one for girls at a cost of £55,000.   [B07]

A contract for erection of the Senior School was awarded to Messrs. Creer Bros. Ltd., at a cost of £75,030.9.2d.

Newly built during 1939, the school was quickly requisitioned by the Royal Navy at the onset of WW2 for the duration of the war. Renamed 'HMS St George', the school was used as a shore-based school for boy entrants to the Royal Navy.

Re-opening as a normal school took place during Sept 1946 with a formal opening on Oct 28th 1946.

In 1967 Tynwald approved the purchase of a further plot of land containing 35,861 square yards or thereabouts for the sum of £16,000 as a site for a College of Further Education.

As of Sept 1985 the school was reformed and became an 11 to 18 years "through school" similar to the Douglas High School.

The school is situate on St Catherines Drive and has been well funded for additional construction.

At present the school has 651 boys and 689 girls attending within the age range of 11 to 20; to help them on their way there are 90 teachers. There are two large capacity halls, both of which are undivided.

Plans are afoot for a new "Medway Block" to be erected, possibly, about 2004. The total estimated cost being £1,018k.

BALLAQUAYLE HIGH SCHOOL FOR BOYS.
Opened 27/5/1927.

BALLAQUAYLE INFANT SCHOOL.
Opened during 1971, this school is on Stoney Road. There were 97 boys and 68 girls attending during the year 2000; they were taught by 8.5 teachers and 2 NNEB as well as lunchtime ancillaries. The school has been extended since opening and now has 8 classrooms. There is a hall, approximately 30' X 45' which can be sub-divided. The possibility of a further extension is being considered but nothing has been programmed for the near future.

BUCKS ROAD SCHOOL.
Plans for a new school were approved in Jan 1882 with places for 290 infants, 300 older boys and 300 girls.

CENTRE FOR MANX STUDIES
At present within a three storied terrace house, No 6 Kingswood Grove, near the Museum, this is not a school, instead it is a centre widely used by those wishing to pursue differing Manx studies in depth.

CRONK Y BERRY

A primary school opened in September 1978; there are 15 classrooms and a hall, the hall is not sub-divided other than from the dining area.

Children attending are from 4 to 11 years of age and they include 42 in the nursery, 148 infants, 184 boys and 166 girls. There are no known plans for any extensions.

The school can be found on Hailwood Avenue.

DEMESNE ROAD SCHOOL.

Originally planned as a mixed school, the specifications and plans were approved during 1904/5. The site cost was £1,159 and building costs were quoted as being £3,860.

The school opened during January 1908 with accommodation for 398 boys who were transferred from Athol Street and Tynwald Street schools. The boys school was closed in 1973 and the building was then re-furbished and re-opened as the BALLACLOAN INFANT SCHOOL.   [M29]

DOMESTIC SCIENCE COLLEGE - see KINGSWOOD GROVE.

DOUGLAS ACADEMIC SCHOOL -see DOUGLAS GRAMMAR SCHOOL (II)

DOUGLAS GRAMMAR SCHOOL (I) (St Matthews)

Originally established in Dixon House, New Bond St, under the care of the new chapel of St Matthews. The first Master was reputed to be William Walker in the early 1700s. The Chaplain and Master of the Grammar School were always the same person until closure about 1876, this was because of the endowments given for both the Church and the Schoolmaster.

After the 1876 closure the rival MIDDLE SCHOOL (founded 1758) became DOUGLAS GRAMMAR SCHOOL and continued as such until its closure and replacement by the modern GRAMMAR SCHOOL. The 'old' Grammer School was sold in 1878 for £300.

(Also see DOUGLAS MIDDLE SCHOOL)

DOUGLAS GRAMMAR SCHOOL (II)

The early school changed title in 1804 to become the "ACADEMIC SCHOOL". A Mr Barton opened an establishment known as the 'Grammar School' but he changed the name to the 'HEYWOOD HOUSE ACADEMY', upon which another person said that they would open a Grammar School in Duke St !

Within a short time the mantle fell, once again, on the St Matthews School which continued as the Grammar School until eventual closure by 1837.

John Cubbon, in 1853, revealed that the Grammar School and its extensive library had been shamefully neglected, the library being kept in a corner whilst the building was let as a dwelling place and vault. (See also DOUGLAS PETTY SCHOOL)

DOUGLAS HIGH SCHOOL FOR GIRLS.
(see PARK ROAD and ST NINIAN'S)

DOUGLAS LANCASTRIAN SCHOOL. (1)
The LANCASTRIAN SCHOOL was started in Muckle Gate during 1810. During Jan 1811 the school moved to Athol St leaving the Muckle Gate premises to be used as a girl's school.

DOUGLAS LANCASTRIAN SCHOOL. (2)
The site for a new Lancastrian school in Athol St was provided by John Moore and his wife on two lots or parcels of land numbered 16/17 in Taggart's map or plan of the same street.
The site backed on to Shaw's Brow.
The Deed was dated 23rd May 1811 in favour of the trustees for "Establishing a Sunday and Day School to be conducted on Mr Joseph Lancaster's plan."
Amongst other things, the deed stated that the school was to be built upon the plan revised by Joseph Lancaster and that the school and land was to belong for ever to the Town of Douglas and the Neighbourhood.
The Trustees were to pay the Chief Rent annually and an alienation fine to the Lord every five years and to John Moore, his heirs and assigns a ground rent of one shilling annually - and,......"the contents of the dunghills or midden stands as shall or may be made upon the premises to be removed or taken away by the said John Moore, heirs and assigns every half year also permitting John Moore, his wife and heirs and assigns from time to time for ever to send 12 children to the school without charge."

The foundation stone for the new school was laid on June 4th 1811. The school cost £111/8/8.
Sometime after 1813 the premises were renamed as a 'DAY AND SUNDAY SCHOOL'
In 1821 the school had 119 boys and 137 girls attending.

The school was closed at some time in the late 1880s, eventually being re-opened by Douglas Board on June 1st 1895 with accommodation for 200 boys and 200 girls.

Closed again on January 10th 1908 because the building was considered to be no longer satisfactory, it re-opened on Sept 18th 1908 but with a greatly reduced capacity for 75 children.
On Jan 10th 1910, a girls' department was opened for 150 girls and, on July 6th, certain portions of the school were re-opened for up to 90 boys.
The Athol St School finally closed during October 1915.   [M12e] [M29]

DOUGLAS MIDDLE SCHOOL

Situate on Dalton St and opened in 1858, the school was linked to St Thomas' Church and became the new DOUGLAS GRAMMAR SCHOOL when renamed as such in 1873. In June 1888 the will of Mrs Hall left the dwelling house, school and large playground, jointly, to the Vicar-General, the High Bailiff of Douglas and the Vicar of St Thomas's together with £300 to buy property, the rent from which was to provide an income for the Headmaster.

DOUGLAS PETTY SCHOOL

A free school was probably in existence before 1649 but was definitely established under Bishop Barrow's inheritance. The school was still known as such in 1675 and 1694 although by 1705 the GRAMMAR SCHOOL had been grafted onto it.
See also GRAMMAR SCHOOL (I)

DOUGLAS SCHOOL OF ART

Built in Kensington Rd durin 1880. On the 20th of May 1884, the Board of Education gave a grant of £196 toward the cost of construction. Designed and built by Philip Christian, it wasn't long before there were 50 students on day courses and about 200 on night courses. In 1908 mention was made that the school was likely to be closed on financial grounds but, instead, it soldiered on and, in 1926 it was extended by the purchase of an adjoining gymnasium.
The building was taken over as a girl's school in 1926/7.
(see also RAPHAEL ROAD)

DOUGLAS SCHOOL OF SCIENCE

This school was run in the PARK ROAD SCHOOL for a few years but had faded out by 1904. Science subjects continued to be pursued in evening classes.

DOUGLAS SECONDARY SCHOOL

Strangely, this school was first mentioned by the Board of Education as a 'Secondary School, mixed" during 1904. The report stated that the school operated on the second floor of a two storey building but, in the relevant report the Board made no mention of where this secondary school actually was !
Presumably it was within PARK ROAD SCHOOL.
Pupils were paying fees of one shilling a week or ten shillings a quarter, the average attendance being 148.
In 1908 HMI reported :-**The Douglas Secondary School has been improving year by year, and the success of the school has proved its need and value very conclusively. The school has outgrown its accommodation, and the question of providing a permanent home cannot be delayed. The number of pupils is now too large for the buildings and five of the seven classes in the school contain larger numbers than the Board are prepared to recognise as a permanent arrangement."**
[B03]

DRILL HALL

DRUMGOLD STREET (1)

A temporary school in use for a short period from 1886 to July 1889 pending construction and completion of the HANOVER STREET BOARD SCHOOL. There was accommmodation for 131 boys and 114 girls. This school was one of the first to have a Penny Savings Bank for the children.

DRUMGOLD STREET (II)

BOURNE HALL was opened as a temporary school in September 1895.

FAIRFIELD JUNIOR SCHOOL

Opened in 1874. (See TYNWALD STREET)

HANOVER STREET BOARD SCHOOL

The site for this school at the corner of Hanover Street and Barrack Street cost £4823. There was also a small sum payable as compensation for the displaced tenants.

A foundation stone was laid on July 4th 1888 and the school was opened on August 26th 1889. Total cost of the school building was £10,218 and funding was mainly from loans, £8656 at three and threequarters percent from the Prudential and £1125 from Dumbells Bank at the same rate of interest.

Capacity was for 320 infants on the ground floor, 256 girls on the first floor and 244 boys on the second floor.

In 1890 there were 271 infants. 229 girls and 271 boys on the register and it was in this year that the school started to run a Penny Savings Bank for the children.

Converted to be a COLLEGE OF FURTHER EDUCATION in 1960, the college moved to Willaston in 1972.

The building is now known as being the Government Offices in Lord St and is used by the EDUCATION MUSIC CENTRE and by the Office of Fair Trading.

GLENCRUTCHERY. Willaston.

This site was proposed during the 1960s for a College of Further Education, becoming so in 1972. Removal of the college has enabled the premises to become the home of the Education Department's Special Needs and Psychology Service.
(see also ISLE OF MAN INDUSTRIAL SCHOOL)

ISLE OF MAN COLLEGE
(Holmefield Avenue. Willaston)
I suspect that the majority of people on the Isle of Man are completely unaware of the sheer size of this college and the number of students that pass under its wing. Post Secondary Courses of Study were introduced during 1959/60.

Progressively extended in 1990, 1994 and 1998, the College now caters for 650 full time and 9,000 part-time students in the age range of 16 plus. The College has 78 classrooms and possesses an undivided hall which is 45' X 70'. There are 100 full-time and 204 part-time teachers.

Plans are in the pipeline for a refurbishment of the college by 2004 at an estimated cost of £732,000. An extension on a new, additional, site has been mentioned but, at present, there is no committed capital for such a scheme although funding has been approved for pre-contract design fees of £59,000.

ISLE OF MAN INDUSTRIAL SCHOOL
A place of correction. In later years this school became known as the ISLE OF MAN CHILDRENS' HOME. The Childrens Home was in Glencrutchery Road before moving to Knottfield in Woodbourne Avenue. Glencrutchery, as a school, closed in 1997.
(see Onchan)

KINGSWOOD GROVE DOMESTIC SCIENCE COLLEGE
Following removal of the College to become part of the SCHOOL OF TECHNOLOGY, ARTS AND CRAFTS in 1947, the building now houses the Government Laboratory.

MANOR PARK PRIMARY SCHOOL.
Situate on Pulrose Road, this school was opened during Sept 1973 as a junior school. Infants joined from PULROSE SUNSHINE SCHOOL in 1986, The school was built on the 'open' plan and has an undivided hall. Two classrooms were constructed during 2000 for Y5 and Y6. There were 163 scholars, 84 boys and 79 girls; they have 9 teachers, including the Head, as well as 4 ancillaries.

MONA TERRACE COLLEGE OF DOMESTIC SCIENCE.
Also known as the MANX RESIDENTIAL AND DAY TECHNICAL COLLEGE FOR WOMEN. In 1922 the Council of Education bought No 9 Mona Terrace, to be adapted for instruction in "Cookery, Laundry and other Household matters designed to help the Tourist Industry".

The purchase was made possible by a grant from Henry Bloom Noble Trustees, the first teachers being Miss Lindsay and Miss Birch.

MUCCLESGATE SUNDAY SCHOOL
(Also known as Mucklesgate)
Established in 1786, this was the first Sunday School on the Island. The teachers were paid, but such a bold experiment did not last and the school closed eighteen months later.

Hugh Stowell is credited with establishing the next Sunday School in 1808.

MURRAYS ROAD SCHOOL (I)
The site for a new school on the Murray's Estate was purchased for £1906/15/3. The area extended to 4,032 square yards. A foundation stone was laid on June 23rd 1896 and the school was opened on Sept 4th 1899. The school was able to absorb children from DRUMGOLD and SALISBURY ROAD schools.

This was the first Manx school to be provided with hot water radiators. There were 17 classrooms, 9 on the ground floor. The hall dimensions were 80' X 30', the height of ground floor rooms being 15', those on the first floor were 20'

Accommodation was for 50 babies, 350 infants and 100 juniors on the ground floor and 500 senior and junior on the first floor.

In 1926 a centre for the instruction of 12 myopic children was established within the school.

MURRAYS ROAD SCHOOL (II)
The Education Dept intended to give a complete renovation to the original MURRAYS ROAD SCHOOL during the mid 1960s, this was because the school was not all that old in relative terms and had good overall accommodation. Following an examination, contractors found that the place was severely affected by rot and the scheme for modernisation had to be dropped.

The first estimate put to Tynwald requesting funding for a replacement school was submitted on May 16th 1965 for £87,375. This estimate was on the assumption that the new school would be built on the playground area of the old school to be followed by the subsequent demolition of the rot affected building.

Work commenced in October 1965.

MURRAYS ROAD SCHOOL (III)
The new school opened on the same site during Sept 1967, the cost was £116,500.

Now known as the MURRAYS ROAD JUNIOR SCHOOL, the main entrance is on Laureston Avenue. There are 10 classrooms and a hall which is 10m x 13.77m. The hall is sub-divided so as to create a dining area of 6.13m x 10m. There are 10 teachers, including the Head, for 124 boys and 124 girls within the age range of 7 to 11.

At present there are no extensions within committed schemes by the Education Dept but consideration may be given to the development of an existing underground area as a library/ computer suite by, say, 2005/6.

PARK ROAD ELEMENTARY SCHOOL
A site was obtained on the corner of Melbourne St and Farrant St at a cost of £934, this was in May 1888. Subsequently the site was extended by the purchase of land fronting on to Park Rd for £550. The total area became 4730 square yards. Amongst other funding, the school received a building grant of £450.

Classed as a Higher Grade School it also housed the DOUGLAS ORGANISED SCIENCE SCHOOL for a few years.

In 1894 Douglas School Committee opened a Secondary School here as a single class of 24 students. Progress of this SECONDARY SCHOOL was so good that on August 1st 1919 the school ceased to be used as an elementary school and became the EASTERN DISTRICT SECONDARY SCHOOL.

Extension followed in 1922 so as to provide accommodation for at least 400 girls, this cost £15,000. Messrs.W & J.E.McArd next submitted a tender for £16,485 for further extensions which were completed in 1929; the whole of the premises then became the :-

DOUGLAS HIGH SCHOOL FOR GIRLS.
(previously PARK ROAD ELEMENTARY SCHOOL)
During 1929 the fees were 6 guineas. Out of a total of 303 scholars, 108 were granted free places.

A new assembly hall and gymnasium were built during 1936.

In September 1985 the school was reformed as an 11 to 18 years of age 'THROUGH SCHOOL' and renamed ST NINIANS HIGH SCHOOL.

There are 22 classrooms and a gymnasium, the hall is 30m x15m.
(see ST NINIANS)

PULROSE INFANTS SCHOOL
It was in 1932 that consideration was first given to provision of an infant school for the Pulrose district. Unfortunately, money was scarce in the early 1930s and it was not until 1935 that an estimate of cost was put at £12,000.

Work started in 1936 for a school sufficient for 250 children.

Opening took place on July 12th 1937, with Miss M.M.Creer as Headmistress and with 73 pupils. The school became well known as THE SUNSHINE SCHOOL.

Closed as a school in 1986, the building now houses the Pulrose Community Centre.   [B07]

RAPHAEL ROAD HANDICRAFT CENTRE.
Boys from Demesne Road, St Thomas's and St Mary's schools went to this centre. In 1929 it was reported that 10 separate classes of about 20 boys received instruction every week.

RAPHAEL ROAD SCHOOL FOR DEAF CHILDREN

Because of the travel and other costs involved in obtaining tuition in England within the specialised schools for the deaf, an experimental SCHOOL FOR THE DEAF was established for Manx children in the gymnasium premises of the school.

A qualified teacher was appointed and in 1933 seven children were attending.

The school ran for just over five years until, following the resignation of the teacher and the near impossibility of finding another suitably qualified person as a replacement to work on the Island, it was decided not to continue, instead, the children were sent once again to recognised schools in England.

ROMAN CATHOLIC SECONDARY SCHOOL.

A proposal was put forward in 1956 seeking a Roman Catholic Secondary School which should be maintained by the Education Authority as an Aided Voluntary School.

The Authority objected on the grounds that it would involve unreasonable public expenditure and would be contrary to the best educational needs of the Island.

The Board disapproved of the proposal on the ground that it did not provide for efficient instruction and training.

ST BARNABUS INFANT SCHOOL

Opened under the church in Cattlemarket St in 1837 at a cost of £500. The school then moved to Fort Street and, in 1845 was enlarged with the help of a Parliamentary Grant of £85.

In the late 1880s the Managers offered the school to the Douglas Board so that it could continue in use for educational purposes subject to certain conditions. The Board refused to accept the proposal because it would have had the effect of placing a Board School supported by the General Rate of the town under the auspices of one particular relgious denomination.

ST BARNABUS SCHOOL closed in June 1888.

ST BRIDGIT'S SCHOOL.

St Bridgit's was the first chapel to be opened for Roman Catholic worship on the Island in 1814 and was situate about a mile from Douglas on the old Castletown Rd.

A school was built beside the chapel in 1824. The Master, Mr John Kelly, taught allcomers, Catholic and Protestant alike, there was only one classroom and children paid their weekly fees in kind as well as in coin. The school did not remain open long.   [M12j]

ST GEORGE'S SCHOOL. (I)

The church of St George's had a sequence of three schools. The first, an infant school opened on Jan 12th 1810, in a room off Callow Slip in Mucklesgate, under the auspices of St George's. The school was for 25 scholars up to the age of eight.

ST GEORGE'S SCHOOL (II)

The school was moved to temporary accommodation in an Athol Street club room on Jan 21st 1811. This was followed by the laying of a foundation stone for a new school on June 4th 1811.

By 1831 the range of children accepted was from 18 months to seven years of age.

ST GEORGE'S SCHOOL. (III)

A new school for boys and girls opened on February 10th 1813 and, during 1838 an infant school was provided on the corner of Barrack Street and Kelly's Court. In 1890 there were 221 boys, 191 girls and 94 infants on the register.

At short notice and in what might be regarded as a fit of pique, the Managers decided that the infant school should close during June 1894. They then gave notice that they intended to close the Boys and Girls schools in November 1894. These were two precipitate actions which displaced a large number of children at fairly short notice and caused considerable problems for the Douglas School Board.

ST MARY'S RC SCHOOL. (I)

First established in 1824, it moved in later years into the basement of St George's Hall.

ST MARY'S SCHOOL. (II)

Opened within premises on Stanley Mount in 1861. By 1890 there were 117 infants and 183 mixed on the register. A new elementary school was opened on the same site by Father Edmund Walsh in 1894.   [M12j] [M29]

ST MARY'S SCHOOL. (III)

(St Mary's Road/ Somerset Road.)

It was on June 16th 1964 that Tynwald approved the transfer of St Mary's mixed and infant school to a new site off Somerset Rd. Tynwald authorised grants toward the cost of land and buildings. The buildings had been estimated as costing £74,000 but the overall cost turned out to be £113,653.

The estimate for the School Managers' proportion, made in 1966, was £60,080, of which they were entitled to a 50% grant. It was agreed that the Managers be given a loan of £30,000 repayable over 30 years. The estimated cost to the Education Department for providing the site, playing areas, medical room and meals facilities was £45,573.   continued >

St Mary-Douglas

St Mary's Church - Not a school but the place from which the Roman Catholic schools on the Island were primarily controlled. Drawn November 1997.

St Mary's Schools, cont.

Opened for pupils by September 1967, the new school was officially opened on March 7th 1968, the old school was sold to the Isle of Man Government for £12,500.

[B08]

Further extension has taken place although, at present, no further extensions are being considered.

The school has an undivided hall and 13 classrooms for it's pupils, all between the ages of 4 and 11. About 316 in total. There are 15 teachers and 3 ancillaries.

ST MATTHEWS SCHOOL
(see DOUGLAS GRAMMAR SCHOOL)

ST NINIANS HIGH SCHOOLS
(Schoill Ard Noo Ninian)

Opened under these names in Sept 1985 following a restructuring of secondary education in the Douglas area but using schools which had existed on the same site for many years.

There is a LOWER SCHOOL at Park Road and an UPPER SCHOOL at Bray Hill. Altogether there are about 75 class rooms excluding the sports halls, halls and library.

The age range is from 11 to 18 years and there are 89 teachung staff for the 594 boys and 600 girls in attendance.

A new extension came into use on the Bray Hill site during Sept 2000, it is a Post 16 unit known as the Barbara Cottier Centre, the cost was £1,117m. The LOWER SCHOOL at Park Road caters for the years 7 and 8 in Stream 3; there are 213 boys and 219 girls attending. (Included within the figure in para 3).

Consideration is being given to an extension of the dining room and an extension of the LOWER SCHOOL playground by about 2006, the cost is likely to be £951,000. plus design fees.

ST THOMAS'S INFANT AND PRIMARY SCHOOL.

The foundation stone was laid by Mrs Hutton, wife of the Vicar, Rev F.Hutton, on July 31st 1874. The school is on Finch Road and was opened in 1875/6. By 1890 there were 124 mixed pupils on the register and by 1892 the fees were 2d a week.

At the time of writing this is the only C of E school still in operation on the Island. There are three classrooms as well as a hall.

Children from the age of 4 to 11 years of age attend and in 2000 there were 20 infants, 25 bays and 35 girls attending. There are four teachers and one classroom assistant. The school suffers through being overshadowed by a hill one side, St Thomas's church on another and on a third side by a massive concrete multi storied car-park from which litter and rubbish - even including supermarket trollies - have been maliciously thrown from a height on to the playground below.

SALISBURY STREET SCHOOL.
Originally a Wesleyan Chapel which was opened as a school for a limited period from April 1896 to 1899/1900. Accomodation was provided for 180 infants. The school was disbanded in 1900, the children going to Murrays Road School.

In 1910 the building was again re-opened on a temporary basis as a school to relieve overcrowding at Park Road.

SOMERSET ROAD BOYS HIGH SCHOOL.
A site for a new school had been purchased in 1913 but it was not until November 1921 that the Council of Education submitted a scheme for a new Secondary School with accommodation for at least 400 boys. Tynwald voted £53,410 to cover all the costs.

The school opened in 1927, the cost being £47,500.

In 1929 the fees were Six Guineas but there were also 121 free places out of 346 pupils. Extended in 1958.

STRATHALLAN HALL. See Onchan.

THOMAS STREET SUNDAY AND DAY INFANT SCHOOL.
The Thomas Street school was within a Methodist Chapel. The Sunday School opened on Jan 26th 1837. These premises served for girls and infants until the school in Well Road was opened in 1841. During 1843 there were 120 boys and 193 girls in the Sunday School.

By 1890 there were 353 mixed and 174 infants on the ordinary school register. The school fees for 1892 were 1d for standards I to IV, and 2d for standards V to VII.

The school closed as from August 1898 but the premises were immediately rented by the Douglas School Board for a further year so as to gain time during which to relocate the children.

Rather surprisingly, these premises were brought into use as a school once again in May 1922 so as to provide accommodation for some of the lower forms of the Douglas Secondary school.

The school was on the corner of Thomas Street and Wellington Street - between King Street and Drumgold Street - where Victoria street now is.

(See also WELL ROAD.)   [M25] [M29]

TYNWALD STREET
A school existed here in 1874. The present school was built in 1882 and £5,800 was borrowed to defray costs.

TYNWALD STREET SCHOOL was one of the first to start a Penny Savings Bank scheme for the children.

During 1906, the boys were transferred to DEMESNE ROAD so that TYNWALD STREET SCHOOL could be converted into a school for girls and infants only.

By 1908 the conversion was complete. Later, the school was converted to a mixed junior school and became known as FAIRFIELD.

WELL ROAD WESLEYAN CHAPEL
SUNDAY AND DAY SCHOOL.

During 1837 this was a boys school but, from 1841, the school concentrated on infants and girls.

In the earlier days any child wishing to enrol for the Well Road School had first to be recommended by the Representative Committee or by a subscriber to the upkeep of the Sunday School before admittance to the roll.

The normal minimum age was 6 and the fees were One penny a week or, if the child could write, Twopence.

There were 132 infants on the register in 1890.

WELLINGTON BOARD SCHOOL.

This was the first Douglas Board School, in fact, the first on the Island. Opened within a converted printing works in Wellington Street on August 26th 1873.

The school catered for children between the ages of 7 and 13 at a fee of Twopence every week.

Closed when the purpose built Bucks Road School was opened in 1882.

WILLASTON PRIMARY SCHOOL.

The site for this infants school was purchased from Douglas Corporation for £5,586 during 1953 and, at the time, the overall cost of the school was estimated at £30,005, a remarkably good estimate because the final cost was £29,170/7/5.

Entrance to the school is from School Road, Willaston.

The school opened on January 5th 1955; there was a Head Teacher and two staff.

Now, there are eight classrooms, a hall and two double mobile units for the 192 scholars, there are 76 infants among the 103 boys and 89 girls. There are 10 teachers, including the Head.

No major extensions are planned although some internal alterations are being considered.

*   *   *

"Whom are you ?' said he, for he had been to night school."

(George Ade 1866-1944)

*   *   *

Chapter twenty
From East Baldwin to Onchan

EAST BALDWIN SCHOOL.
Opened in 1764, the school was built upon land sold for the nominal sum of one shilling by John Cain and Robert Creer.

FOXDALE PETTY SCHOOL 1833 ?
Stuart Lambie the Head Teacher of the present Foxdale School, discovered a reference in the Patrick Parish records of 1833, which names the Master of Foxdale Petty School as being John Quirk, a man who was 'generally moral' and had 'qualifications sufficient for the situation'. This was at a time when, if all the children attended, they numbered 'about twenty'.

(LOWER) FOXDALE C of E VOLUNTARY SCHOOL.
"Patrick, Lower Foxdale Mission Room School has been placed on HMI list for an annual grant. Accommodation 50 children."
(Detail from a Department of Education minute.)   [B01]
Foxdale Voluntary School was in a Mission Hall about half way up the hill from Lower Foxdale, on the right hand side from St. John's. It remains as an example of a clergyman creating and maintaining a school by himself for the benefit of local children.
In 1888 there were 53 pupils but the school was supported almost entirely by the Rev E.W.Cochran who was the first Vicar of Foxdale, from 1879 to 1900. Unfortunately when he left the district there was no other source of income which might have enabled the School Board to meet the essential expenditure of maintaining the school other than the small annual grant.
The School was transferred to the Patrick School Board in 1901 and almost immediately closed after the summer holidays of that year, it was never reopened.

FOXDALE NATIONAL SCHOOL.
Built on land at Ballamanagh in 1846 with a grant of £100 together with £200 from the Isle of Man Mining Company, the company also paid the teacher's salary of £100 p.a. for a while.
From about 1850, the school was also used for church services and was known locally as the "Mines Chapel" this continued until Foxdale Church was built in 1881.   [2]
The school was transferred to the Patrick School Board in July 1902.

Foxdale National School cont.,

In 1909 the average attendance was 188 but, following closure of the mines in 1910, and the resultant disastrous effect on the local community, many families left the district to find work elsewhere and the numbers attending Foxdale school fell steadily.

By 1915 the average attendance had fallen to 84, by 1920 it was down to 57 and in 1952 only 33.   [B04]

This was one of those occasions when the Education Department showed compassion; despite the low numbers, the school was allowed to remain open and, somehow, it managed to struggle through the leanest of years.

Closure eventually came in 1991 when the new 'Mines Road' school was opened.

At present the old school building is a private residence and is situate on the A 24 road.

FOXDALE PRIMARY SCHOOL. Mines Road.

Opened in September 1991, on land reclaimed from the old railway sidings, the school has 4 classrooms and a hall measuring 10m X 15m, a dining area is within the hall. There are 5 Teachers including the Head and their pupils are aged from 4 to 11 years of age; there are 41 boys and 41 girls, this figure includes 13 infants.

If the present rate of growth continues in the Foxdale catchment area then the possibility of an extension to the school might be considered but, at present, the school is not among the forecast list of committed schemes.

GLENMOIJ PETTY SCHOOL
(Glenmay)
School location unknown.

GREEBA WESLEYAN SCHOOL.
Opened in 1868, date of closure not known.

GRENABY NATIONAL SCHOOL. (Malew District)
Was transferred to Malew School Committee in 1879. Date of closure not known but re-opening of the school was still being requested in February 1912. Was on the B 41 road.

ISLE OF MAN INDUSTRIAL SCHOOL.
(see Douglas)

JALLOO.
(see Maughold)

JURBY PAROCHIAL SCHOOL.(1)
The Parish received land in 1766 for a schoolhouse and a dwelling for the master. Originally the teaching was in Manx but it had swung over to English by 1786. During 1833 the school was described as being 'insufficient'.

JURBY NEW PAROCHIAL SCHOOL.(2)
An assessment was made in 1860 for funds with which to build a new school. £260 was raised, £100 borrowed and £228.06.00 was provided as a Parliamentary Grant. The tender accepted for a new school was £523 from Mr W.Corlett of Ramsey.

This school was named Jurby New Parochial School on Feb 2nd 1862.

The school was closed from 1874 to 1877 and then re-opened.

By 1937 the school only had 20 children on the roll, five being between 11 & 14, all of whom remained at school for their midday meal. There was a Headmaster and a trained, certificated Assistant Mistress and the cost of maintaining the school, including salaries, came to £635 per annum.

The Education Committee decided that it was in the best interests of all concerned, including the children, that the school close and the remaining pupils be transferred to Andreas School. It was estimated that a special bus service closely approximating to the actual hours of the opening and closing of the school could be provided for the children at a cost of £225 per annum. Closed in 1938 , the school was not sold until 1952/3 when the proceeds were £1573. [B07]. *It is more than likely that this school was reopened during the intervening years.*

The school was situated where the present (empty) Jurby garage stands at the junction of the B3 and A10 roads.

JURBY INFANT & PRIMARY SCHOOL.
Opened on the Royal Air Force camp, January 1970. Despite the departure of the RAF from the area in the late 1980s the school continued to thrive until closure in 1981.

Situate on the A14 from Sandygate to Sartfield

JURBY COMMUNITY SCHOOL
The main entrance is on a private road off School Close. This new school was opened in 1982 and has 54 boys and 44 girls; there are 34 infants and 12 in a nursery; ages range from 3 to 11.

With 7 classrooms and an undivided hall measuring approximately 9m X 22m, the school has 6 teachers, including the Head Teacher. There is also one Special Unit teacher. No extensions have been necessary to date but if further large scale housing development takes place by 2006, then the possibility of an extension will have to be considered.

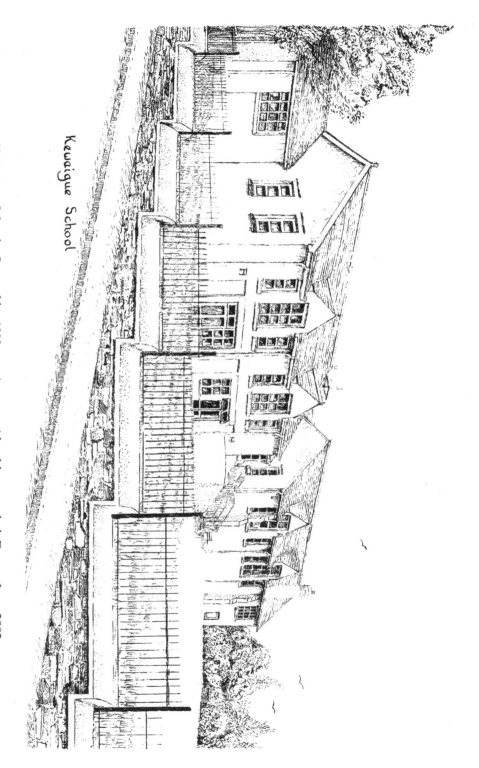

Kewaigue School

Kewaigue School - Opened by 1893 ans since considerably extended. Drawn June 2002.

KELLY'S (or the Mountain) SCHOOL. Lezayre.
(See SULBY)

KEWAIGUE SCHOOL.
(Braddan District)
Opened by 1893, the school is on the A6/A24 road.

In 1907 HMI reported :- **"The seats in the Offices are all too high for the youngest children. Attention has been drawn more than once to the unsatisfactory state of the playground. It is not likely that strewing the playground with cinders will produce any satisfactory result. At the visit the children were doing their drill exercises in long wet grass."**

In February 1953, notice was given that the school would be temporarily suspended at the end of the summer term but there were strong protests and the school remained open; this was probably a good thing because in 1999, the school had to be considerably extended.
83 children were attending in the year 2000.
Unfortunately the school now has its own horror story following the discovery of a man's body within a car in the Kewaigue School car park during November 2000. Apparently he had committed suicide.

KIRK MICHAEL PETTY SCHOOL.(1)
A schoolmaster's and a schoolmistresses house were recorded in 1764.

KIRK MICHAEL SCHOOL. (2)
(Michael District)
This school was opened in 1841 with the aid of a Parliamentary grant of £67.10s. Transferred to the local school committee in 1875/6.

KIRK MICHAEL SCHOOL (3)
A new Board School was opened on Dec 26th 1894; this is the original building which is still in use. The Education Dept. awarded a building grant of £380 in 1895 toward defraying part of the expenses.
There was some consternation caused during 1896, when it was announced that, during May, a 'Private venture' school was to open in Kirk Michael; at the time, the Board School staff thought that they would lose several of their pupils to the private school with a consequent threat to their own jobs, but this did not occur. As from Sept 16th 1946, the school was dedicated to infants and juniors alone, the older children being transferred to Ramsey.

Kirk Michael School cont.,

Because of the steady increase in the numbers attending Kirk Michael School over recent years, an extension was proposed during 1990, work started in 1991, and new classrooms were brought into use during 1992.

The school is currently known as Michael Primary School. Further information is given under that heading.

KIRK RUSHEN SCHOOL. (1734).
(see RUSHEN)

*   *   *

LAXEY AND LONAN

Lonan Church was consecrated on March 25th 1735; the consecration deed forbade use of the church as a school.   [2]

LONAN PETTY SCHOOL.
By 1782, English was being taught in Lonan Petty School but,in 1872, the school was reported as being " Hardly satisfactory ". Within the report an extension was recommended. This report was followed up by a new school being built at South Cape.

LAXEY INFANT SCHOOL
An infant school was built in 1836 at Rencell Hill.
Closed 1929, the building was sold for £180.

LAXEY GLEN SCHOOL.
Built in 1868, with the Laxey Mining Company donating £339, the National Society £110 and the Commissioner of Woods and Forests, £100. The School was for mixed boys, girls and infants.

On January 1st 1908, the Laxey Glen Schools were taken over on a lease by the Lonan School Board.

Closed when Minorca School opened, the property was then sold for £200, but the sale fell through; after being put up for public auction no bids were received.

The building still stands within the Glen, converted to restaurant/dance hall.

LAXEY MIXED AND INFANT SCHOOL - SOUTH CAPE.
Built 1868 as a replacement for the old Lonan Petty School.

In 1925, it was proposed that the South Cape School should be closed, the pupils to go to a new elementary school being built at Minorca but the closure was delayed until 1929.

The South Cape school building was then sold for £275 and is now a fine private residence; the alterations have been such that the structure is hardly recognisable as ever having been a school.

LAXEY NATIONAL SCHOOL.
Built 1834, given grant of £38. This was, possibly, the infant school mentioned previously although the dates do not agree.

LAXEY PRIMARY SCHOOL

LAXEY ELEMENTARY SCHOOL
(Minorca).
Approval to build a new school intended to replace the Laxey Mixed, Laxey Infants and South Cape Schools was given on May 14th 1925, and Tynwald voted £17,500 to cover the capital cost. The contractor was Mr Wm. McArd whose tender was for £13,450. The site cost £546. Opened 1927, the overall cost was £17,500.

This was the first school on the Island to have its' own electricity - from its own generator.

On opening the Headmaster was Mr E.Killip.

The school stands on Quarry Road which is off Minorca Hill.

Major extensions were completed during 1999 and the school now has 10 classrooms, an undivided main hall and a sports hall. The cost was put at £1,858m.

Teaching staff number 12 including the Head Teacher. There are 236 scholars, 122 boys and 114 girls, amongst the total there are 83 infants.

When the official opening ceremony for the new extension took place, a booklet was produced which listed all the people needed to run the school; the list is reproduced here as being a fair representation of the staffing levels of similar schools.

Head Teacher. Deputy Head Teacher. Teaching Staff (10).

Nursery nurses (3). Secretary. Caretaking & cleaning staff (3).

Dining room assistants (2). Ancillary staff (4).

LONAN - BALLAGAWNE
Opened Monday Oct 8th 1877, under John Wallace, the Master; he stayed in post until 1901.

On the first day of opening there were 31 children, but by January 1878 there were 79.

The Master described the children thus :-

"The majority of the children are such as have never attended any elementary day school and are consequently on a par with infants both in intellect and attainments."

In 1903, there was a critical HMI report which concluded :-

"The classroom of this country school is far too small for any practical purpose, and is often overcrowded. The School walls are not weather proof, and the latrines are not yet satisfactorily drained."

Partial reconstruction followed in 1906 and whilst this work was going on the school was moved out into temporary premises which were far from suitable for the purpose.

Lonan - Ballagawne cont.,
The Master reported :-
"Moved to temporary premises on May 18th, we then had 11 weeks of futile attempts at work under most miserable and adverse conditions. One small room for 67 infants and senior children with caps, hats, coats and cloaks hanging around, poor windows, floor very seldom brushed out, the seldom emptied offices in close proximity to the windows, cars (tramcars) stopping outside the window, passengers and pedestrians all gawping in like a side show."

The enlargement was designed to allow the school to cope with 40 infants and 80 older children although by the time the school re-opened average attendances had fallen to 68.

The school reopened on Sept 17th yet within a couple of weeks the builders had to be called back to try and rectify numerous faults !
It fell to Jessie Blanche Callin to be in charge when the school finally closed; in the last couple of years, numbers on the roll had fallen to between 27 and 30 and, despite strong protests from local parents, the school was closed at 4pm on the 22nd July 1932.   [M31]

*   *   *

LEZAYRE DHOOAR SCHOOL
(see Dhooar)

LEZAYRE MOUNTAIN (or Kelly's) SCHOOL.
(See Sulby)

LEZAYRE SCHOOL.
In 1698, Bishop Thomas Wilson's commission to William Crow, who was probably the first schoolmaster for Lezayre, as distinct from the Vicar, included the following :- "..you are impower'd to demand sixpence for each quarter .. for each child you instruct. (Whose parents are of the ability to pay it.)"
If a child was being taught Latin, Mr Crow was entitled to claim 9d per quarter if the parents could afford it, otherwise 6d.
A schoolhouse was recorded as in being during 1722.
In 1757, it was reported that :- "The Master of the Lezayre Parish School is a foreigner and therefore unable to teach.".
By 1766, apparently, he could do so !
In 1782, the school was being taught in English.

Ruins of Lezayre School to the left of the picture. Built before 1722.
Drawn January 1989.

Lezayre School. cont.,
During the incumbency of Henry Maddrell, in 1803, the old church became ruinous and the school was roofless.

A similar state of affairs existed in 1820, when the question of repairing or building a new school on another site caused a stir in the parish; at this time it was suggested that a house should be provided for a schoolmaster but nothing was done about it. Henry Maddrell was reported as having been a miserly, parsimonious character - but this may have been just a co-incidence !   [2]

The Lezayre school was situate on the side of a hill at the bottom of the church yard alongside what was, at the time, the main road between Ramsey and Sulby, it was also the route from Ramsey to Douglas by way of Sulby Glen or Kirk Michael.
On the slopes above the school hundreds of people were buried and, supposedly, " the air was tainted with a disagreeable stench - not only disgusting to human beings but also very unwholesome."

Those who suggested the erection of a new school on another site would seem to have had good cause. Instead, by March 1821, the old school was repaired and put back into use.

In 1856 the Vicar and Churchwardens were authorised to pull down the school and erect a new school together with a Master's dwelling house in some more suitable place and, as if to emphasise the point, during the next year of 1857, the school was declared to be:- "..insufficient in size and...very unhealthy..." T h e s e critical comments made not slightest difference to the Lezayre Parochial School Board; none of these worthy changes were carried out.

In August 1863 a report suggested that :- **"There was no Parochial School, nor had there been one for a considerable time. — Education is much neglected and unattended to in the said Parish."**
The report must have caused immediate reaction because in September of that same year the incumbent, Rev Edward Snepp, was able to say that a schoolmistress was now teaching in the old school, albeit unrepaired as it was.

In 1874, the Vicar and Wardens declared that they had entered upon the site for a new school but this was far too late for it to be seen as the start of a progressive new era so far as they were concerned because, in March 1875, the old school was transferred to the School Committee absolutely, and, as soon as a new National School had been built, the old school was closed.

Lezayre School.cont.,
This closure allowed the old school to be converted in due course into the Lezayre Reading Room and Billiards Room, the conversion was made for the Rev Arthur Bridgeman at his own cost and remained in use by local people until 1930, when it fell into disuse.

In 1954, the structure was being used by the sexton as a store house, although at present - in 2003 - the building is, once again, in a roofless, overgrown and ruinous condition).

LEZAYRE NATIONAL SCHOOL.
This was a brand new school, built in 1876, on a site of 2420 sq. yds. with half the cost being paid for by the Manx Govt.

The costs were :- School		£195.00.00
Walls & outbuildings		58.10.00
Desks, benches, fittings		20.00.00
Architect's fees		7.10.00
Drainage		5.15.00
	Total	£285.15.06.

As built, the schoolroom was 25'long x 16'wide and from 11' to 22' high, the associated classroom was 13' long, 13'wide and from 11' to 14' in height.

The school was transferred from being a National school during the following year of 1877, and was, thenceforth, a Board school.
Closed on July 29th 1921, and sold in 1929.

A portion of the school's boundary wall was sold to the Vicar and Wardens for £33.12s - presumably for the benefit of the adjoining cemetery - and the remainder of the property was sold to another for £200.

The property has since been converted into a private residence. This conversion was fairly sympathetic and the basic outline of the school can still be seen in Churchtown, Lezayre, opposite the present Vicarage..
Of interest is a high wall with iron gate which divided the school playground. Toilets for the children were separated from the school, that for the boys to the left of the school the girls to the right.

LHAGGAN SCHOOL
(see Maughold)

LHEN,or THE LHANE SCHOOL.
Within the Andreas district; the original opening date for this school is not known but by 1880, it had been closed.

The school was re-opened in 1885, by the Andreas School Committee and the appointed teacher was Miss Cormode Auduas at £26 p.a.

The number of scholars in 1888, was 26 but, in 1889, it was decided that no child above 9 should be allowed to remain at the school, children who were over that age were transferred to Andreas School.

Plans were put in hand during 1901, for the provision of a new school (which did not materialise), the Lhen then continued as a junior and infant school until closure in 1933, by which time the number on the roll had fallen to 5.

MALEW RURAL SCHOOL.(1)
The first school, was founded in 1660.

MALEW PAROCHIAL SCHOOL AND CHAPEL.
Both were built in 1772 and, in 1782, the school was still using Manx as the norm for Catechism and prayers.

A separate school was provided in 1795 and this was transferred to the Board of Education in 1886.

MALEW.
The site for a new school to accommodate 80 children was proposed by the Malew School Committee on July 13th 1885, as being at, "The Old Smithy on the East side of the road."

On October 15th a tender submitted by John Collister for a new school was accepted and a site purchased from Miss Quayle :-

"100' along the High Road from North to South and back from the High Road to the boundary of Mr Mylchreest's land from East to West." The surrounding walls were to be built by the Committee at their own expense.

Money for the work was obtained as a dual purpose loan totalling £350, this was to pay for the new school and an additional classroom at Ballasalla. The loan was raised by way of a mortgage with the Isle of Man Insurance Company Ltd at a rate of 5%, the principal to be repaid within four years. Repayments to be from the local school rate, which was 3d in the pound.

The actual cost of the school was £210, being £186 to Mr Collister and £24 to Mr Kelly who did some additional work - possibly the surrounding walls ?

Miss Eliza Harrison was appointed to teach at Malew from May 1st 1887, and, at first, her salary was £30 in lieu of the Government grant, together with the childrens pence.

The new school was placed on the list for inspections in 1888, and by 1894, there were 76 children in attendance.

School closed on December 31st 1940.   [M12r]

MAROWN PETTY SCHOOL.(1)
In 1869, this Parochial school did not provide any 'free' places for children.

MAROWN SCHOOL.(2)
(Parochial) (Marown District)
The Ellerslie gift was granted in 1741, this was a parcel of land on which the school was to be built, and, in 1742, a further parcel of land was donated by Thomas Christian in trust for the use and benefit of a School-house for the said Parish.

There must have been some problems concerning the local school board because, in 1874, the Board of Education appointed a School Committee by reason of default. The school was transferred to the Local School Committee in 1876.

MAROWN SCHOOL.(3)
(Hillside)
Built 1878 (?) with the aid of a Government grant but, in 1880, the school inspector was reporting that one master, without help, was expected to teach two infant classes as well as children in all six standards !

The school closed prior to the opening of Glen Vine school in 1985, but the building still stands on the right hand side of the road.

MAROWN PRIMARY SCHOOL.(4)
Situate off Glen Darragh Road, Glen Vine; itself off the A1 between Union Mills and Crosby. The site was purchased in 1983, and the school opened on October 10th 1985, with 85 pupils.

At the present time there are 91 boys and 56 girls of whom 40 are infants. The age range is from 4 to 11.

The school has 6 classrooms and a subdivided hall measuring 17m X 13m. The teaching staff, including the Head Teacher, number 7 and there are 2 ancillaries.

An extension was completed during 2002. The cost was estimated in 1999 at £528,000, it actually came to £706,000.

MAUGHOLD - DHOON BRIDGE SCHOOL.
There was an old school which stood "at the junction of the Curlerd Stream with the Dhoon River at the arch of the Dhoon Bridge"; this may have been built about 1836.

For many, many years it was a dual purpose building, being used as a church by the people of Dhoon and Ballaragh in the days before Dhoon Church was built in 1855.

In modern day terms the school was near the little bye road from Dhoon Glen Railway station.

Dhoon Bridge School could hold 30 children although the average was about 15.

Closure came about in 1876 and the property was sold by 1921.

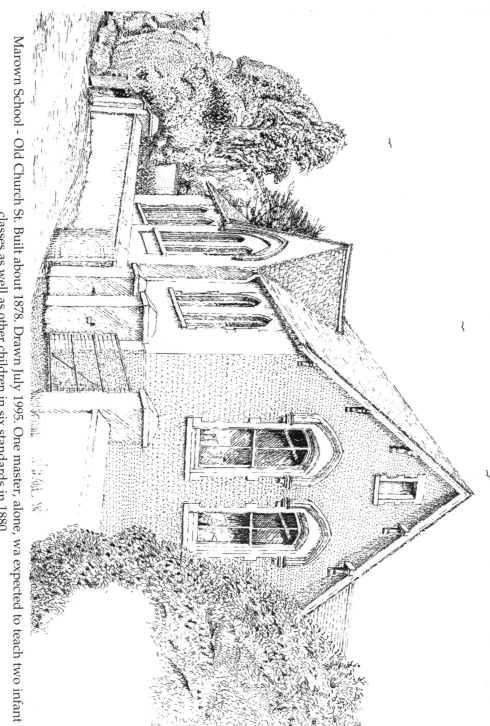

Marown School - Old Church St. Built about 1878. Drawn July 1995. One master, alone, wa expected to teach two infant classes as well as other children in six standards in 1880.

MAUGHOLD JALLOO SCHOOL.

It was the Rev Henry Allen, Vicar of St. Maughold's (1727 to 1746), who secured the land at the Jalloo on which this, the first parochial school, was erected.

Built in 1740, but goodness knows what happened because by 1747, the school was being reported as "out of repair" !

A school was maintained in these premises almost continuously until closure in 1886. (but see "Mary's House" below.)

The school had a capacity for 40 children although the average was about 25. Several parents chose to send their children to this school instead of the 'new Central School' during winter months because Jalloo was much easier to get to and more protected from the elements.

Jalloo was closed when the new Dhoon school opened, although the building remained in church use until finally being sold in 1962. The old school is now part of a private residence.

Situate on the A 15 Ballajora to Maughold Road on the left hand side and certainly not recognisable as a school !   [M12q]

MAUGHOLD - MARY'S HOUSE

During the early 1770s there were occupancy problems in the Parochial School of Jalloo which prevented the building from being used as a school. To overcome this minor disaster, Edward Corkhill, the Parish Clerk, leased one of the cowhouses in Churchtown, among a row of property known as 'Mary's House', for a period of eight years from 1778 for use as a schoolhouse for the Parishioners' children.

MAUGHOLD LHAGGAN SCHOOL.

(or Allagagh - or Mountain School.)

This school had a collection of names; it was also called the LHARGAN or LHIAGGYN SCHOOL. (Maughold District)

Rather a small school, it was built in 1794., having been paid for by a sum of £40 bequeathed by John Kermeen of Ballig in a will dated 1793. The land cost £15 and a further £19 was raised by subscription for the support of the school.

The school was situate in the Ballig area and during 1830, between twenty and thirty scholars were attending but, in 1852, it was closed for a while without a master: The re-opening date is not known but by 1863, there were 40 pupils.

Ceased to be a school in 1876, when the pupils were transferred to the new Dhoon School. Sold out of 'church' use in 1908.

MAUGHOLD CENTRAL SCHOOL.

(Carn School, Maughold District)

The name should not be confused with the much later grading of schools on the Island when some became known as Central Schools. Maughold Central was so called because of its central position within the Parish of Maughold.

Maughold Central School. cont.,

This parochial school was opened in 1852, as a replacement for the old Jalloo Parochial school although, in fact, Jalloo remained open until 1896.

Ground for the new school had been conveyed for £9 and the building costs were £401/6/0.

The accommodation was designed for 80 boys and 80 girls, there was also a house adjacent for the Master and Mistress.

In 1872 the parish committee was replaced by an elected body.

A critical report was made by HM Inspector in 1883, which found particular fault with the very exposed position of the school, which often led to the absence of children in inclement weather.

The Managers gave thought to moving the school elsewhere but at a public meeting their proposals were outvoted by a relatively small group of prominent people who did not want the school to be moved and who, by so voting, sentenced the majority of children attending the school over the next three or four decades to years of unnecessary exposure as they made their way to school through the fierce elements which often raged around the high hill top position on which the school had been built.

Central remained the Parochial school until closure on April 31st,1922, when its few remaining pupils were transferred to Dhoon School. In 1922, it was the proximity of the Manx Electric Railway to Dhoon School that influenced the decision to close Central rather than Dhoon School.

The school was sold for £300 and is now a private residence situate on a bye road from the A2 leading toward Ballasaig and Dreemskerry.

MICHAEL PRIMARY SCHOOL

(See also 'Kirk Michael' for detail of other schools in the area.)

This school is on the Ramsey - Ballacraine Road,(A3), just to the south of Kirk Michael village.

There are 51 infants. 48 boys and 52 girls within the overall age group of from 4 to 11, and their Teachers are 7 in number including the Head.

The school has 6 classrooms and an undivided hall 45' X 120'.

Further major extensions commenced during November 2000, these works included the provision of a new Sports Hall, Community Facilities and 2 classrooms. Provisional costings were for £796,000. but the final cost was £1.274m.

NOBLES SITE NEW PRIMARY SCHOOL

Obviously anticipating growth in this area, a new school is planned for the future - starting probably in 2006. A major project, the estimated cost in 2003 is for design fees of £537k and construction costs of £6.452m.

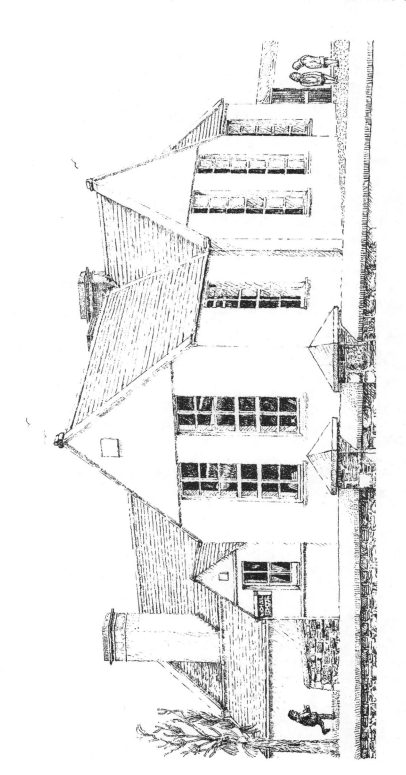

Michael Primary School - Opened 1894. Drawn 1999 before the school was considerably extended.

OAKHILL SCHOOL.
- see BRADDAN, opened 1860. Now a chapel. Situate on the A25.

ONCHAN SCHOOL.
William Christian was licensed as a Teacher and started the first school within the church but, in 1734, the Parish was told to provide a decent schoolhouse, which they did in 1736.
The building could not have been very good because by 1745, it was in need of repairs. This school is believed to have been near the top of The Butt and was sold when the new Parish School was opened in 1845.   [M12k]

ONCHAN INFANT SCHOOL.
An infant school was built in 1842, at the bottom of The Butt. It was closed when the new school in Bar Beg Road was opened in 1876, but reopened for a relatively short space of time in 1877, at the request of the Vicar, Rev J.Howard.
When sold it became known as Welch House.   [M12k]

ONCHAN PARISH SCHOOL.
Was built in The Butts in 1845. An Inspector's report of 1860, was highly critical, describing the unsuitable site as being :- **"in a low, damp, and unhealthy situation, and the whole inadequate in extent.**
Closed as a school on August 23rd 1876; the property was eventually sold and became a private residence in 1956.   [M12k]

ONCHAN BOARD SCHOOL.
Built on Bar Beg Road (now School Road) at a cost of £1058, this new school opened for lessons on September 25th 1876, with 60 attending. By October there were 151.
In 1907/8, the school was given two extra classrooms and a bookroom and whereas the School had previously accommodated 228 children, it now catered for 210 in the mixed and 110 in the infant departments, a total of 320.

By 1952, the school was so overcrowded that a further extension was proposed and in 1954, three extra classrooms were added together with toilet facilities, a Headmaster's room and a boiler house at an estimated cost of £25,588.
Accommodation was now for 360 pupils.
The school is now known as :-

ONCHAN PRIMARY SCHOOL
In 1967 the school was enlarged even further with six extra classrooms and a new school hall, the anticipated cost had been £80,530. This new extension made Onchan the largest Primary School on the Island with 450 scholars.   [M12k]

Onchan Primary School. cont.,
There are now sixteen classrooms and a special unit, the main hall is multi purpose whilst the smaller hall is a dining hall.
The teaching staff number 19.5.
One extension is now being built and a further small extension may possibly be needed by 2006/7, a provisional estimate of cost suggests £296,000.

ONCHAN.
ASHLEY HILL SCHOOL.

Work started on this school in 1971, and the opening took place on April 17th 1972. By September there were 97 on the roll.
Growth in the area was rapid and by 1976, a double mobile classroom was needed; by the end of 1977, there were 292 on the roll, over half of whom were infants.
Further new classrooms were added from 1980, and by 1983, the roll had increased to 382.
It was in 1988 that a further block was built for the physically disabled, most of whom are integrated into other classes as much as possible.In 1992, the Ashley Hill roll stood at 444 and the staff numbered 20.   [M12k]
At present the school has 15 classrooms including one special unit, there are also two undivided halls.
The childrens' ages range from 4 to 11 and their teachers number 15 together with 3 NNEBs. At lunchtime help is given by 6 auxiliaries with a further two for the   special unit. Altogether there are 297 scholars, 152 boys and 145 girls.
Phase 1 and 2 extensions may be completed round about 2005, the overall cost is likely to be £592,000.

ONCHAN.
STRATHALLAN HALL INDUSTRIAL SCHOOL.
As from 1912 the title Strathallan Hall was dropped and the new designation of ISLE OF MAN INDUSTRIAL HOME was substituted; later still it became known as the Isle of Man Childrens'Home.
In 1939 the Isle of Man Homes for Orphan and Destitute Children had 16 female students attending evening classes here.

ONCHAN. NEW SECONDARY SCHOOL.
The outline plans for this brand new school are subject to a lot of negotiation at present concerning the site which is on land to the rear of the Governor's Residence.
If approval to the scheme is given this will be one of the biggest capital schemes ever envisaged for education purposes on the Isle of Man. Provisional estimates suggest £17,477,000.

ONCHAN VILLAGE HALL AND SUNDAY SCHOOL.

This attractive building was never envisaged as being an ordinary school, it is included here because it was designed so that the hall could be used as one large Sunday School classroom whilst two more classrooms were provided beneath in the basement.

Designed by Baillie Scott and built by W.McAdam, having a Voysey tapestry for the curtain and platform, this fine building was opened by the Lieutenant Governor, Lord Henniker on 26.11.1898.

(Lord Henniker's full name was John Major Henniker-Major and he sat in the House of Lords as Lord Hartismere. He was appointed Lt Governor in 1895.))

If the original design had been followed through the main hall would have had a much grander interior, it would have looked more like a baronial hall than a church hall. This design was rejected as being too costly - as it most certainly would have been.

[M12i]

"That's what education means - to be able to do what you've
never done before !"
(G.H.Palmer 1842-1933)

*   *   *

Chapter twentyone
Schools from Patrick to Port St. Mary

PATRICK SCHOOL.
The first school was built in 1716 although both school and school house were reported as existing in the years from 1715 to 1720.

PATRICK SCHOOL.
(Patrick District)
A new school was opened in 1854 having been paid for with an assessment of £147 and a Parliamentary Grant of £200.
The School closed in July 1986; the building continues in use as a Sunday School and stands but a short distance from the Parish Church of Kirk Patrick at the junction of the A30 and A27.

*   *   *

PEEL
Population growth.

year	number
1726	475
1821	1909
1851	2342
1891	3631

PEEL PAROCHIAL SCHOOL.
This School was, in fact, provided for the Parish of German and was centred at St.John's Chapel. (See St.John's)

PEEL ENGINEERING SCHOOL
Was situate in Market Place. Peel.   [M12d]

PEEL SCHOOL OF NAVIGATION. (Gawne's)
Largely the inspiration of John Gawne who became the Master.
The School was housed in a building just off Douglas Street but was closed shortly after the death of Mr Gawne.
The building still stands although it has been modified; at first sight the condition of the walls leave a lot to be desired but I suspect that with judicious repair and repointing the appearance could be greatly improved.
Douglas Street car park is the best place from which to view.   [M13a]

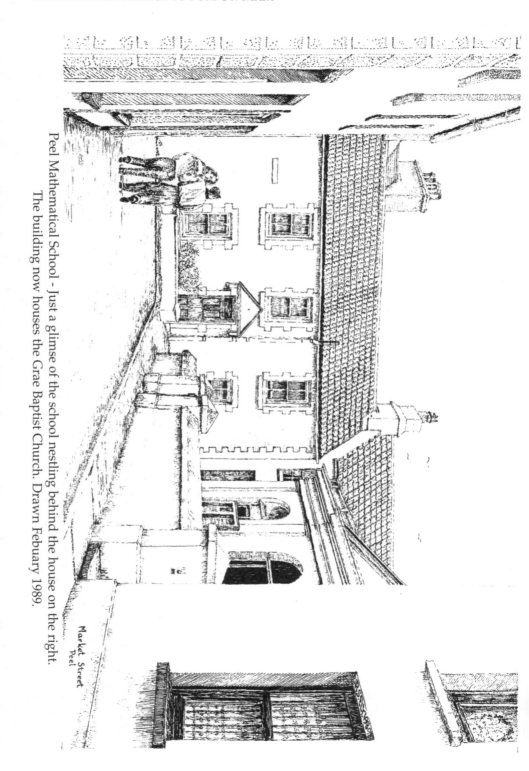

Peel Mathematical School - Just a glimpse of the school nestling behind the house on the right. The building now houses the Grae Baptist Church. Drawn Febuary 1989.

Market Street
Peel

PEEL GRAMMAR (or LATIN) SCHOOL.
Situate at 31 Castle Street and bounded by Court House Lane, the School was founded in 1746 as a gift from a private donor.

The donor also provided an endowment of £500, the income from which was to be paid "unto a proper schoolmaster qualified to teach Latin and such other learning as may fit youth for the service of the country in Church or in State."

Opened in 1760, the school continued in use and Vicar James Gelling became master of the School in 1811; within a few years he was neglecting the school and by 1822 it had only one scholar whilst the schoolroom had been converted into a barn and slaughterhouse !

The school was later combined with the Mathematical School (founded in 1763) which specialised in Navigation.

By 1863 the premises had become the Grammar School and Master's House. The premises were sold in 1892.   [M12d]

PEEL INFANT SCHOOL.(1)
Opened in 1861 with a grant of £315 and gifts of £291.

During 1937 an architect suggested that considerable sums would need to be spent to keep the school in repair. The war years prolonged the life of this antiquated school, the last day being March 30th 1953, when the children and staff were transferred to the new Junior & Infants school at the top of Derby Road. At this time, in 1953, there were 110 on the roll.

PEEL INFANT SCHOOL.(2)
In 1935 an estimate of £7000 was made for a new Infant School - plus £230 for the land

Land for the school was bought on Derby Road Lane, this extended to approx. 1.57 acres, and at the time it was proposed that the school entrance should be from Albany Road.

In 1952 the estimated cost was £17,825.

The new school opened to accept the 110 pupils transferred from the old school by March 30th 1953.

PEEL MATHEMATICAL SCHOOL.
It was the Rev James Moore of Dublin who left money in his will for the erection and endowment of a School of Mathematics in the Isle of Man.

Sir George Moore bought the land and had the school built from a set of plans that cost £6/16/6d. Sir George, with his brother Philip, had the privilege of nominating the scholars.

The school was built in Market Street during 1763, and had the rare distinction of having George III sanctioning a grant from the Inland Revenue of Thirty Pounds a year to support the school.

The first Master was appointed in 1765 when the school opened.

Peel Mathematical School cont
From 1798 to 1801 the school was run jointly with the Grammar School but in
September 1801, the school was re-opened as a separate establishment.

By about 1822 the school was reported as being in decay and, by 1824, the
premises were being used for sales and as an auction house, even as an ale house,
which possibly explains why, in 1827, it was in a state of dereliction.

PEEL MATHEMATICAL SCHOOL (II)
A new school built on a plot appurtenant to the original school was started in 1844
but not completed until the latter part of 1847. Opened in January 1848, it had to be
closed within three months due to the virtual desertion of the Master.

The school re-opened during May 1848.

Under the terms of the endowment the Master had to teach 14 free scholars, the
remainder paying fees. By 1876, the fees were from 12/6d per quarter for those
under 10 years of age, to One Guinea a quarter for those over 12, an extra fee was
charged for music, drawing and French.

Closure eventually came about in 1892 because the Trustees were no longer able
to guarantee payment for a Master; in that year there were only six pupils.

[M12d] [M13a] [M14]

The school building has been maintained in good order and is now the home of
the Grace Baptist Church.

PEEL CLOTHWORKERS' SCHOOL.(1) (Philip Christian School)
Philip Christian was a Manxman who went to London and prospered: It was in
December 1653, that he made his will in which he bequeathed property to The
Clothworkers Company., the income from which was to be used toward the
maintenance of a Free School in Peel.

Philip died in 1654, but the school was not founded until thirty years later because
the legacy could not be claimed if a Free School already existed - and there was such
a school.

The bequest lay dormant until it was revived by Bishop Baptista Levinz who
founded the first Clothworkers' School in 1689; a little cheating was undertaken so
as to take advantage of the will ! To do so, the existing Free School was allowed to
lapse for a while and was then re-started as a new foundation with the bequest to
back it up !   [M12b]

PEEL CLOTHWORKERS SCHOOLS. (2)
In 1875, High Bailiff Robert Moore sold two acres for a new Clothworkers' School
at the low valuation of £300 per acre and, on December 6th 1878, a new school was
formally opened at a cost of £2382 plus £917 for fittings.

Peel Clothworker's School. cont.,
For a good resume of the convoluted methods of funding and the various additions to this school over the years, please read Hinton Bird's two books entitled, "An Island That Led".
(see also Peel. Christians National School)

PEEL CLOTHWORKERS SCHOOLS. (3)
The present school is off Derby Road, the A20. The first of the new schools was opened in 1952 and during 1972 a further new building was provided for the infants. A Special Unit was added in 1999 at the same time as a Staff room/Library.
Altogether there are 17 classrooms and two halls, the halls are not sub-divided; their respective dimensions are 14.3m x 10.9m and 11.5m x 9.6m. There are 19 teachers.
The ages of the children range from 4 to 11 and they are in K stream 1 and K Stream 2. In 2002, boys and girls are almost equal in numbers, a total of 410 compared with 363 in 1984.

Further extensions are being considered, possibly commencing about 2004/5. If the work goes ahead, provision will be made for a link building to join the two existing separate ones, there will also be a new hall, kitchen and dining hall. The provisional cost, inc fees, is estimated at £1,903m.

PEEL CHRISTIANS NATIONAL SCHOOL.
To help toward the cost of this new school the old Clothworkers School was sold for £90, the Clothworkers Company gave a gift of £20, as well as income of £130. There was also a Treasury Grant of £130 toward the cost of £352. The school opened in June 1843.
In 1905 the Managers gave notice to the Board of Education that they would cease to carry on the School; this despite the Trustees (The Clothworkers Company) stating that they would be prepared to hand over a sum for educational purposes amounting to about £248 p.a.
This action by the Managers was similar to that of a number of Manx National School managers during the early 1900s. It does suggest that in the background there was some form of semi- political decision.
What makes it even harder to understand their decision to close the school is the annual report which HMI had just made, in which he said :-
"A really first rate school. Some of the work I have not seen equalled in any other school."

The school ceased to exist under its' original name on 31st March 1905, and opened the following day as the Peel Derby Road Board School.

PEEL DERBY ROAD BOARD SCHOOL

The Peel Christians National School buildings were leased to the Peel School Board at a peppercorn rent for 21 years from April 1st 1905, the lease then continued and the school remained in use as the principle school in Peel until eventual closure in 1953.

The building still stands in Christian Street and is now used for differing social purposes including a day nursery.

PEEL WESLEYAN SCHOOL AND SCHOOLHOUSE.

The Wesleyan Chapel in Peel ran a series of bazaars and other events to raise funds with which to buy land and erect a new school building in the town.

In a Trust Deed of 1861 there was a conveyance from Thomas T. Dilks to Thomas Kermode and others of:-

"A parcel of land, in trust, as a school for the education of the children of the labouring, manufacturing and other poor classes of the town and as a residence for a Master and Mistress. The School to be a Wesleyan Methodist Weekday and Sabbath School belonging to the religious denomination of Protestants of the People now called Wesleyan Methodists.".

The school was built in Tynwald Road during 1861/2 at a cost of £838/15/3d and gained a grant of £395 from the Parliamentary Council of the Committee.

Opened in 1862; by 1869 there were 150 pupils, all of whom paid quarterage.

The school closed on May 5th 1905, with 102 children still on the register, the children being transferred to the Peel Derby Road Board School.

The school buildings are now privately owned and used as a private residence. They are situate on Tynwald Road, part of the A1.   [M13a]

PEEL. ST. PATRICK'S ROMAN CATHOLIC VOLUNTARY SCHOOL.

Father Walsh, Rector of St. Mary's, built a schoolroom annexe to St. Patrick's Chapel of Ease in 1891; it was recognised as a school by 1893, the teacher being Miss McNamara. The school closed in June 1901, due to a lack of pupils, only 5 being on the register, three of whom were due to go another school.

St. Patrick's is on the road from Peel to Patrick.   [M12j]

PEEL. QUEEN ELIZABETH II HIGH SCHOOL.

The 'Topping out' ceremony for this new school took place in 1978, the school being officially opened by Queen Elizabeth II during July 1979. By 1984, the school had 657 pupils on its roll.

Progressively extended, an I.T. Block and an SEN unit were added in 1990, these were followed by a post 16 unit opened on September 22nd 2000, at a cost of £1.064m.

Peel.Queen Elizabeth II High School cont.,

The latest extension block comprises a 90 seat lecture theatre and six classrooms with miscellaneous accommodation; it will be known as the Forster Building.

At present the school has 41 classrooms and a large undivided hall.

The scholars are from 11 to 19 years of age, 389 boys and 411 girls, 120 are in 6th form; they have 58 teachers, including the Head Teacher, there are also 3 ancillaries.

Provision is being made in the estimates for the construction of a "Humanities" block from 2006 onward. Cost £1.053m.

The school is situate on the A1 Douglas Road, on the left as you leave Peel.

*   *   *

PORT ERIN INFANT SCHOOL.

(Rushen District)

Opened in 1899. By 1911, there were two teachers.

During the year ending 31/3/1927, the average attendance was 23 and, being so low, the Board of Education decided to close the school.

This was a decision which angered local residents who protested because of the distance that the infants would need to travel so as to get to the new Rushen School; unfortunately for the youngsters, the protests proved ineffectual and the school was closed in 1927.

The school was on Bay View Road and the premises were sold for £1370.

PORT ERIN SCHOOL.

Mr William Milner, the benefactor of Port Erin, died in 1874. In his will Mr Milner left money for the erection of a church and school for the village but, in the event, the trustees decided that a school was not needed. A new church was the only beneficiary, this was St. Catherine's, completed in 1880.

PORT GREENAGH ?

Vague mention has been made of a small school in this locality but I have no further detail.

PORT ST. MARY NATIONAL SCHOOL.

(Rushen District)

When built, this school received a grant from the National Society of £75. It was opened in 1835. In 1876 the school was transferred to the Board of Education and, following completion of the Board School in 1880, the National School was closed.

PORT ST. MARY BOARD SCHOOL.
Built to replace the old National School, this new school opened in 1880. When the school was closed during the year ending 31/3/1927, the average attendance was 86 boys and infants.

This was another closure which led to considerable bad feeling locally. It seemed to the parents as if no thought had been given to the distances that their infants, in particular, would need to travel so as to get to their new school at Four Roads, Rushen. Once again their protests availed them nothing.

The school and the adjoining Master's house were sold for £1500. The building has since been sub-divided and is used by various shops and flats. It is on the corner of Bay View Road and the Promenade.

PORT ST. MARY - SCOOIL PHURT LE MOIRREY.
After having removed the two infant schools from the centres of Port Erin and Port St. Mary in 1927, the building of this new school on Station Road, Port St. Mary, is an interesting reversal of policy by the education authority.

Opened in September 1994, the school has 8 class bases on an open plan and part of the hall is sub-divided for Dining purposes.

There are 10 full time teachers, 1 part time, 2 full time N.N.E.Bs' and 1 part time N.N.E.B.
The school is for infant and primary children and there is a Special Unit. In K stream 1 there are 30 infant girls and 37 boys whilst in K Stream 2 there are 54 junior girls and 31 boys. During the year 2000 the Special Unit cared for 1 girl and 6 boys.

PORT ST. MARY.
Mention is made of a "school on the prom" which had two rooms each of which had a teacher who controlled two classes but I do not know where, presumably it was the original National School ?

PORT ST. MARY.
(Harley's College)
Round about 1880, a Miss Jane Harley conducted a primary school for younger children in premises opposite the Police Station.   [M21]

"Four things come not back - the spoken word, the fired bullet, the past life, and the neglected opportunity."

*   *   *

Chapter twentytwo

RAMSEY SCHOOLS

THE SCHOOL OF THE BALLURE CHAPEL OF ST. CATHERINES.
Ballure Chapel was completely rebuilt by 1640, as such it was a Chapel of Ease to Maughold as well as being the 'RAMSEA' school. A reader was appointed who was also to act as the Schoolmaster. In 1680, a Miss Hannah Bennett was keeping the official school and teaching English, while, from 1700, James Knipe was the Schoolmaster.

The quality of workmanship on rebuilding projects in Ramsey seems to have been rather poor because the Chapel had to be extensively rebuilt yet again in 1706. Unbelievably, by 1716, it needed further repair and, by 1746, was described as being in a ruinous condition.
Rebuilt yet again in 1747, Bishop Wilson would not allow the school to continue within the Chapel; nevertheless, the school did continue somewhere, Thomas W.J.Woods being appointed Reader and Schoolmaster.

Despite not being used as a school the chapel was, once again, in a poor state of repair by 1758, and, this time, the chapel did not last very long. A complete restoration took place in 1851, at which time the place was dedicated to St. Mary. The Chapel is just off the tramway level crossing over Walpole Drive.

RAMSEY GRAMMAR SCHOOL.(I)
In 1762, a small parcel of land known as Croit Vess was bought for the erection of a Grammar School together with accommodation for the Chaplain. Once erected, the building was also used as the Court House until the present one was built. This school was reported as being in disrepair by 1805, yet it continued in use until the 1860s.
Not very large, the school was on a plot of land behind where Lough House stands, just off Waterloo Road.

RAMSEY BOWRING ROAD SCHOOL.
On January 20th 1849, the Vicar of Lezayre, W.B.Christian., equipped and opened at his own expense, Taggart's Barn, just off Bowring Road to be used as a Chapel of Ease to Lezayre. This was the predecessor of St. Olave's.

Ramsey, Bowring Road School cont.,
The Chapel was on the first floor, the ground floor being occupied and in use as a schoolroom. The teacher was the Curate of Lezayre in charge of North Ramsey, one of whom was Rev George Paton. The premises remained in use until 1870.

RAMSEY GRAMMAR SCHOOL.(II)

A bazaar was held in Ballure Glen in 1860, to raise funds for the building of a new Grammar School in Ramsey. £600 was raised, which, together with other funds, allowed a site to be bought. Work started on a new school in Waterloo Road in 1863, the foundation stone being laid on May 10th 1864.

The school opened in 1865, with Edward Barton as Headmaster and Catherine Stringer as Mistress.

From 1872 to 1873, the school was renamed :-
RAMSEY COLLEGIATE GRAMMAR SCHOOL
and in 1888, Rev Alfred Newton took over as Headmaster.

During 1892, the school was transferred into two large houses on the Mooragh Promenade where it stayed until 1906. when it returned to the Waterloo Road School. (The National Infant School was in occupation during these intervening years)

By the 1920's the Grammar School was becoming overcrowded and, following the closure of the Wesleyan School in Albert Road their vacated school buildings were taken on lease and the 'maintained' Grammar School moved in during 1922.

The Waterloo Road School buildings then continued in use as the Grammar School laboratories until 1933. It was during these years that the Wesleyan School in Albert Road was used as the main teaching block for the Grammar School. (See Ramsey Wesleyan School) At present the old Grammar school building is being used as a Youth Centre.

RAMSEY CHARITY SCHOOL

This school was variously known as the Grammar or Petty School. At first, from 1812, it was in a rented room, being formally opened on June 20th 1812. The school followed the principles of the National Society.

Neither the name of the Master or the actual location is known and it seems likely that the School moved between premises.

Fortunately, the Trustees of the National Schools of Ramsey were offered land slightly to the north of the 1762 Grammar School, the Trustees had a new School built thereon which opened in 1831, this was to become the :-

RAMSEY NATIONAL SCHOOL.(1)

Opened in 1831, the new School proved to be too small within twenty years and in 1849, permission was sought, and obtained, to sell the building and use the proceeds to refurbish and renovate the nearby St. Peter's Chapel which was disused at the time.

RAMSEY NATIONAL SCHOOL.(2)

St. Peter's Chapel was presented to the Trustees by the Lord Bishop for conversion into a National School with girls on the first floor and boys on the ground floor.

Funding for the conversion came from proceeds of the sale of the old school together with a Council of Education grant of £155. The School opened with 100 boys and 95 girls.

The Chaplain of Ramsey was to supervise moral and religious instruction and a Committee of Management appointed a Master and a Mistress. The previous (1831) building was then used to house the Grammar School, which it did until the new Grammar School was built in Waterloo Road during 1864.

Prior to 1873, there was no separate department for infants and this led to complaints being made by the School Inspectors who also complained about overcrowding. As a result of these complaints the infants were moved to a converted house which then served as an infant school.

The infants were taught in the house until 1895, (see Old Cross Hall, below) when they were moved to the Waterloo Road ex-Grammar School where they remained until absorbed into the Albert Road School in 1905.

The National School was extended in 1884, but this had the negative effect of reducing the yard space available for use at playtimes. Technically the school closed on March 31st 1900, but, in fact, it continued in use until final closure on February 28th 1905 when the last of its pupils were transferred to the Albert Road School. There is now no trace of the school buildings, they were demolished as part of the Queens Court redevelopment scheme.

RAMSEY, OLD CROSS HALL INFANT SCHOOL

The Curate of St. Paul's, George Paton, did much for the town of Ramsey and in 1875, Robert Corkhill rebuilt a house belonging to the La Mothe family for Mr Paton. This became the Old Cross Hall, an infant school.

The numbers taught in the school seem phenomenal with an average attendance of 139, peaking at 234 in 1890. Unbelievably, the school did not have a playground.

The building was condemned as a school during 1895 by HM Inspectors, (see Ramsey National School and Ramsey Grammar School above), but continued in use for several years as a concert hall.

In 1910, the building was re-fitted and re-opened as Ramsey's first cinema, 'The Picturedrome'.   [2] [9]

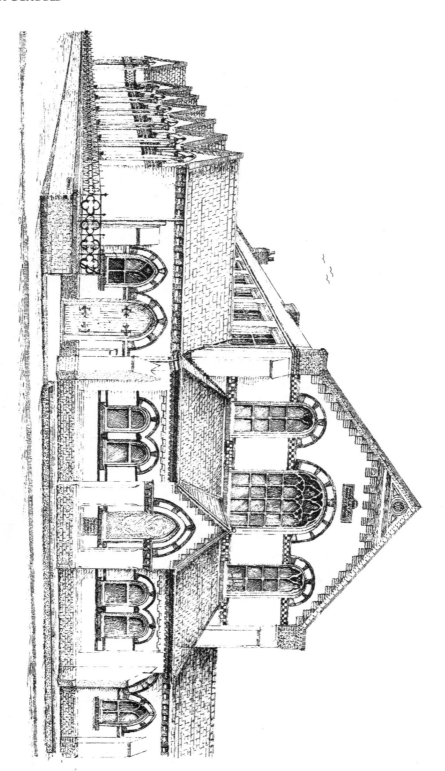

Ramsey Wesleyan School - Opened 1888, last used as a school in 1974. Had a huge hall, but tiny classrooms. Drawn January 1988, just prior to demolition.

RAMSEY, QUEEN STREET METHODIST SCHOOL.

This, the first Methodist School in Ramsey, opened within what had been the Queen Street Chapel in March 1850. It was not a success and closed due to lack of support in February 1853.

RAMSEY QUEEN STREET SCHOOL.

Queen Street School reopened in 1857, with Mr C.H.Moxey as Master. In 1860, it was reported that the School was being kept by Edward and Mary Macauley. Eventually the school must have closed once again.

RAMSEY WESLEYAN PUBLIC ELEMENTARY SCHOOL.

In January 1874, Queen Street opened its doors to scholars yet again, this time under the Wesleyan persuasion.

There are no traces of this school, the building was demolished as part of the Queens Court redevelopment scheme.

EDUCATION IN RAMSEY AND DISTRICT.

In 1883, a proposal was made for a United School District of Ramsey. Jurby. Andreas. Bride. Lezayre. Maughold. There was a strong protest from Ramsey which considered the new district to be too large for efficient working. Nothing came of the idea.

RAMSEY WESLEYAN SCHOOL.

On May 25th 1888, a memorial stone was laid on a site for a new Wesleyan School in Albert Road. Ramsey. From the start it was intended that this new Wesleyan School should be a fee paying school, the aim being to provide a middle class education at low cost. The School opened on November 24th 1888, with lessons commencing on the 26th.

Built on the central hall system, the School was quickly in trouble with the HM Inspectors who commented that:- **" the school had been built more with an eye to having a fine hall than to being a good school building"** !

Furthermore, the Inspector considered that ventilation was poor and the classrooms too small. Notice was given that the grant would be withheld unless better conditions were provided.

The Trustees must have been shattered at these findings because the cost of the required alterations was going to be considerable. I don't believe that they intended to be rushed but by the end of the century the required 'modernisation' had been satisfactorily completed. !

The peak attendance was reached in 1898 when there were 299 scholars, from then on there was a gradual fall until, by 1921 there were only 115.

Ramsey Wesleyan.cont.,

During early 1922 the School closed as an independent establishment but the building continued to be used for school purposes. Over the years it was leased by the Education Department to outhouse pupils from either the Grammar School or Albert Road School.

As an example, from July 14th 1922, a lease was obtained for five years so as to provide class rooms for 153 Grammar School pupils. The lease was then further extended until, in 1931, the new Grammar School in Lezayre Road was opened. During these years, the school was renamed "Ramsey Grammar School".

In 1924, the number of 'Free' grammar school places in the Grammar School was increased from 10 to 12, candidates to be not more than 12 years of age. During October 1925, there were 91 boys and 117 girls attending, of whom, 56% were from Ramsey.

Ramsey Wesleyan was last used as a school in the 1970s' when it was used as an overflow for Albert Road School pending completion of the Auldyn Infant School which opened in 1974.

In its later years the building was used by different trades for business purposes, none of great note. Eventually, during 1995/6, the property was demolished and the site converted into a car park. It has since been developed for housing purposes.

RAMSEY BOARD SCHOOL. ALBERT ROAD.

A new school was opened in Ramsey on March 14th 1905, with accommodation for 225 infants and 500 older children in an age range from 5 to 14.

In fact it started its career by serving 225 infants, 100 junior and 400 senior pupils; the Infant School maintained its own log books and the School had provision for cookery, laundry and manual work rooms.

The school has two halls, one on the ground floor the other on the first, their respective dimensions are 7.5m X 13m and 7,5m X 18m, both are undivided and the number of classrooms is 12.

By 1928, the school was considered to be inconveniently full.

RAMSEY, ALBERT ROAD JUNIOR SCHOOL

This is the school's present name, the main entrance is on Albert Road. There are now 177 boys and 134 girls attending within the ages of 7 and 11 and for to help with their education there are 15 teachers, including the Head Teacher, and 3 ancillaries.

Being nearly one hundred years old, the school is now considered to be time expired and talks are taking place which will attempt to solve the problem of how best to provide a replacement for this school and to decide the future educational requirements of the Ramsey area. (see Ramsey North)

RAMSEY NEW GRAMMAR SCHOOL.

On February 28th,1930, Tynwald voted £26,500 to provide new buildings and equipment for the Ramsey Grammar School. The President of the Royal Institute of Architects was invited to suggest a suitable assessor to conduct the architectural competition and adjudicate on the plans. Seventy-two designs were submitted and 1st place was awarded to C.B.Pearson.Son & Duffy., of Lancaster.

The successful tenderer for the construction work was Wm. McArd & Son with £20,685 and they took possession of the site on Feb 1st 1932.   [B07]
Opened off Lezayre Road during September 1933; an extension soon proved   necessary and a newer school was built a little further along Lezayre Road in 1939, with Messrs. W.McArd & Sons, Port Erin.,being awarded the contract for £25,596 10s.

In 1940 the new extension was requisitioned by the Royal Air Force and throughout the war it was used as a sector control of Fighter Command. This was the World's first Area Air Traffic Control Centre and as such was the forerunner of all the major civil systems that exist throughout the world today.

After the war, formal opening as a School took place on September 14th 1946, and the two sets of buildings became known as Ramsey Grammar School East and Ramsey Grammar School West. The school became the first inclusive, comprehensive (non-streamed), mixed school in the British Isles. The sexes were not segregated in any way as they were at other Manx Schools.
Both sets of school buildings have since needed considerable extension, the latest works being completed in 2000/1. Whilst retaining the title Grammar School, the two schools really do justify their combined role as one, large, fully comprehensive mixed school.
The entrances to both the East and West sites are from the Lezayre Road.

Scholars in the year 2000 numbered 398 boys and 424 girls within the age range of 11 to 19, they were accommodated within 76 classrooms, had 2 halls and were taught by 57.5 teachers.
Yet further extensions are anticipated for the year 2006 onward, present estimated costings suggest £1.350m.

RAMSEY, ST. MAUGHOLD'S ROMAN CATHOLIC SCHOOL.

Father Richard Barton was appointed Parish Priest in 1900 and Ramsey's Roman Catholic school came about largely due to his devotion to the cause of specific fundraising for the new church and a new school. Sadly, he died just before completion of the school in 1910.

St Maugholds Roman Catholic School - Opened 1910. Drawn August 1991.
This school was demolished with haste after completion of a school term.

Old Ramsey
St Maughold Junior school - Ramsey,
demolished 1990

Ramsey, St Maugholds. cont.,

The school provided accommodation for 40 mixed older scholars and 36 infants and the school remained in constant use until a relatively sudden closure during 1991.

St Maughold's School was on the opposite side of the road to Albert Street School; the site remains but within weeks of the last pupils leaving the school the buildings were demolished, with what seemed to be unseemly haste..

RAMSEY, AULDYN INFANT SCHOOL.

This school was well overdue when built in 1974; it was needed to relieve chronic overcrowding in the Albert Road School.

Opening took place in 1975.

From the outside the school has an unimpressive, almost prefabricated appearance but this is belied by a bright cheerful atmosphere within the school, there are plenty of windows and the school has been built on a spacious site with open green space on two sides.

There are 10 classrooms but, at present, in 2001, there are also two mobile classrooms in use. There is an undivided hall.

The children are all infants from age 4 to 7, the boys number 103 and the girls 98. There are 12 Teachers as well as 5.5 N.N.E.B. but within these figures there is the staffing for what is known as The Albert Tower Room, a unit for Special Needs children who require 1 teacher and 2 N.N.E.B.

Because of continuing growth in the catchment area the school does require a permanent extension and the fact is realised. There was a problem facing the planners however, how best to proceed knowing that the present school is not all that old ? Several options were considered, the final decision being that a new school will be built slightly to the North on the present playing fields. A start on building work will probably be made during 2003/4. The overall estimate is £2,697,000.

At present the entrance to the school is from the Lezayre Estate not from Lezayre Road but this will be changed for the new school.

RAMSEY NORTH NEW SCHOOL

A replacement for Albert Road School is at present in the early design stage with a possible construction date of 2005. The estimated cost is £6,417.000 and the school is likely to be built on the Clifton Park site.

THE CAARJYS CHILDREN'S RESOURCE CENTRE

This centre is in Grove Mount and is specifically for children with learning and physical disabilities together with family if need be. The centre is under the aegis of the Department of Health.

"This above all, to thine own self be true,
And it must follow, as the night the day,
thou canst not then be false to any man."

*   *   *

Chapter twentythree

The schools from Rushen to West Baldwin

RUSHEN ABBEY INFANT SCHOOL.
Part of the lands of Rushen Abbey were bought for an infant school in 1855. (Kewaigue)

RUSHEN ABBEY BOARDING SCHOOL.
This was a private girls school run by Ellen Stowell and her sister Bellane in the 1850s.

RUSHEN CHURCH - THE GATE SCHOOL
The original school was built at the church gate so as to take scholars out of the church as required by the Bishop; it was built with the help of Bishop Wilson in 1734, and the Parish Clerk was the Master.
When a new Rushen school was built in 1861, the Rushen Church Gate School was demolished to make space for graves.

RUSHEN PAROCHIAL GIRLS' SCHOOL.
Opened 1798, and rebuilt between 1873 and 1880. Closed April 1927, when the scholars were transferred to Rushen School

RUSHEN PAROCHIAL BOYS' SCHOOL.
Building date not known but it might have been 1861, the school was certainly recorded as being in regular use by 1871.
Attendances during the final year averaged 65 boys and 93 girls, the boys being transferred to Rushen School.
Upon closing on Mar 31st 1927, it was agreed that the school be sold by auction, the net proceeds to be divided equally between the Vicar and Churchwardens and the Educational Council; the sum received was £940.

THE RUSHEN SCHOOL
(Rushen District)
(I regret that I have not been able to positively identify which school the detail below refers to, presumably it was the pre-decessor of the Rushen School mentioned on page 210)
This school was built in 1858, with a Parliamentary Grant of £334 and donations of £253. Opened in 1859.
Memo - if this was the original CENTRAL SCHOOL, it closed on 31/3/1927 when the average attendance was only 31.

RUSHEN SCHOOL / RUSHEN PRIMARY SCHOOL

The site for a new Central School was purchased in 1923, and plans were approved on Dec 21st 1923; a tender for £14,799 was received from the successful contractors, Messrs. W and J.McArd in 1924.

Rushen School was completed in 1927, at a cost of £16,250.

Opened to pupils on April 4th 1927, with 332 on the roll, the school replaced six others, Rushen Parochial Boys School, the Rushen Parochial Girls School, Port St. Mary Boys School, Port St. Mary Infants School, Port Erin Infants School and Rushen Central School.   [M21]

Now known as the Rushen Primary School, the school is situated on Church Road, Port St. Mary, on the A29. There are 16 classrooms and the school has the good fortune to have two undivided halls, one being 22m X 12.5m, the other 15m X 11m.

With 15 teachers, including the Head, there are also 7 ancillaries for the 163 boys and 155 girls. There are 134 infants and the school teaches in the age range of 4 to 11.

The school has been considerably extended recently and no further extensions are foreseen, at present.

RUSHEN HIGHER EDUCATION SCHOOL (Rushen District)

Built on the 'Four Roads' site and opened on Nov 1st 1910. The wood and iron building was paid for by way of a loan for £500 at 4% over ten years.   [B04]

RUSHEN PRIMARY SCHOOL. PORT ST. MARY.

Closed 31/3/1927.   (See Port St. Mary)

SANDYGATE SCHOOL FOR GIRLS.

On Feb 27th 1875, the Mistress of St. Judes School, Miss Eliza Radcliffe, reported the opening of a girls school at Sandygate which she feared would absorb some of her pupils. I can only imagine that it was a private school, there was no further mention of such a school and the date does not coincide with the opening dates of any other nearby northern schools.

SANTAN PAROCHIAL BOARD SCHOOL.(1)

A petty School seems to have existed in Santan in 1669, but a further school was probably built because, on February 22nd 1848, the Santan Vestry bought an acre of land at Ballakissack on which a schoolhouse was to be built funded by a grant from Parliament of £100, the National Society £30, £208 from various donations and £101 from the sale of the old school.

The new school was opened on 2/3/1855, and was transferred to the School Board in 1875.

SANTON. Llannon Shee (2)
A new school, known at the time as the Kirk Saint Anne New Schoolhouse, was provided about 1880. During 1974 this school had a mobile schoolroom in use but by the 1980s the roll was down to the 30s, closure was inevitable because there was no likelihood of any increase in the number of local children at that time.

ST. JOHN'S.(1)
The Rev James Wilks was born in Santan in July 1719. As Vicar of German he obtained a piece of land at St. John's to build there the first school in the neighbourhood. Provision was made for a school and schoolhouse in 1743; these premises were in use until the new parochial school was opened in 1845.

ST. JOHN'S.(2). THE VRANEY SCHOOL.
THE VRANEY is mentioned in the Isle of Man Charities as an estate in the parish on which was built a school subsequent to 1781. The school was still in use in 1831.
 The word Vraney derives from Brainagh - a grinding mill.

ST.JOHN'S PAROCHIAL (?) SCHOOL.(3)
This school was opened on February the twelfth 1845, in the building now used as St.John's church hall. The school was built before the present St. John's Church, which was not opened until March 7th 1852.

ST. JOHN'S BOARD SCHOOL. MAIN A1 ROAD.(4)
Funding of £1,798 for a new school on a site almost opposite Tynwald Hill was authorised 23/3/1901 and opening took place on Feb 1st 1898. (see chapter six) Closure came in Dec 2002.
The school had 5 classrooms and an undivided hall for its children, all of whom were between four and eleven years of age.
There were 6.8 teachers and two ancillaries for the 110 children attending the school, of that figure over 40 were infants.
From Sept 2003 this building will be used as a Manx Gaelic medium centre with two classes of reception, Year One and Year Two children being taught through the medium of Manx. A Manx Language officer and team of 3 peripatetic Manx teachers will also be based there.

ST JOHN'S PRIMARY SCHOOL. STATION RD.
Construction started Aug 2001. The foundation stone was laid 11/3/2002. Completed 22/11/2002 at a cost of £5million, which was £200,000 below the budget figure. The school opened 10/3/2003.
In addition to the teachers there is a Nursery Nurse, caretaker and secretary. There are 6 classes. By Sept 2003 it will also have a 40 place pre-school class, a Special Unit for pupils with Special Educational Needs, nursery, hall, youth and community room, play areas, a sensory garden and amphitheatre.   [19]

ST. JUDE'S SCHOOL.(1)
(Andreas District)

St. Jude's church was consecrated on 25th November 1841, the first Chaplain being Rev William Drury; it was mainly through his efforts that the first school was built near to the church.

In 1865, Rev Benjamin P.Clarke started evening classes in the school where workmen could learn the elements of education for a small fee.

Closed for some unknown reason in 1876, the school re-opened in 1881, it was a popular school and soon became overcrowded.

In 1894, HMI reported :-

" **The school is now becoming overcrowded. As there are children in all the seven standards and as the mistress has no suitable assistance she cannot without neglecting the older children afford the time necessary for the proper instruction of the infants. If the Managers wish to make the school thoroughly efficient they should build a classroom, fit it up and appoint a qualified Assistant Teacher."**

Instead, a new school was provided.

The old school can still be seen as a private residence on just past St Jude's Church on the right of the A13 from Ramsey.

ST. JUDE'S BOARD SCHOOL.(2)

Built almost opposite St. Jude's Church, a new school opened on Sept 20th 1897. In 1953 a public notice warned of a temporary closure at the end of the summer term but there were many petitions against the closure and a reprieve was gained.

The school eventually closed at the end of the summer term in 1982, mainly because of the opening of a brand new school at Jurby. The premises are used at present by a Manx Language group, both the school and its grounds are well cared for.

ST. LUKE'S BALDWIN. CHURCH AND SCHOOL.

Opened 14th May 1836. The school portion remained in use until 1870. (see BALDWIN, St. Lukes.)

ST. MARK'S SCHOOL.(1)

Bishop Hildesley petitioned the Governor persistently until, in 1771, some land was made available for the erection of a Chapel of Ease and School in this part of the Island. The chapel became St. Mark's church which was erected by June 1772. The foundation stone for a school was laid in 1774.

ST. MARK'S SCHOOL.(2)
(Malew District)

Helped by Bishop Short, a new schoolhouse and schoolmaster's house were built in 1845/6 together with two cottages whose rent would form a repair fund for the school.

St Mark's cont.

Rev John Thomas Clark was Chaplain at the time and he obtained £70 toward the cost of the school from the National Society for Education in London, this was done by persuading them to alter their charter which, previously, had confined their work to England and Wales; he also got £30 from the British Government. There was a proposal to close the school in 1953 but it was not until 1954, when only two children remained on the roll, that closure was effected.

The school buildings can still be seen on the B30 road.

SCOILL PHURT LE MOIRREY
(see Port St. Mary)

SCOILL VALLAJEELT
(see Braddan)

SMEALE SCHOOL
(Bride District)

Closed by 1880, this tiny one roomed school building was offered on lease to Andreas Schools Committee but they had no use for it, they considered the Lhane School was adequate for the needs of the locality and the Committee rejected the offer.

SPOYT VANE SCHOOL. MICHAEL.

Part of the Ballaveigh Estate near Glen Mooar (off the A3 road from Kirk Michael) was conveyed for the purposes of a school, which was built in 1860.

SULBY GLEN BOARD SCHOOL.
(Lezayre District)

SULBY, LEZAYRE MOUNTAIN (or KELLY'S) SCHOOL.

Built in what was then the remote and almost inaccessible Tholt-y-Will valley of Sulby Glen.

The site is indeed remote and was chosen because it was at the meeting point of several pathways from the surrounding mountainous hillside farms and lands. Nowadays the best way of describing the location is to say that it is only a short distance from the foot of Sulby Reservoir Dam embankment which, at the time, had not been constructed.

Funded in 1746, the School was known locally as Kelly's School because John Kelly of Marown left in trust the sum of £60 and by a codicil in his will the sum of £11 toward the funding of a school in the Mountains of the Parish of Lezayre.

Philip Quayle and William Kelly, parishioners of Lezayre, likewise endowed land in Ballaugh and Lezayre to support the school which, when erected, included a house for the Master.

These were given new slate roofs in 1829.

Sulby Glen Cont.

In 1831, the Master was Ewan Crow and about ten or eleven scholars were attending but, by 1887, no school was being held because of the infirmity of the aged Schoolmaster.

The School was rebuilt and reopened on Oct 10th 1888, the Mistress recording the size of the Schoolhouse in the school log book as being :- Length 25', Breadth 16', Height to the eaves 10'7", height to collar beam 12'10" and to the ridge 17'.

In 1890 the average attendance was 15 out of 19 on the register, nevertheless, the school was classed as efficient..

By 1900, there were only a few scholars and the School finally closed on March 11th 1907, when two remaining pupils and the last teacher, Miss Molly Bannister, were transferred to Sulby. (see chapter twelve for further detail.)

The school buildings were sold in 1921 and have had several owners since. They have been converted into a private residence of distinction but the alterations have been extensive and, apart from the bell tower - minus original bell- very little remains to suggest that it was once a school.

SULBY TREEN SCHOOL.(1)

The first School was built on a small plot of land, ten yards square, on land bestowed by John and Margaret Garrett at their Claggach on June 30th 1715. Even as late as 1755, William Curphey of Castletown, bequeathed £10:-

"To be laid out at interest at the discretion of the Vicar and Wardens which interest is to be paid yearly to the Schoolmaster or Schoolmistress at Sulby School".

This was one of several small legacies to benefit the School and/or its Master or Mistress.

In 1757, it was recorded that:-

"The Master is a foreigner and therefore unable to teach in Manx.", but, by 1766, he was another person who could do so !

The school must have passed under the control of the church quite early on because moneys from different endowments, which were specifically for the upkeep of Sulby School and for the provision of a teacher licensed by the Bishop, were soon being attended to by the Vicar and Wardens of Lezayre.

It is quite possible that this was another school which suffered from the procrastination of the Vicar and Churchwardens of Lezayre, who would probably have argued that the upkeep of Sulby School was the responsibility of the inhabitants of the Treen of Sulby in accordance with the original deed because, in later years, the building was suffered to go to ruin.

When a land conveyance was made in 1771, for a new school, this earlier school was recorded as, " being in decay ", and the School (now known as Mrs Margaret Christian's School) was vacant for several years before 1776.

{Note :- See 'Lezayre School' for further examples of procrastination by the Vicar and Churchwardens, there are more examples in "The Annals of Kirk Christ, Lezayre." by R.D.Kermode.

SULBY DAME (or TREEN) SCHOOL.(2)
(Lezayre District)

The replacement, or new school, stood at the corner of the Claddagh and Sulby Glen roads on a portion of the croft known as Sulby Big Miln Croft. It was built on land sold on the 26th of February 1771, to the Vicar and Churchwardens of Lezayre for the sum of 5/-, "for the use of a school house for the benefit of the children of the Treen of Sulby."

The date on which the new school was opened is not known but, by 1782, English was being taught. In 1831 the number of scholars attending varied between thirty and fifty.

The building still stands on its own corner site but another floor has been added to the original single storied structure.

SULBY, ST STEPHEN'S CHURCH AND SCHOOL.
(Lezayre District)

Bishop William Ward's combined church and school for Sulby was built on land given from the Staward Estate by Major Caesar Bacon on June 4th 1838. A condition of the conveyance was:-

"That the premises shall be used exclusively as a church and schoolhouse, otherwise the premises are to revert to the Grantor, his heirs or assigns".

A grant of £100 was made by the Treasury toward the cost of construction of the school as well as £100 from the National Society. During a visitation in 1845 it was reported that there were 134 scholars, an amazing figure for a small hall. !

A house in Sulby Glen was provided in 1848 for the Schoolmistress at a cost of £30, £10 of which was granted by the Commissioners of Woods and Forests and £20 by subscription.

St. Stephen's remained in use as a combined church and school until the new elementary Board school was built on adjoining land in 1879.

The church and church hall were largely rebuilt in 1879/80; both remain in use, the hall now being used by the Sunday School. To get a good impression of what St Stephen's church/school was originally like you should go to Dalby and visit St. James' Church, where the hall still has sliding screens which extend to the full height and width of the hall and can be used effectively to divide the hall into two.

Sulby School and Schoolhouse 1988.

Sulby Board School - This view includes the house provided for the master or mistress at the far end of the school. Hasty demolition of the house shortly after being drawn December - January 1998-9 caused offence. School open from 1879 to 1991.

SULBY ELEMENTARY SCHOOL.

Land for a new school was donated by the trustees of the late Caesar Bacon on June 26th 1879; it had formed part of the Staward, or Ballabrooie Estate.

A School was built, together with a nearby teacher's house, and the Board of Education made a grant of £397.08.00d toward the cost. The opening date was December 2nd 1879.

In September 1961, the School was made into a "one teacher" School with all children over eight years of age being transferred to Ramseys Albert Road School. At the time there were 27 children on the roll, 12 juniors and 15 infants; it was thought that numbers would fall further over the years.

By the mid 1980s, however, the picture had changed radically and the Education Department approached the owner of land adjoining the school to see if additional land could be obtained on which they could extend the facilities. The result was unexpected and very welcome; see below, under Sulby Primary School, for details.

The teacher's house was demolished with what local people considered to be undue haste in or about 1989, and the School was closed on July 31st 1991, the children being transferred to a new Sulby primary school.

The Education Department then sold the old school buildings, together with the land attached to a private person, an act which was considered immoral by local residents who understood that the Department should either have returned the school and site to the original donors, heirs, etc., or alternatively converted the listed building into a centre for further studies of one description or the other.

Located on the A3 near Sulby Village.

SULBY PRIMARY SCHOOL.

Plans for this new school were submitted to Lezayre Parish Commissioners during 1988, and the School was finished in 1991.

Built on land given by Dr. Daniel MacDonald of Ballamanagh during his lifetime, he laid the foundation stone in July 1990. In addition to the land, Dr. MacDonald gave £1,200,000 to pay for the school; regretfully, he was never to see it completed because he died in February 1991, at the age of 85.

The School was completed during August 1991 and opened to pupils on September 1st; an 'Official opening' took place on October 21st.

Despite being much larger than the previous school, the new School proved to be inadequate by 1999 and in December of that year a mobile temporary classroom was erected alongside.

Entrance to the spacious grounds of the Sulby Primary School is gained off Sulby Glen Road, the A14.

Sulby Primary School cont.,

At present there are 5 classrooms (including the mobile). A large hall 20m x 12m, includes provision for a dining platform. *There are 6.5 teachers including the Headteacher for the 53 boys and 67 girls of whom the infants number 46.* The age range catered for is from 4 to 11.

Plans were thought to be in hand for a permanent extension, possibly in 2005 at an estimated cost of £292,000 but the work has been dropped from existing capital forecasts.

THE LHANE SCHOOL.
see LHEN.

WEST BALDWIN SCHOOL.

"Pressing people to learn things they do not want to know is as unwholesome and disastrous as feeding them on sawdust."

G.B.Shaw.

*   *   *

Chapter twentyfour

PRIVATE SCHOOLS

A report produced by School Inspectors concerning Private Schools on the Isle of Man in July 1929, was critical in several respects; natural lighting, space for physical education, and floor space per child were, in almost all of the Private Schools, considered to be below acceptable standards. (excepting the Secondary Schools)

The general conclusion of the report was :-

"Material conditions vary with the individual schools. Some defects have been pointed out which do not apply to all schools, but in each case the proprietors of the school know, through the special reports in their hands, whether his or her school is open to the criticisms offered.

Educationally, in the narrow sense of the term, it may be fairly said that, up to the age of thirteen plus, quite fairly good work is being done in private schools. Children get a good grounding in fundamentals, and those who pass on to other schools make good progress. But beyond the age of thirteen plus, conditions are much less satisfactory.

Children who remain are certainly as well and possibly better educated than if they had gone to an elementary school; but, comparing children of the same ages, the standards of sound secondary school work are not even approached,

There must always be some special and peculiar reason to justify the parent in keeping his child at a private school after the age of thirteen."   [B06]

*   *   *

A SELECTION OF PAST PRIVATE SCHOOLS IN DOUGLAS

Albert Terrace Ladies Collegiate (Miss Emerson)
Athol Academy. Crescent.(N.Forrester)
Bradda Mount (Reid)
Byrn Villas for Day Pupils and Boarders.(Miss Jane Dutton)
Carlton House School (Gallard Mason)
Cleveland, Woodbourne Road (Miss Oldham)
Collegiate School (Reid)
Crescent Academy (A.Steele)

Past private schools cont.,

Crescent Seminary (Misses Parry)
Derby Square (Misses Stowell)
Derby Square (Mr Pierpoint)
Derby Square High Schools (G.Green)
Eastleigh (Miss Newton)
Ellesmere Prep School. Recognised as from 1927. Fees were from 9 to 15 guineas. For Boarders the fees were from 66 to 81 guineas including tuition. The Head Mistress was Mrs E.A.Garrett and there were 57 scholars.
Falconcliff (Dr. Gough)
Finch Road Convent School, opened about 1890.
Glen Lyon (J.McMullen)
Greens High School
Ingleby (Garrett and Cowan) closed 1977.
Mathematical Academy. Odd Fellow's Hall.
Mount Havelock,Park Road (H.Hemmings)
New Douglas Grammar School (Pearce/Poole)
St. Francis (Miss Chapell/Mrs Stansfield).
    Opened in Derby Road, 1929 closed 1977
St. Josephs Convent School closed 1978.
Strathallen Park (Steele)
Victoria College (Richard Farrell)
Villa Marina (Misses Dutton).
    Opened 1834 and, following the retirement of the two ladies was closed by 1861.
Woodbourne House (Misses Kayll)
Woodville (Miss Parkin)

*   *   *

RAMSEY PRIVATE SCHOOLS

THIS SHORT LIST DOES NOT PRETEND TO BE COMPREHENSIVE

RAMSEY, LEZAYRE HOUSE SCHOOL FOR GIRLS.
A private School which opened in 1876; from 1900 it was run by the Misses Brown and Phillips.

RAMSEY, LEZAYRE GRAMMAR SCHOOL.
Under Rev Thomas Millington, this school was being advertised in 1845 with fees at One Guinea a quarter for the under 10s' and £1.11.6 over. Boarders were five Guineas a quarter plus fees.   [M14]

Ramsey private schools cont.,

ALBERT ROW SCHOOL.   Richard Mark.   1857.
                              (Later at 56 Waterloo Road.)
ALBERT STREET SCHOOL. Edward Macauley. 1852.
BOYS SCHOOL.   Mr W.Corlett.   1820.
    "   "   Mr Joseph Hetherington. 1824.
    "   "   Mr Smith.   1828.
DARTMOUTH HOUSE SCHOOL. (The Shore) Joseph Coates 1857.
                       (Thence to Beach House by 1861.)
LYNDOCK COTTAGE SCHOOL. (Sandy Road) Rev R.Airey. 1851.
                       (Thence to Belgrave House in Coburg Road by 1857.)
THE OLD CROSS SCHOOL. Joseph Reardon 1852.

                         *   *   *

PAST PRIVATE SCHOOLS
- other than in Douglas and Ramsey.

This short list does not pretend to be definitive. Many private schools came and
went as a will-o'-the-wisp, but it does give some indication of the wide variety of
locations.

        BALLAKILPHERIC PRIVATE SCHOOL
        BELMONT ABBEY. Opened 1867.
        CROSBY HOME SCHOOL.
                (Rev G.C.Stevens)
        GREEBA CASTLE - THE STANLEY HOUSE ACADEMY.
                (Mr Ash and Mr Appleton). This school closed by 1870.
        HOME SCHOOL FOR THE DAUGHTERS OF GENTLEMEN. MILNTOWN.
                (Mrs Christian)
        MILNTOWN BOARDING SCHOOL
                (Christian)
        RUSHEN ABBEY SCHOOL FOR YOUNG LADIES.
                (Misses Stowell)

                         *   *   *

Independent Schools
(formerly known as Private Schools)

(FROM A REPORT)

"At 31st March 1957, there were 69 boys and 168 girls attending six independent schools."

The registration of Independent Schools on the Island came into operation on September 30th, 1957.

These Schools then had six months in which to apply for registration, provisional registration would then be accorded to all who applied and supplied the necessary particulars. H.M Inspectors would then visit all the provisionally registered Schools to advise the Board whether to confirm their registration.

The various grounds on which the Board had power to find an independent school "objectionable" could be appealed against by the Proprietor in front of a Tribunal."   [B08]

*   *   *

PRESENT DAY HAPPENINGS

There is a private school/college devoted to the training and teaching of pupils wishing to progress in the catering and hotel trades.

At present the school is within premises which were built in 1894; for most of their existence these buildings formed part of a well known collection of Port Erin sea front hotels.

The school is known as The International Hotel School and the address is :- Windsor House, The Promenade. Pt Erin.

Started in 1984, the school is well established and offers its intending resident students a wide range of courses which can lead to Advanced and Higher Diplomas or, in association with Glasgow Caledonian University, to graduation with BA Degree.

Apart from the other extensive training and instructional facilities the school has 6 classrooms and, at present, has 120 students, 80 boys and 40 girls within the age range of 16 to 24.

There are 16 teachers and 3 ancillaries.

Thought is being given to an extension of the school.

*   *   *

There are two other independent establishments on the Island but they are not schools in the normally accepted sense :-

The Brightlife Educational Establishment.
                    (Ballavoden Manor. Andreas.)

The Manx Academy of Performing Arts.

*   *   *

An interesting development has arisen over recent years as a direct result of the large number of women now engaged in full time employment, namely, the provision of a large number of "Nursery Schools".
There are, for example :-

Beehive Kindergarten & baby wing. Hillberry Road, Onchan.
Footsteps Day Nursery. Queen's Pier Road, Ramsey.
Hopes and Dreams Day Nursery. 91 Woodbourne Road.Douglas.
Palm Tree Nursery. Park Road, Douglas.
Park House Nursery. Cooil Rd., Braddan.
Puddleducks Nursery School. Raphael Rd., Douglas.
Roslyn House Kindergarten.
Sandcastles Kindergarten. Queens Promenade Douglas.

These and several others cater mainly for babies from one to five years of age. Altogether, there are at least twenty-five such privately run establishments on the Island.

PRIVATE SCHOOLS

" The role of the teacher revolves round the transmission
of knowledge and the transmission of values; particularly by virtue of the second function, teachers play a part in the socialization of the child."
(C.Cannon. May 1964)

*   *   *

Chapter Twentyfive

RECENT EVENTS

To bring the tale up to date:-

During the year 2003 there were 47 schools in use on the Isle of Man serving a
population of over 71,000 inhabitants.

Almost all of the schools on the Isle of Man are operated and controlled by the
Manx Department of Education; the C of E has hardly any involvement other than
in the infant school of St. Thomas's. The Roman Catholic Church does still
continue to be involved with the operation of the St. Mary's mixed and infant
school.

These year 2003 figures should be compared with the number of schools recorded
in 1910 by A.W.Brown when there were :-

42 Board schools and 11 denominational schools serving 55,600 people.

The denominational schools in 1910 were:-
Roman Catholic (2), Wesleyan (3) and Church of England (6).

*   *   *

In addition to the Department's nurseries at Jurby, Manor Park, Ballacottier and
Cronk-y-Berry there are nurseries in partnership with private contractors at
Castletown, Ramsey and Peel.

*   *   *

During 2003 the Manx schools continuing in use were :-
Albert Road Mixed School. Albert Road, Ramsey.
Anagh Coar Primary School. Darragh Way. Douglas.
Andreas School. Andreas Village.
Arbory School. Main Road, Ballabeg.
Ashley Hill Primary School. Ashley Hill, Onchan.
Auldyn Infant School. Lezayre Estate. Ramsey.

Manx schools cont.,

Ballacloane Infants School. Demesne Road, Douglas.
Ballacottier Infants School. Clybane Road. Douglas.
Ballakermeen High School. St. Catherine's Drive. Douglas.
Ballaquayle Infant School. Stoney Road. Douglas.
Ballasalla School. Douglas Road. Ballasalla.
Ballaugh School. Station Road. Ballaugh.
Braddan Primary School. Braddan Road. Braddan.
Braddan. Scoill Vallajeelt. Meadow Crescent.
Bride School. Cranstal Road. Bride.
Buchan School. Westhill. Castletown.

Castle Rushen High School. Arbory Road. Castletown.
Centre for Manx Studies. 6 Kingswood Grove. Douglas.
College of Further Education. Homefield Road. Douglas
Cronk-y-Berry Primary School. Hailwood Ave. Douglas.

Dhoon School. Glen Mona. Dhoon, Maughold.

Fairfield Junior School. Tynwald Street. Douglas.(?)
Foxdale School. Mines Road. Foxdale.

** Glencrutchery Special School. Glencrutchery Road. Douglas.**
** Glencrutchery School is now used by the Special Needs and Psychology
Department. There are no pupils in this school.**

Jurby School. School Close. Jurby.

Kewaigue School. Kewaigue. Douglas.
King William's College. Douglas Road. Castletown.

Laxey Primary School. Quarry Road. Minorca, Laxey.

Manor Park School. Pulrose Road. Douglas.
Marown School. Glen Darragh Road. Glen Vine.
Michael Primary School. Main Road. Kirk Michael.
Murray's Road Junior School. Laureston Ave. Douglas.

Onchan Primary School. School Road. Onchan.

Peel Clothworkers School. Derby Road. Peel.

Queen Elizabeth II High School. Douglas Road. Peel.

Ramsey Grammar School. Lezayre Road. Ramsey.
(The Grammar School is housed in two school building complexes known as 'East'

and 'West', they are about a quarter of a mile apart.)
    Manx schools cont.,

Rushen Primary School. Church Road. Port St. Mary.
St. Johns Manx Gaelic Centre. Main Rd. St John's. (Open 9/2003)
St. John's Primary School. Station Rd. St. John's.
St. Mary's RC. Mixed and Infant School. St. Mary's Road. Douglas.
St. Ninians Lower School. Park Road. Douglas.
St. Ninians High School. Bray Hill. Douglas.
St. Thomas C of E Primary School. Finch Road. Douglas.
Scoill Phurt Le Moirrey. Station Road. Port St. Mary)
Scoill Vallaveelt. (see Braddan.)
Sulby Primary School. Main Road. Sulby.

Victoria Road School. School Lane. Castletown.

Willaston School. School Road, Willaston.

                    *   *   *

DEVELOPMENT PRONOUNCEMENTS MADE IN THE YEAR 2003.

AULDYN (RAMSEY) - EXTENSION OR REBUILD ?
A feasibility study took place to determine whether to completely refurbish and extend the present School or to build new. New has been decided upon at a provisional cost of £4.918m with design fees expected to be £289,000.

BALLAKERMEEN - NEW MEDWAY BLOCK.
A new block needed to provide an increased capacity. Work will commence in 2004 (possibly) at a cost of about £946,000. Approved design fees for 2002 were £179,000.

BRADDAN - SCOILL VALLAJEELT - EXTENSION.
Design stage work might have commenced for an extension to the SCOILL VALLAJEELT, probably for eight extra classrooms.
    Such a scheme is likely to cost £1.123m.

BRADDAN SCHOOL - EXTENSION.
Long term plans are being prepared for an extension round about the years of 2005/6.
At present the cost is forecast at £280,000.

DHOON SCHOOL - EXTENSION.
Costing about £1.587m, a permanent extension was under construction in 2002 for completion in 2003, this allows the two mobile classrooms to be dispensed with as well as permitting an improvement to the playgrounds. Other costs were £316,000.

Manx proposals cont.,
ISLE OF MAN COLLEGE - REFURBISHMENT.
A major refurbishment of the College in Homefield Road is being forecast for 2003/4 at an estimated cost of £732,000
Design fees forecast for a new teaching block were £59,000 and construction costs £710,000. Possible start in 2004   [Ba]

ONCHAN. NEW SECONDARY SCHOOL. BEMEHAGUE.
Proposals are being considered for a new Secondary School within Onchan on a 17 acre site at Bemehague. Design fees are expected to be £1.323m.
Estimates suggest the cost of the school might be £17.029m with a start in the years 2004/5 provided that the necessary approvals are given and the planning applications are granted.

RAMSEY NORTH - NEW SCHOOL
A new school will replace the present, time expired, Albert Road School. Preliminary plans are proceeding in anticipation of the school being built in the Ormly Hall area of Ramsey. If there are no unexpected problems the work of construction will probably be started 2006/7 at an estimated cost of £4.918m. (preliminary design fees possibly £289,000.)

ST. JOHN'S SCHOOL - REPLACEMENT.
During July 2000, an announcement was made that a new school was to be built at St. John's on a site in Station Road,to the rear off the main road, in a location near to where the old railway station once was. The estimated cost was £3.178m with planned completion in 2002/3.
Work began in August 2001, and the foundation stone was laid by the Education Minister, Steve Rodan, on March 18th 2002. At that time the estimated cost had risen to £5.2 million. The work was completed by November 22nd 2002, the cost being £5m.
See also chapter 23.

*   *   *

ASHLEY HILL. With building work starting in 2003, extension design fees of £22,000 and construction costs of £367,000 are expected.

MULTI-SITE Extension Scheme due 2004/5 costing £2.956m. fees probably £177,000.

PEEL CLOTHWORKERS' SCHOOL extension starting 2004 is likely to cost £1.765m plus design cost of £138,000

RAMSEY GRAMMAR. Provision of a Medway Block is likely in 2005 at £1.254m plus fees, at present £96,000

CASTLETOWN VICTORIA RD SCHOOL extension starting in 2004 will cost £73,000 in fees and £917,000 for construction

In addition to the schemes listed on the preceeding pages, the following projects are provisionally included within the Capital Estimates. Work on these projects is unlikely to start much before the years 2004/5.

CASTLE RUSHEN HIGH SCHOOL	EXTENSION
ONCHAN SCHOOL.	EXTENSION
SULBY SCHOOL.	EXTENSION
ST. NINIAN'S.	EXTENSION AND DINING ROOM
QUEEN ELIZABETH II, PEEL.	HUMANITIES BUILDING
NOBLES SITE.	NEW PRIMARY SCHOOL

[Ba]

*   *   *

One further educational project received major practical help from the Manx Government and has been implemented. This was the establishment of the Isle of Man International Business School.

The provision of such a school means that Manx students will, for the first time, have an opportunity to study full or part-time toward a degree taught entirely on the Isle of Man.

Students began degree programmes in Sept 2001 and the first results announced in April 2002 were six percent above those at the John Moores University in Liverpool.

Sponsorship is being actively sought for Bursaries and Scholarships.

The location of the new School is the Nunnery, near Douglas, just off the Old Castletown Road.   [17]

*   *   *

EDUCATION FOR DISAFFECTED CHILDREN.

Whilst not being schools in the accepted term, educational facilities are being provided for young people between 10 and 19 years of age in establishments such as the new 5 bedded CHILDREN'S SECURE HOME at White Hoe in the Isle of Man. The facilities are being co-ordinated by 'INCLUDE', a charity, which is part of CFBT, a non-profit organisation based locally at Agriculture House, Ballafletcher Farm Road, Cronkbourne Village.

*   *   *

UNIVERSITY OF LIVERPOOL

The University provides various courses based on the Centre for Continuing Education within the Centre of Lifelong Learning courses held in the Isle of Man. Some of the courses carry accreditisation which may be used toward degrees.

MANX SCHOOLS - PAST, PRESENT AND PROPOSED.

Bibliography

[1]   A history of the Isle of Man   A.W.Moore
[2]   A history of the Manx Church   John Gelling
[3]   An Island that led. (two volumes)   Hinton Bird
[4]   Centuries of childhood   P.Aries
[5]   Our heritage. Did you know ?   Kate Rodgers
[6]   Portrait of the Isle of Man   E.H.Stenning
[7]   Poverty and the Industrial Revolution   B.Inglis
[8]   Ramsey 1600-1800   Constance Radcliffe
[9]   Shining by the sea   Constance Radcliffe
[10] The Annals of Kirk Christ Lezayre.   R.D.Kermode
[11] The story of the Isle of Man   C.W.Airne
[12] Manx Museum Manuscripts
       [M12a] MM ref 5443 - date 1848
       [M12b] MM ref 2069b   D.Kermode Parr
       [M12c] MM ref 9321/26. 1861/1879.   re Jurby.
       [M12d] MM ref F74/159
       [M12e] MM Lancastrian School papers.
       [M12f] MM MS 5132c
       [M12g] MM 5124   log book for Bride school 1873/98
       [M12h] MM 5125   "   "   "   "   "   1898/1924
       [M12i] MM   M.H.Baillie Scott misc 1865/1945
       [M12j] MM E 186   Rev W.S.Dempsey
       [M12k] MM F79/4 The Onchan Story.G.N Kniveton
       [M12l] MM 5443C
       [M12k] MM 5153B   Log Book of St. John's School
       [M12l] MM GO 36
       [M12m]MM D 426/28   Arbory School 1834-1984
       [M12n] MM GO 31/7   Undenominational Schools
       [M12o] MM GO 31/5   Grammar & Public School summary
       [M12p] MM MD 10025   Barragarrow School Log Book
       [M12q] MM D426   Centenary Dhoon School
       [M12r] MM 5184C   Malew School Board minutes
       [M12s] MM 5183c   "   "   "   "
       [M13]   Isle of Man Natural History and Antiquarian Society
       [M13a] Vol IX. No 3.   R.E.Forster. B.A.
       [M13b] An address - 17/4/26 - Early Schools.   W.Cubbon
       [M14]   Filmed record   Manx Sun 1848/9
       [M15]   Log Book Albert Road Infants School
       [M16]   Log Book Cronk-y-Voddy school
       [M17]   MM5046   Log Book Lezayre Parochial School

Bibliography cont.,

[M18]	MM5043	Log Book Sulby Glen Board School.
[M19]	MM D426/1/3	Report on schools. Rev H.Moseley
[M20]	MM D426/6	Castletown National Schools
[M21]	MM 75.15	Our Heritage
[M22]	MM D154 6x	Accounts of Govt Treasurer 1868/88
[M23]	MM5159/b	Log Book Kirk Andreas
[M24]	MM MD12552	Schooling in the Isle of Man
[M25]	MM E240/32X	Thomas St Sunday School. Douglas.
[M26]	MM 5153B	Log Book St. John's. 1889-1922
[M27]	MD 12511	Andreas Sch Brd Minutes. 1872-94.
[M28]		Log Book St. Judes. 1874-1910
[M29]	D426/9	Douglas Sch Comm. 1884-1903
[M30]		Lhane Log Book. 1886-1932
[M31]		Ballagawne Log Books 1877-1932

[13] Laxey as I remember it   G.E.Kermode
[14] Manx Society. Vol 1 Abstract of laws, customs & ordinances.
[15] The Isle of Man - History.   Rev J.G.Cumming.
[16] Manx Memories & Movements.   Samuel Norris 1938.
[17] International Business School prospectus 1999/2000
[18] English Social History   G.M.Trevelyan
[19] Dept of Education memo 24/4/2003 John Cain

BOARD OF EDUCATION REPORTS

[Ba]	Estimate of capital payments 2000 to 2005.	
[B01]	Sixteenth	y/e Mar 31 1888 to 1895
[B02]	Twentyninth	y/e Mar 31st 1901 to 1905
[B03]	Thirtyfourth	y/e Mar 31st 1906 to 1910.
[B04]	Thirtyninth	y/e Mar 31st 1911 to 1915
[B05]	Fortyfourth	y/e Mar 31st 1916 to 1920
[B06]	Fortyninth	y/e Mar 31st 1921 to 1930
[B07]	Fiftyninth	y/e Mar 31st 1931 to 1946
[B08]	Seventyfifth	y/e Mar 31st 1947 to 1968

INDEX

CLERGY
(CARDINALS)

*   *   *

SCHOOLS

In some cases the Manx name is given, a duplication may sometimes occur.
This is a generic listing, the different descriptions, such as Petty, National, Board
School etc., are within the text.

Schools cont.,

St Jude's	71 81 114 129 212
St Luke's Baldwin	212
St Mark's	40 42 212
Scoill Vallaveelt	(see Braddan) 224
Spoyt Vane	213
Smeale	70 82 213

SULBY

Sulby	23
Sulby Dame's	215
Sulby Elementary	216
Sulby,St Stephen's	20 21 23 215
Sulby Mountain (or Kelly's)	122 124 213
Sulby Primary	216 217
Sulby Treen	23 214

Surby	?
The Lhane - see Lhen	
West Baldwin	217

*   *   *

NURSERY SCHOOLS

Beehive Kindergarten and Baby Wing.	222
Buchan Kindergarten	"
Footsteps Day Nursery	"
Hopes and Dreams Day Nursery.	"
Palm Tree Nursery	"
Park House Nursery.	"
Puddleducks Nursery School.	"
Roslyn House Kindergarten	"
Sandcastles Kindergarten.	"

Department Nurseries	223

*   *   *

MISCELLANEOUS SCHOOLS/ESTABLISHMENTS

Brightlife Educational Establishment	222
International College	221
Manx Academy of Performing Arts	222
School for disaffected children	227
University of Liverpool	227
Learning disabilities	28

TEACHERS

*   *   *

MANX SCHOOLS

Schools Past, Present and Proposed.

The End